E. McKNIGHT KAUFFER
a designer and his public

from WINTERS GLOOM
to SUMMERS JOY

E. McKnight-Kauffer

E. McKNIGHT KAUFFER
a designer and his public

Mark Haworth-Booth

Additional research by Graham Twemlow

V&A Publications

First published by V&A Publications, 2005
V&A Publications
160 Brompton Road
London SW3 1HW

This edition fully revised and updated from original edition published
by Gordon Fraser in 1979

Distributed in North America by Harry N. Abrams, Inc., New York

Work by E. McKnight Kauffer © 2005 Simon Rendall

Text © Mark Haworth-Booth
Appendix © Graham Twemlow
Checklist of posters © Graham Twemlow, Alan Howell,
Mark Haworth-Booth

The moral right of the author has been asserted.

ISBN 1 85177 466 1

Library of Congress Control Number 2005925453

Every effort has been made to seek permission to reproduce those
images whose copyright does not reside with the V&A, and we are
grateful to the individuals and institutions who have assisted in this task.
Any omissions are entirely unintentional, and the details should be
addressed to V&A Publications.

Designed by Janet James
New V&A photography by Paul Robins

Front cover illustration: *Soaring to Success! Daily Herald – the Early Bird*,
1919, poster (detail)
Back cover illustrations: BBC Handbook, 1928, book jacket;
American Airlines – Chicago, 1950 (plate 89); *BP Ethyl Controls
Horse-power,* 1933 (plate 68)
Frontispiece: *From Winter's Gloom to Summer's Joy*, 1927, poster,
London Underground. Circ.408-1971
Contents page: *Look! Under that broad beech tree …*(Walton), 1932,
poster, London Underground. E.3341-1932
Page 6: *London History at the London Museum*, 1923, poster, London
Underground. E.2-1924

Printed in China

V&A Publications
160 Brompton Road
London SW3 1HW
www.vam.ac.uk

CONTENTS

Look! under that broad beech tree I sat down when I was last this way
IZAAK WALTON

Preface   7

1 THE CALIFORNIAN   9
2 PAINTER INTO DESIGNER   13
3 THE EARLY TWENTIES   30
4 THE LATE TWENTIES   46
5 THE THIRTIES (1)   59
6 THE THIRTIES (2)   76
7 NEW YORK, 1940–54   96

Appendix: The role of the lithographic
artist in poster production by Graham Twemlow   110

Notes   112

Select bibliography   117

Checklist of posters by E. McKnight Kauffer   118

Index   126

E. McK. KAUFFER. 22

LONDON HISTORY AT THE

LONDON MUSEUM

DOVER STREET
OR ST. JAMES'S PARK STATION.

171. 1000. 8·2·23.   VINCENT BROOKS DAY & SON LTD. LITH. LONDON. W.C.2.

PREFACE

I first came across the name and work of E. McKnight Kauffer by chance – at Embankment Station in London in 1966. That was the year of the four hundredth anniversary of the Great Fire of London. London Transport reissued Kauffer's 1922 poster for the London Museum – which featured the Great Fire. It was and remains an astonishing image. It still seems extraordinary that a public company commissioned it and displayed it throughout London's vast Underground railway system. I thought it odd, too, given the originality and brilliance of the design, that Kauffer's unusual name should be so completely unfamiliar to me. Those thoughts gave rise to this book, which was first published 25 years ago.

I was lucky to begin studying Kauffer in the 1960s, when many of his friends and associates were still alive and delighted to talk to me about him. I was particularly fortunate, when my book was finished, to receive the following characteristically generous letter from Sir John Betjeman: 'There never was so good a poster-designer as that tall red-haired American Ted Kauffer. This book shows how he made the whole world his studio. He could make a picture out of autumn leaves or blotting paper. He showed how there was no such thing as commercial art. People are either artists or they are not. Ted Kauffer was an artist. This book is too good to be Art History, it has no jargon. Anyone can enjoy and understand it as they could enjoy Ted's posters and pictures'.

The first edition, published by Gordon Fraser in 1979, has been out of print for many years. Collections of Kauffer's work have changed since 1979. For example, the archives of Shell-Mex, which I consulted at Shell-Mex House beside the Thames, were transferred from there first to Warwick University and then to Sotheby's, where they were sold and dispersed in 2003. Also, the top third of the 'Early Bird' poster, which Kauffer gave to the Museum of Modern Art, New York in 1937, was de-accessioned by that museum in 1992. It seems that no public institution in the land of his birth now holds an example of Kauffer's masterpiece. I am delighted that the Victoria and Albert Museum, where I served as a curator from 1970 to 2004, consistently acquired Kauffer's works from the beginning of his career in England in 1915 and throughout his life. Kauffer was appointed to the V&A's Advisory Council in 1935 and after his death the museum mounted a grand memorial exhibition in his honour which was opened by his close friend T. S. Eliot. In the years after that exhibition, held in 1955, the V&A's Kauffer collection continued to grow. The Museum has a splendid tradition in the field of poster art and graphic design. The remarkable Brian Reade, who created influential exhibitions of Mucha and Beardsley in the 1960s, has been followed by Margaret Timmers, who created the landmark exhibition and book, *The Power of the Poster*, in 1998 and has immeasurably expanded and enhanced the collection. In 2004 the American Friends of the V&A received a major donation of some 2000 posters, a gift of Leslie, Judith and Gabi Schreyer and Alice Schreyer Batko. This significantly improved even the V&A's outstanding Kauffer collection.

I was delighted that the V&A decided to bring out this revised edition of my book. Errors have been weeded out, the checklist of Kauffer's posters has been much expanded and there are many new illustrations and far more colour plates. In addition to the generous support of many individuals and institutions acknowledged in the first edition, I am indebted to Graham Twemlow – a Kauffer scholar of great dedication and thoroughness – for sharing the task of updating the book. Finally, thanks are due to Simon Rendall, a typographer and designer of whom his grandfather – E. McKnight Kauffer – would have been proud. We are most grateful to him for his support for this new edition and for all his insight and advice.

Mark Haworth-Booth, Honorary Research Fellow, V&A

London History at the London Museum, designed 1922, issued 1923
poster, London Underground
E.2-1924

THE CALIFORNIAN

Edward Kauffer was born in Great Falls, Cascade County, Montana on 14 December 1890, the only son of John and Anna Kauffer. His parents were first- and second-generation immigrants to the United States, his father of Hanseatic German stock, his mother of Swedish stock. John Kauffer was better known as Johnny Kifer, his professional name as violinist and trap-drummer with the Beach and Bowers Minstrels and various showboat bands. Edward Kauffer resembled his grandfather on the Kauffer side in hair and build.[1] A friend who met him in his early twenties described him as 'a very tall, lanky, good-looking man, with a slightly curved nose, blue eyes, a shock of red hair and the very light complexion that often goes with red hair'.[2]

Kauffer grew up in the small brewing town of Evansville on the Ohio River in Indiana, where the Kauffer grandparents had settled. Johnny Kifer was away for long periods with theatre orchestras and the marriage was unsuccessful, ending in divorce when the child was three. As his mother was obliged to go out to work the boy was placed in an orphanage for two years. As a man of 60 he recalled with distaste the 'clipped hair, uniforms and impersonal dormitory methods'.[3] He grew up solitary and reflective in temperament, 'very much to myself always'. Like other children of poor families he was errand boy, soda jerk, grocery clerk and even factory hand before his twelfth birthday. He remembered his early life as 'lonely, nostalgic and uninspiring', typified by dingy hallways, drab houses and a monotony punctuated only by the ritual of a bath in a tin-tub every Saturday night. By the age of four or five he had begun to draw, and while other children played he would sit in the backyard drawing from flowers or copying reproductions of the dashing Wild West paintings of Frederic Remington.

1. *Caricature of Kauffer* by Thos Keane, 1913
pencil
Simon Rendall collection

His mother remarried, this time very happily, in 1899. Her second husband was John M. Rees, a miner. They lived together in Evansville for the next thirty years and Kauffer recalled that his stepfather had encouraged his artistic aspirations. Kauffer left school at the age of 12 or 13 to be helper to the scene painter at Evansville's Grand Opera House. He was clearly precocious and by the age of 17 – unusually for a minor – he is listed as a painter in the City Directory.[4] The first listing, in 1907, probably coincides with Kauffer's departure from the town as scene-painter, barker and general help to a travelling repertory theatre. Looking back on his Evansville childhood late in life Kauffer said 'An environment like that has a propelling force to certain kinds of natures. You want to get out of it.'[5]

While he was with the travelling players he met the character actor Frank Bacon (1864–1922), who later became widely known as co-author and star of *Lightnin'*, a Broadway hit in 1918 and later a John Ford film. Bacon took to Kauffer and invited him to emigrate to California where he owned a fruit ranch. At least part of the time Kauffer seems to have worked on the ranch – probably in exchange for the time to paint. In 1910 Bacon left for the East Coast but first settled Kauffer in a position with the San Francisco bookseller and art dealer Paul Elder. Kauffer's time on the ranch – perhaps a year – was later celebrated by an unusual portrait of him by the painter Maxwell Armfield. The picture, titled *The Californian*, shows Kauffer galloping naked over the plains on horse-back.[6]

Kauffer was taken on by Elder on condition that he would, within one month, 'learn the English language sufficiently to approach customers without his slangy stage jargon'.[7] In the Elder Bookshop and Art Rooms at 239 Grant Avenue Kauffer acquired not only a speaking voice of marked attractiveness and distinction but also a life-long passion for books. He continued his studies as a painter by receiving his first formal training at evening sessions at the Mark Hopkins Institute, a centre of the 'Californian Style' in easel and mural painting.[8]

A good customer of the bookshop was Joseph E. McKnight (1865–1942), Professor of Elementary Education at the University of Utah. The story of Kauffer's meeting with Professor McKnight and the subsequent momentous result is told in a long letter Kauffer wrote to his parents on 1 August 1912. As it is the earliest surviving letter from Kauffer, and discloses something

of his ardent and innocent nature, the letter is quoted here almost in full:

My dear Mother and Father
Can you believe it, that I'm going to Paris, France, to study. Its really and truly so. I'm so happy for it means that now at last the time has come and will be short for our being together for good for just as soon as I return we shall make a home and a studio. Now I'll tell you how it all came about, *oh so* sudden. About two years ago a professor of the University of Utah came into the store, we became quite friends and corresponded, it seems as though at the very beginning he took a deep interest in me and my work. Of course nothing was said in particular, only that I had great talent. Last year during vacation he came in with his wife and daughter who is about ten years, and visited quite often, noting my progress, still time went on and I never gave Paris a thought. He returned again this year and visited a few times and saw my late advancement. Well yesterday he came in and said, 'I want to talk with you'. Said he: 'Do you want to study?' 'You just bet I do', said I. Said he, 'Then you will, for I can help you'. Well – my goodness, what could I say – my life's dream come to life, and it seems like a fairy story. Its absolutely true and I will be home for a while to see you both, about October, if all goes well. Think of it dear ones, it doesn't seem possible does it? I know Mr McKnight well and that it is just his love of art to persuade a talented fellow along. Now of course this is a loan in a measure, that is, when I have made good I pay it back as I can, no hurry nor limited time, just when I'm successful – everyone is so certain that I am going to be a great painter that I know I will or else the way and means would not have opened up to me. He is a Christian Scientist, having overcome a great illness. Therefore I know his desire is purely that of humanity to progress – and a pure thought, for when I have paid it back it goes to some other struggling youth, who dreams of a great future, such as I have done. I know this is going to make you both happy, for it surely means that at last the sun is shining for us three. I attribute it to Science and my mother's great teaching to know the truth. God bless you mother dear, you have done it all, and He is going to let us three have the happiest days imaginable. I can't question your confidence in me, for I feel sure you know and feel that I will be successful, and the money borrowed will be a trifle compared to being successful. I figure on two years in Paris and that twelve hundred dollars or less will be the amount. I shall be economical, knowing full well that in that I'm helping another to

gain his point. I shall study right along in my Science knowing that it will point the truth always and always. I don't want you to ever feel alarmed of the environment of Paris, for that is prevailing everywhere and a strong character knows the good from the bad. I am sure you don't question that, for I shall always stay the boy you wanted me to be, for I know the struggle that you, mother dear, went thru. I can see your face just beam with joy when you read the news, for it is the event of events, and the beauty of it is, it is just a loan, to be repaid whenever I can and when I have gained success.

Already the art critics from the *Call* and *Bulletin* have been in and received my story and also viewed what sketches I have and before I leave S. F. no doubt there will be quite a story, which all helps to make me known. Everyone is glad. Miss Taylor is away yet and does not know, but she will be too – I give my notice about the fifteenth of August – quit about September 20th. Stopover in Salt Lake City when Mr McKnight is to make the final arrangements then on to home to see you for a month and then the Red Star Line from Philadelphia for Paris, France, second class cabin. Write me soon and tell me how happy you are …

Ever your devoted and affect. son,
Ed[9]

A small exhibition of Kauffer's paintings was held at the Elder Art Rooms and Porter Garnett wrote an enthusiastic notice for the *San Francisco Call*.[10] In homage to his patron Kauffer adopted the name McKnight and was soon on his way to Europe. He stopped for a few months, however, in Chicago – and by chance saw one of the epoch-making exhibitions of the twentieth century.

Kauffer was a student in the 'antique' programme at the Art Institute of Chicago from October 1912 to March 1913. He took classes in painting, anatomy and the history of painting.[11] Perhaps he wished to improve his basic skills before he began the precious two years in Paris. He conserved his funds by 'stoking the lodging house boiler in the morning, clearing dishes in the student refectory at lunch and carrying a spear in the opera at night'.[12] At the end of the year he exhibited an oil painting, *The Inlet – California Note*, and a chalk drawing, *Blackstone Hotel*, at the annual exhibition of the Art Students' League. The following March the great 'Armory Show' came to the Art Institute on tour from New York City. The 634 works in this exhibition introduced America at one blow to almost everything of major importance in European painting from Delacroix to Marcel Duchamp, whose *Nude Descending a Staircase* was only one of many masterpieces shown. America was already familiar with Impressionism, which was eagerly collected, but here were Cézanne, Gauguin, van Gogh, Matisse and other Fauves, the progress of Cubism up to 1912 represented by Picasso and Braque, Kandinsky and a group of German Expressionists, and recent sculptures by Brancusi and Duchamp-Villon.

Kauffer came upon the results of 40 years' experimentation in painting all at once, and in a tense and embattled atmosphere. No art exhibition in America had ever aroused such passions as the Armory Show. The press and public figures felt obliged to proclaim their opinions – and the prevailing general feeling was of sheer outrage. Even museum curators, teachers and students joined in the orgy of condemnation. One of the painters who had organized the exhibition wrote back to New York from Chicago: 'The students are a lot of rowdy roughnecks … All the instructors at the Institute are mad through, one even went so far as to take a big class of the students into the French Room and threw a virtual fit condemning Matisse.'[13] On the last night of the showing in Chicago members of the Art Students' League staged a mock trial and ritual stabbing of a dummy labelled Henri Hairmattress followed by the burning of travesties of Matisse's *Le Luxe* and *La Femme Bleue*. He later spoke of his response to the exhibition as 'intuitive': 'I couldn't have spoken about it then. I didn't understand it. But I certainly couldn't dismiss it. I felt a kind of quickening.'[14] He took a boat from Baltimore which put in at Algiers and Naples, and he reached Venice by June 1913. He made for Paris by way of Munich, where he stayed for a month or two.[15]

At this period the Bavarian capital was a centre of experimental activity. Paul Klee noted in his diary some events of 1913 – an exhibition of Italian Futurism, a Nolde exhibition, Nijinsky and Karsavina dancing with the Ballet Russe, but 'the measure is still not full!! Even Schönberg is being performed, the mad melodrama *Pierrot Lunaire!* Burst, you philistine, methinks your hour is struck!'[16] How much of all this Kauffer witnessed is not known, but in Munich he came across something of specific importance for his later work. This was the poster art of Ludwig Hohlwein (1874–1949).

Hohlwein was the outstanding poster designer of the period between the Art Nouveau flourish of the 1890s and the rise of Functionalism after the First World War. A correspondent from the London art magazine *The Studio* wrote of the posters of Munich in 1912:

Posters summon you to the different beer-restaurants for concerts or carnival revels, announce some special brew, or the great drinking feasts of the Spring or the fairs of Autumn, the joyous Kermesse. These posters are, for the most part, characterised by sober elegance and fine harmony of tone, they do not 'shout' at you from the walls nor are they crude in colour – they attract by their undoubted good taste, and fix the attention of the passer-by with their excellent colouring.[17]

Hohlwein was himself a notable bon viveur and an aficionado of hunting and the turf. His first success was a poster advertising a fashionable Munich tailor, Hermann Scherrer. This shows a young man with riding crop, saddle, riding boots, and breeches in grey and white check – a bulldog at his feet. It is an image of international elegance based on English tailoring and fashion – Scherrer indeed chose to use the English words 'Breeches-Maker and Sporting Tailor' to describe himself. Chic of fashion is equalled by chic of advertising. A French correspondent for the Paris magazine *Art et Décoration* observed that copies of this poster were taken home by the young French and English dandies who visited the city.[18] *Das Plakat*, the influential poster magazine, devoted an issue to Hohlwein in May 1913, and posters such as 'Marco-Polo-Tee' (1910) (plate 2) directly influenced Kauffer's early style as a poster designer.

In posters, programme covers, trade-cards and other ephemera Hohlwein publicly defined a particular kind of elegance, and became 'well-known and deservedly appreciated, not only by an élite of artists and sportsmen, but by the general public' as the *Studio* writer observed. *Art et Décoration* went further,

declaring that Hohlwein was conceivable without Munich, but not Munich without Hohlwein. At the time of the Armory Show Kauffer would have seen the quality that could be achieved in poster art, for the exhibition included Toulouse-Lautrec's *Le Divan Japonais*. Munich, however, would have provided his first opportunity of seeing the contribution a master poster artist could make to the surface of life in a cosmopolitan city.

Kauffer reached Paris in the autumn of 1913. Like other students he worked in the museums, in the afternoon sketch schools, and at the Académie Moderne. Given the immense amount of activity in all the arts in Paris at this date it would seem impossible to know what particularly impressed Kauffer. Fortunately a friend he made at that time, the Englishman Colin Hurry, was able to recall this.[19] Kauffer was interested in *everything*: 'Now he would be influenced by a friend, now by a book, now by the work of another painter, now by some aspect of nature.' More specifically, however, Hurry remembers that Kauffer talked of Matisse, Derain, Vlaminck and Chagall but that 'van Gogh was his hero-figure at this time'. In the spring of 1914 Kauffer went off to Normandy on a painting trip, taking with him van Gogh's *Letters*. A small oil painting of the Seine survives from this period and establishes Kauffer's discipleship to the milder aspects of van Gogh's style.[20]

On 7 July 1914 Kauffer married a gifted American concert pianist, Grace Ehrlich. She had been a pupil of Edward MacDowell in New York and was then studying under Isidore Philippe at the Paris Conservatoire. A close friend from the Paris period, Maria Zimmern Petrie, described Grace Kauffer as 'highly intelligent, warm-hearted, a strong personality with a genius for teaching'.[21] Only a month after their marriage the young couple were obliged to leave Paris. War conditions made survival there impossible. By then Maria Zimmern Petrie had settled in Durham and they left for England to join her in August 1914.

2. *Marco-Polo-Tee*, Ludwig Hohlwein, 1910
poster, E.361-1921

PAINTER INTO DESIGNER

'I do not remember how he came to England', Sir Francis Meynell wrote after Kauffer's death, 'but when he came he was already the exquisite, the son of a hundred kings.[1] Kauffer himself wrote that he felt at home for the first time. He liked the tranquillity of the landscape, the sense of roots and tradition.[2] In later notes he wrote he made it clear that he had come to England on his way to America – but 'liked the look of England and decided to stay'.[3] His personality soon won him friends among painters and writers but his first years in Britain were hard. Maria Zimmern Petrie wrote:

We lived together for two or three months and Teddy tried hard to find a market for his beautiful textile designs or posters, tramping the streets of Newcastle for days. He painted and sketched at Durham, but a stop was put to that also, for the boys thought he was my brother and a spy [Maria Zimmern Petrie was German-born; her husband Eric had already enlisted on the British side] and boys began to throw stones at him. There seemed no possible chance for the couple to settle down anywhere in northern England and find a living, so we decided that they must try their luck in London.[4]

An oil painting by Kauffer of the Petries' house in Durham from this time shows that he was still under the spell of van Gogh.[5] In London the search for work was still hectic and living conditions difficult. Grace had of course no piano, so could neither play nor teach.

Teddy had to spend hours every night dishwashing to earn a living, and again tried every avenue to find a post as designer or artist or get commissions.[6]

3. *E. McKnight Kauffer, c.1920*
photograph by Maud B. Davis
Simon Rendall collection

Kauffer had tried over 25 London companies unsuccessfully when he met John Hassall, one of the best-known poster artists of the day. Hassall advised him to try Frank Pick, the Publicity Manager of the London Underground Electric Railways.[7] Pick had been obliged, like every other publicity man, to cut back his programme because of war shortages of paper – but he gave Kauffer a commission. Kauffer's first posters appeared for the London Underground Railways in 1915. Over the next 25 years the company became his major client and he their major poster artist. The company gave Kauffer an audience of millions – in return he gave the company a succession of designs of sparkling originality and widespread influence. This important partnership owed much to Frank Pick – but also to the tradition of which Pick was a part. Tracing this is essential to the understanding not only of this one client but of the climate of opinion in which Kauffer worked in England.

Frank Pick and Advertising

Frank Pick (1878–1941) came from non-conformist Lincolnshire stock and trained as a solicitor before joining the London and North Eastern Railways.[8] He rapidly became the golden boy of the company and when his chief, Sir George Gibb, became head of the Underground Electric Railways Co of London, Gibb shrewdly brought his assistant with him. They began work in 1906 and two years later Pick was put in charge of publicity. This was a department in which railway companies in general had a bad name. Speaking at a meeting on poster advertising in 1893 one commentator accused the London railway companies of spoiling the newly laid-out Embankment Gardens between Charing Cross and Temple stations beside the Thames. The new vistas were closed by ugly painted boards which were useless as advertisements because 'no one sees them unless he sees the station, and those who go in quest of it certainly do not need this dirty kaleidoscope to embitter their approach'.[9]

More graphically, Rudyard Kipling likened the hoardings lining the London and South Western Railway to 'an Army and Navy Stores list in a nightmare'.[10] The speaker at the meeting in 1893 was Richardson Evans (1846–1928), one of the unsung heroes of advertising history, and the meeting resulted in the formation of SCAPA – the Society for Checking the Abuses of Public Advertising. This exemplary organization came into being

to discipline the *laissez faire* outgrowth of advertising which occurred in all industrialized countries in the second half of the nineteenth century. In 1872 John Ruskin wrote from Florence:

the fresco-painting of the bill-sticker is likely, so far as I can see, to become the principal fine art of Modern Europe: here, at all events, it is now the principal source of street effect. Giotto's time is past, like Oderigi's; but the bill-poster succeeds …[11]

In England the photographer Frank Meadow Sutcliffe, who was internationally admired in the 1880s and '90s for his pastoral landscape work, also trained his camera on advertising:

We have sometimes photographed ugliness for a lark, and have made lantern slides of bill-posting hoardings … of painted advertisements in beauty spots of somebody's pills, or someone's pianos, and have talked by the hour to big congregations, pointing out how much easier life would be if all such abominations were done away with, but all to no purpose.[12]

SCAPA, however, was very purposeful and very effective. It is familiar that in the 1890s many artists worked in the poster medium and that, in the hands of a Cheret, a Mucha or a Lautrec, posters became a great new medium of expression. It is a much less well-known fact that in the same years artists, architects and designers of equal distinction were deeply involved in posters from a quite different point of view. William Morris, Alfred Waterhouse, C.R. Ashbee, William Holman Hunt, Sir John Millais, Lord Leighton, Sir Edward Poynter, Walter Crane, George Bodley, Halsey Ricardo and C.F.A. Voysey – the backbone of the Royal Academy and the spearhead of the Arts and Crafts movement – were all members of SCAPA. Morris's last public appearance was made in support of SCAPA.[13]

SCAPA's President, the architect Alfred Waterhouse RA, made two specific proposals for the improvement of advertising on London's Underground railways:

1. The spaces let for advertising to be clearly defined and to have some harmonious relation to the general [architectural] scheme.
2. The display on the main walls and the platform and fences to be confined to the more artistic forms of poster: and provision to be made for their frequent change.[14]

The London and North Eastern Railway had been more sensitive to SCAPA's proposals than any other line – even completely banning advertising in some country stations – and when Frank Pick took charge of publicity at the London Underground Electric Railways he did something quite simple. He put the Waterhouse proposals into effect. He disciplined the actual arrangement of the poster advertising within and without his stations, restricting them to partitioned areas, and, although he was not in a position to control the quality of advertising issued by other companies, he set about creating a standard for his own.

Frank Pick's example provided a pattern which other businesses followed, and this made possible Kauffer's brilliantly successful work in British advertising over the 25 years from 1915 to 1940.

Kauffer's first posters

Looking back at Pick's work much later, Kauffer discounted the philanthropic intention – he argued that Pick was creating goodwill for the company by respecting the public and that he was 'selling traffic'.[15] Kauffer's first posters are essentially gouache or poster paint landscapes, indicating open spaces relatively distant from central London but served either by the company's trains or buses. *In Watford*, *Oxhey Woods*, *Reigate: Route 160* and *North Downs* (the last two dated 1915 but issued in 1916) offer a fascinating view of Kauffer's stylistic impressionableness at the outset of his poster career. The boldly painted outlines of *Oxhey Woods* can be attributed to Kauffer's continuing interest in van Gogh – black lines describing a yellow path, blue lines for the outlines of a brown tree. The van Gogh notes are augmented,

4. *In Watford*, 1915
poster, London Underground
E.4729-1915

5. *Oxhey Woods*, 1915
poster, London Underground
E.4728-1915

however, by touches from a milder tradition seen in the system of gentle, late Art Nouveau curves which runs through the scheme, and the child-like treatment of trees and toadstools. This almost recalls the children's books of Mabel Lucie Attwell, but these features and the lettering are probably due to contact with Maxwell Armfield, who painted two portraits of Kauffer in 1915, and suggest influence from the Birmingham Group.[16] *In Watford* is a purer manifestation of van Gogh in design, drawing conventions and a colour treatment, notably in the blue trees, which is well on the way to becoming Fauve. The wooden foot-bridge over the lake at Watford strongly recalls similar constructions in Japanese pleasure gardens and suggests that Kauffer had returned to one of van Gogh's sources of inspiration – Japanese colour woodcuts. This supposition is borne out by a change in Kauffer's style of signature. *In Watford* and *Oxhey Woods* are signed in a way which loosely recalls Ludwig Hohlwein's style of signature. The 'E. McKnight' is on one line, 'Kauffer' below it on a second line, the two joined by a diagonal flourish. In *Reigate: Route 160*, in which the tree trunks are pure scarlet, and fields yellow and red, Kauffer has arrived at poster-Fauvism – but now the signature is an orientalizing 'E.K.' enclosed in a box, much in the manner of a Japanese woodcut master's monogram. Kauffer recognized Japanese prints as the inspiration of Toulouse-Lautrec's innovations in poster design – 'his admiration for the Japanese print amounted almost to worship'.[17]

This classic source reappears, breathtakingly transformed, in at least two of Kauffer's finest designs, although in both cases the original models are masked by Kauffer's interest in a new and local style – English Vorticism. Nothing could be further from the 'Earthly Paradise' idylls of the Birmingham Group which seem to touch Kauffer's *Oxhey Woods* than Vorticism. The temper of Vorticism could be summarized as urban, abstract and short – defining itself at the premises of the Rebel Art Centre, in two issues of the magazine *Blast*, in polemics by Wyndham Lewis and Ezra Pound – whose Imagist aesthetics are the closely related by-product in poetry – and at a controversial group exhibition held at the Doré Gallery in London in 1915. In the catalogue

introduction Wyndham Lewis wrote of Vorticism as an antidote to 'an immense commercialised mass of painting and every other form of art … a load of sugary, cheap, anecdotal and in every way pitiable muck poured out by the ton'.

It seems likely that Kauffer saw this exhibition and even more certain that he read Lewis's remarks on how Vorticism would impinge directly on the public:

Let us give a direct example of how this revolution will work in popular ways. In poster advertisement by far the most important point is a telling design. Were the walls of London carpeted with abstractions rather than the present mass of work that falls between two stools, the design usually weakened to explain some point, the effect architecturally would be much better, and the Public taste could thus be educated in a popular way to appreciate the essentials of design better than picture galleries have ever done.

The history of the mutual interaction of advertising design and modern art has yet to be written, but behind Lewis's remarks we can range Marinetti's celebration of posters in a Futurist manifesto in Italy, and an apposite comment by Apollinaire on the painter Fernand Léger in Paris. Much as Vorticism denounced Futurism as mere 'impressionism of speed' the movement was fuelled by Futurist aesthetics. In *War, the World's Only Hygiene* (1911–15) Marinetti urged poets and painters to celebrate 'Multicoloured billboards on the green of the fields, iron bridges that chain the hills together, surgical trains that pierce the blue belly of the mountains, enormous turbine pipes, new muscles of the earth'.[18] In a lecture attended by Apollinaire in 1914, Léger defined a new urban realism in painting. 'Himself a peasant', Apollinaire reflected, 'he knew that peasants who are not shocked to see a poster in their fields have not succumbed to bad taste but have simply learned to savour a necessary reality'.[19] Curiously enough Wyndham Lewis's words seem to be a direct prediction of Kauffer's first major work, *Flight*, which was designed in 1916. This image is also the finest invention of his entire career, became his talisman in the later years of disillusion, and may even provide the key to understanding his personality.

Flight, 1916

Kauffer and his wife stayed in the little village of Blewbury, near Didcot in Berkshire, in the summer of 1916. Blewbury remains as picturesque as its name and has long been an artists' colony. As well as thatched cottages there is a group of wooden summer studios. The Kauffers took the Policeman's Cottage and neighbours during their stay included Alvin Langdon Coburn, the American photographer, Kenneth Grahame and his wife – the setting seems ideal for the author of *The Wind in the Willows* – and Miss S.B. Webster, who (as Susan Beatrice Pearse) illustrated the 'Ameliaranne' books. She wrote of Kauffer over 50 years later:

I knew him fairly well at that time and admired his intense devotion to Art – he saw beauty in everything and his aim was to get to the core of that beauty to share with others. He would follow the flight of birds until he had got the rhythm and harmony of motion which he would interpret in his own way. No detail escaped him. He had a child-like wonder and admiration for nature.[20]

Kauffer's only statement about *Flight* was made in 1950:

The design *Flight* was not invented in a studio. It came after much observation of birds in flight. The problem seemed to me at any rate a translation into design terms of three factors, namely, bird identification, movement, and formalization into pattern and line. Birds in flight and aeroplane formations are singularly alike. The arrowhead thrust is the dominant motif. But wings have a contrary movement – so this too has to be considered …[21]

The design is also Kauffer's homage to Vorticism. Woodcuts were a primary vehicle for several Vorticist artists, notably Edward

Wadsworth and David Bomberg, and were familiar from the pages of *Blast*. A woodcut by Kauffer of *Flight* may be the earliest surviving stage in its design.[22] Another early version was published in an interesting context in January 1917. It appeared in the magazine *Colour* which reserved a page in each monthly issue as a 'Poster Gallery'. Artists were invited to submit designs for free publication on this page and advertisers were invited to buy them for publicity use. The wings in the woodcut are serrated – these are straight in the colour version, which also divides the light and dark areas less geometrically. A third version was adapted for the poster and is dated 1918. The version shown in *Colour* had the disadvantage of making the group of birds into a solid mass which tends to 'drop' through the space below. In the 1918 version the pattern of birds is linked to the borders of the poster. This small alteration emphasizes flat, surface quality and stresses the idea of rapid onward transition.

6. *Flight*, 1917
woodcut
The British Museum

7. *Flight*, 1917
Colour, January 1917

The subject matter was new to Vorticism but not to Futurism. Giacomo Balla painted a series of pictures based on his observation of the flight of swifts in Rome in the late summer and autumn of 1913, and an example from the series was published in Boccioni's *Pittura e Scultura Futurista* in 1914. A comparison of Balla's interpretation with Kauffer's shows the essential difference in aims between Futurism and Vorticism as clearly as it shows the underlying similarities. Balla's work could be regarded as 'impressionism of speed', rendered in large wave-like rhythms. His observations were reinforced by study of E. J. Marey's photographic analysis of bird flight. Kauffer's observations were reinforced from a very different source. Once again he used a Japanese model. It seems likely that a flight of small birds, printed predominantly in green, yellow and grey in an illustrated sketchbook of birds, flowers, insects and fishes published in Japan in 1820, was his model. Kauffer used black and khaki but retained the optimistic flavour of his model by using bright yellow as the ground.[23]

Extraordinarily enough, this revolutionary design actually was used in a poster campaign. Kauffer later said that it was sold – presumably after being seen in *Colour* magazine – to an advertising agent and that he was paid 50 dollars.[24] It seems likely that the agent was T. B. Lawrence, who later commissioned designs from Kauffer. However, it was re-sold to Francis Meynell.

Meynell, later Sir Francis, organized a brilliant poster campaign for the Labour newspaper the *Daily Herald* when it was launched on 31 March 1919.[25] The paper's editor, George Lansbury, promised in the first issue to 'voice the aspirations of Labour. We shall work unceasingly for a revolution, peaceful but complete, which shall destroy the present system of competition and force and replace it by the rule of cooperation'. Meynell recognized Kauffer's image, which he captioned 'Soaring to Success, the Early Bird', as 'a flight of birds that might almost be a flight of aeroplanes; a symbol, in those days of hope, of the unity of useful invention and natural things'.[26] A similar metaphor appears in the pages of László Moholy-Nagy's book *Malerie, Fotografie, Film* published in the optimistic days of the Bauhaus in the mid-1920s: on one page he illustrated a flock of cranes in flight, 'A fine organization of light and shade in itself', and opposite it he showed a flight of seaplanes over the Arctic – 'Repetition as a space-time motif'.

Kauffer's design exactly expressed the aspirations of the radical newspaper and the more general hopes of the post-war period of 'Reconstruction'. A strikingly similar image occurs in a famous poem by Siegfried Sassoon, first literary editor of the *Daily Herald*. The poem, 'Everyone Sang', was written when Sassoon heard that the Armistice had been signed:

Everyone suddenly burst out singing;
And I was filled with such delight
As prisoned birds must find in freedom
Winging wildly across the white
Orchards and dark green fields; on; on; and out of sight.

Everyone's voice was suddenly lifted,
And beauty came like the setting sun.
My heart was shaken with tears and horror
Drifted away … O but every one
Was a bird; and the song was wordless;
the singing will never be done.[27]

8. *Flock of birds*, 1820
Satō Suiseki
Copyright © British Museum

9. *Soaring to Success! Daily Herald – the Early Bird*, 1919
poster, *Daily Herald*
E.35-1973

Sassoon later added, in *Siegfried's Journey: 1916–20*, that 'the singing that would never be done was the Social Revolution which I believed to be at hand'. Kauffer's friend Colin Hurry wrote of him in 1921 that 'He belongs to no political party, unless a fierce pity for the underdog makes him a Socialist. He wants to see equality of opportunity established for everyone else, though he has never asked it for himself.'[28]

As a model of poster design *Flight* even came to the attention of Winston Churchill, who sent for Kauffer with a view to commissioning an emblem for the Royal Flying Corps, later the Royal Air Force. Apparently Churchill's enthusiasm waned on discovering that the artist was an American citizen, and when Kauffer declined to adopt British citizenship at his request the matter was dropped.[29] Many years later, however, one of Kauffer's British disciples, Theyre Lee-Elliott, provided a flying bird symbol for Imperial Airways. Lee-Elliott's symbol (1934) continued in use with British Overseas Airways Corporation and a variant design of it graced the British Airways/Air France Concorde. *Flight* may seem ahead of its time but it fulfils very accurately the idea of the perfect poster as expressed by James Joyce's Leopold Bloom. Towards the close of *Ulysses*, first published in 1922, the advertising salesman Bloom meditates (nocturnally):

upon some one sole unique advertisement to cause passers to stop in wonder, a poster novelty, with all extraneous accretions excluded, reduced to its simplest and most efficient terms not exceeding the span of casual vision and congruous with the velocity of modern life.[30]

Designs and paintings 1916–21

Kauffer later wrote that 'when I began advertising design in England in 1916, the outstanding work then was of the Munich realistic school, more pictorial than poster. My enthusiasm, to counteract that influence, was at first by violent methods, but such designs as I did were confined to exhibition posters for the then modern group of painters known as the London Group, of which I was secretary.'[31] During the five-year period 1916–21 Kauffer was an increasingly exhibited painter who seemed to be at home with all of the different, and sometimes warring, elements of the British avant-garde, but he was also an increasingly successful designer. His remarks above are a little misleading. The *Flight* design was not immediately followed by consistent Vorticist experimentation in poster design. Instead Kauffer actually adopted the style of Munich school realism. Further contributions to the Poster Gallery page in *Colour* can be exactly paralleled in Hohlwein. In the issue of February 1917, for example, Kauffer offered a favourite Hohlwein idea – a servant in period costume offering a box which might contain expensive chocolates or cigars. A month later Kauffer contributed a design of a boy on a donkey. This again was clearly derived from

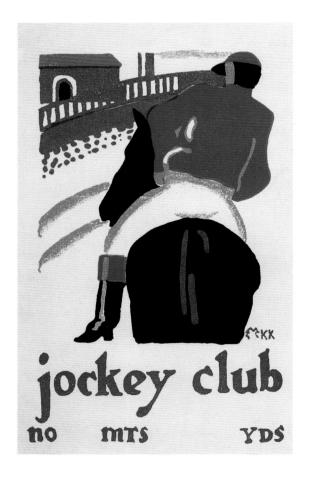

Hohlwein – but this time the poster was bought and duly appeared for the Kensington department store Derry and Toms as *Economy and Smartness in Men's Wear.*

A more interesting commission for which Kauffer produced designs throughout this period was initiated by the Manchester textile company Steinthal & Co. A.P. Simon, head of the firm, was an early buyer of Vorticist paintings and subsequently active in the Design and Industries Association. His partner William Zimmern – a cousin of the Kauffers' friend Maria Zimmern Petrie – commissioned Kauffer in 1916 to design a set of bale labels for use on cotton goods exported by Steinthals to South America. These were colour lithographs which were intended to make identification of the bales easy at a glance. Kauffer's designs were at the outset in his typical early style, but he proved that even ephemeral trade labels could be treated resourcefully and memorably. The series eventually closed, at a total of 36, in 1928.[32] Further landscape posters were commissioned by Pick in 1916, plus a set of season-ticket advertisements for which Kauffer made a series of humorous line drawings. Already he was moving away from the traditional area of the 'art poster' into what is more properly graphic design.

Until 1921 Kauffer regarded himself as a painter. Early British painter friends included the post-Impressionists Robert Bevan and his wife Stanislawa de Karlowska, whose Sunday 'At Homes' in Hampstead the Kauffers frequented. Through the Bevans Kauffer came to know other painters of similar temperament and talent, including Charles Ginner and Harold Gilman. They were all members of the London Group, which had replaced the New English Art Club as the effective meeting-point for new painting and sculpture. Kauffer exhibited with the London Group from June 1916 – when Epstein's *Rock Drill* (which fused a robot-like man, complete with an actual pneumatic drill, with motifs suggestive of a vulture's hooked head) was the principal new work shown. A month earlier Kauffer had his first one-man exhibition in England. This was held at Hampshire House in Hammersmith. The pictorialist photographer M.O. Dell was Secretary and the introduction to Kauffer's catalogue was written by the American Alvin Langdon Coburn, who was the first and only Vorticist photographer. Coburn's distinguished early work included his book of portraits, *Men of Mark,* and he made a portrait of Grace Kauffer for a projected volume – which was

never published – of *Women of Note.* Coburn and Kauffer both made pictures from Coburn's studio looking over the Thames beside Hammersmith Bridge.[33] Kauffer's exhibition included still-life paintings and landscapes from Normandy, Kent, Brighton, Berkshire and London. He also exhibited six of his Underground poster designs. Coburn described the work as 'realistic without ever becoming commonplace, brilliant in colour but never harsh' and valued the paintings for their 'cheerfulness, their intense optimism'.[34]

In the autumn of 1916 Kauffer became a member of the London Group, and he and Grace took on the burden of its administration in the following spring when he became Secretary. He also joined the 'Cumberland Market Group' which included Paul Nash, a talented painter who worked – like Kauffer – in a number of design fields in the next two decades.

10. *Jockey Club,* 1924
cotton bale label for Steinthal & Co
AAD 10/479-1979

11. *Grace Kauffer, c.*1916
photograph by Alvin Langdon Coburn
Simon Rendall collection

12. *Exhibition of Modern Art*, 1919
poster, London Group
E.899-2004

As Secretary of the London Group Kauffer designed exhibition posters, invitations and abstract symbols for catalogue covers. These reflect Vorticist style and take Kauffer beyond his dependence on the Munich school. He was still, however, principally a painter and in 1917 the most influential critic of the day, Roger Fry, provided the introduction to an exhibition Kauffer held at the Birmingham Repertory Theatre. Fry wrote:

He is one of the younger artists working in this country, whose aims may be taken as characteristic of the present phase of the new movement. His earlier work followed closely on the general lines of Cézanne's methods – more recently the influence of Cubism has been apparent, but has scarcely amounted to more than an increasing definition and delimitation of planes, and a slightly more abstract planning of the design. He has not allowed it to interfere with his direct sensibility to the forms and colours of natural objects. He seems to me to be exploring the possibilities in this direction with a view to discovering his own personal equation – the just balance between his acute and delicate sensibility, and his desire for logical precision and completeness of statement.[35]

Fry's support for Kauffer was generous. He kept a portfolio of Kauffer's drawings on sale at his Omega Workshops – a venture which encouraged painters to decorate furniture, pottery, toys and clothes and design mural schemes and carpets – and he included Kauffer's Birmingham exhibition in a larger show he organized at Heal's Gallery in the autumn of 1917, *New Movements in Art*. Fry was incorrect about the Cézanne influence, which only occurred in 1917 after Kauffer's van Gogh period. However, Fry's summing up is a good general description and apt in regard to what was perhaps Kauffer's major painting – a large oil, *Sunflowers* (1917). That Kauffer set special store by this painting is suggested by the price he put on it in the London Group catalogue for the autumn exhibition in 1917: £50 instead of his usual £20 or less (although it is larger than any other surviving painting). He also made a woodcut version of the composition.

13. *Sunflowers*, 1917
oil painting, 90 x 71cm
Government Art Collection

The Kauffers joined Maria Zimmern Petrie in a house she had taken at Edinburgh in 1918. A long letter from Fry shows the kind of painter Kauffer hoped to be:

My dear Kauffer
I was glad to get yr. letter and very much interested in yr. reflections on art. The whole question of groups and competition is very difficult. Art generally seems to flourish only when there are enough people interested in the same kind of thing to create a kind of spiritual high tension: the inspiration seems to come in waves and flourish in groups and yet perhaps the greatest work is done by the solitaries who withdraw like Cézanne when once they have caught the general idea and who work it out in independence. Anyhow the kind of competition of most of our groups, competition in the sense to épater, is worse than useless, and I daresay you will get there quicker for being away from it. Though frankly I shall miss yr. criticism and help. There are so few people in London who care at all seriously or intelligently that I looked on you as a great accession of strength to the little circle of enthusiasts that I am always dreaming [?] of keeping together in London. All the same I think it might really be more necessary for you than for most to work out yr. salvation alone. If I am right I expect you are one of those who will take a long time to discover yr. own artistic personality – I speak feelingly for I doubt if I am more than just beginning to do so at my horrible age. There are some personalities so tight and compact that they stick out at once and never change – often enough they are very small ones and incapable of growth and these do their best work at once, at 30 they have nothing more to discover and can only exploit. But there are others who have a great deal of taste and sensibility and intellect all of which tend to obscure the individual core but make it all the more richer when once the harmony of all these qualities comes to light and I suspect that you are one of that kind, which will mean a slow and laborious development with many doubts and misgivings. But I feel sure you have the character to face all that – it's as often as not lack of some sort of decent morale that ruins our artists here in London and makes them cynically accept a cheap success.[36]

Fry's assessment was borne out by Lord Clark, who remarked that 'Kauffer's personal distinction and integrity cannot be overrated'.[37] The stay in Edinburgh saved the Kauffers' funds – they were desperately poor – but soon they were on the way

back to London, as Kauffer was at last accepted as a volunteer in the American army. On the train from Edinburgh to London they heard the news that the First World War had ended.[38]

The Arts League of Service 1919

Very typical of the immediate period of post-war optimism was the foundation of the Arts League of Service in the spring of 1919. The ALS was founded after a big meeting at the studio of the dancer Margaret Morris: 'energies set free after four years of destruction were seeking a new, peaceable, and above all constructive outlet. The possibilities of the opening of new fields of work were enormous.'[39] The first initiative was a lecture series on 'Modern Tendencies in Art' – Wyndham Lewis on painting, T. S. Eliot on poetry, Eugene Goossens on music, Margaret Morris on dancing. Kauffer was from the first a member of the Artists' subcommittee and wrote on poster design in the opening issue of the *ALS Bulletin*:

Few people realise the importance of the hoardings. It is from them that the masses gather ideas for a great many things that directly influence them. Now that England, after a pause of a dozen years, is again interested in the poster, let this feeling be so genuine and broadcast as to make the hoardings amusingly interesting and vitally important.

Kauffer designed the ALS symbol and took part in an exhibition of *Practical Arts* held at the Twenty-one Gallery in the winter of 1919. He contributed designs for a poster and a cretonne (his first textile design), but more ambitiously a scheme for a 'Model Public House'. Edward Wadsworth sent in a Vorticist 'suggestion for a Building'. This provocative fortress of points and angles was illustrated, with Kauffer's pub, on the front page of the *Daily Mirror* on 18 November 1919. The Kauffer pub is a severe and centralized building, furnished with chairs reminiscent of C. R. Mackintosh, and decorated with murals. The nude figures in these derive from the typical Omega Workshops productions of Roger Fry, Duncan Grant and Vanessa Bell.

A travelling repertory theatre was one of the best-known ALS programmes during the early 1920s and Kauffer regularly provided posters and also sets and costumes. The ALS's call for artists to exercise their gifts 'for the things of everyday life' was

14. *Flowers o'the Corn*, 1920
original design for poster, London Underground, gouache
Circ.363-1925

also taken up by the 'Friday Club' which arranged an applied art display including Bernard Leach pottery, painted tiles by Macdonald Gill, silk designs by Mackintosh, label and poster designs by Albert Rutherston, textile designs by Paul Nash and – by this time inevitably – a group of posters by Kauffer.[40] Kauffer's leadership in the field was established by the *Daily Herald*'s use of *Flight*. Post-war possibilities encouraged Derry and Toms to take a more adventurous Kauffer design than the earlier ones – a *Winter Sales* poster in 1919 which is the first on a theme which drew the best from Kauffer in a subsequent series for the Underground. Vorticism surfaced again in a poster

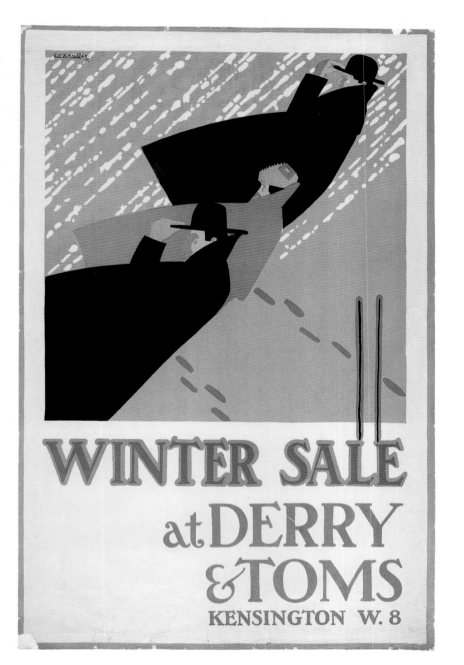

15. *Winter Sale at Derry & Toms*, 1919
poster, Derry & Toms
E.419-1920

for Vigil Silk in the same year – Kauffer's design successfully adapts the style to the patterns of plain stripes typical of the firm's productions. Other Vorticist-derived symbols by Kauffer were used for the important quarterly *Art and Letters* and on the poster of the last London Group exhibition in which he showed in spring 1919 – at least, until a retrospective of the group was held in 1928.

16. *Vigil the Pure Silk*, 1919
original design for poster, Walker Brothers, gouache
E.3222-1980

X Group 1920

Kauffer contacted former Vorticists such as Wyndham Lewis in July 1919, presumably hoping to take up the promise made in the 1915 issue of *Blast*: 'We shall not stop talking about culture when the war is over.' Lewis himself was keen to do some more 'Blasting': 'The present London Group is a bad working collection of individuals and will not improve.'[41] What Kauffer had in mind is clear from a letter Lewis wrote to the New York collector John Quinn: as well as exhibiting together, the group were to take 'a shop or office, where it is proposed to sell objects made by them, paintings and drawings, to a certain extent, and especially to have a business address from which the poster, cinematograph and other industries can be approached'. The business touch is surely Kauffer's, an attempt to advance the synthesis achieved in *Flight* – uniting experimental painting and experimental design.

With Lewis's energy pushing it along a group was formed, a gallery found, the name X Group adopted. The members – of whom there were 10 (a possible explanation for the X) – resigned *en bloc* from the London Group and a minor sensation occurred in spring 1920. Each artist contributed a woodcut self-portrait to the catalogue and these were all reproduced in the *Graphic* for 17 April. 'X' was hardly a unifying symbol and Lewis's evasive introduction to the catalogue did not suggest any real future for the group. The exhibition itself was the last flourish of Vorticism. Lewis's interest in the project seems mainly to have been the opportunity to affront Roger Fry, then influential in the London Group. The resignations were one thing, getting X Group's show into the Mansard Gallery ahead of the London Group was another minor triumph for Lewis. Kauffer's friend Colin Hurry lamely identified, in an article of 1921, the mysterious 'X' as 'the unknown which all artists should be seeking'. Kauffer's client at Vigil Silk, Alec Walker, took the show to Yorkshire and there the matter ended.

For Kauffer himself the exercise revived the memory of his brilliant earlier fusion of Vorticism and Japanese colour woodcuts. Among his finest designs is the Underground poster *Winter Sales* of 1921 (*right*). Roger Fry later wrote of this particular design when he described 'the alacrity and intelligence people can show in front of a poster which if it had been a picture in a gallery would have been roundly declared unintelligible. The judicious

17. *Winter Sales are best reached by Underground*, 1921
poster, London Underground
E.48-1922

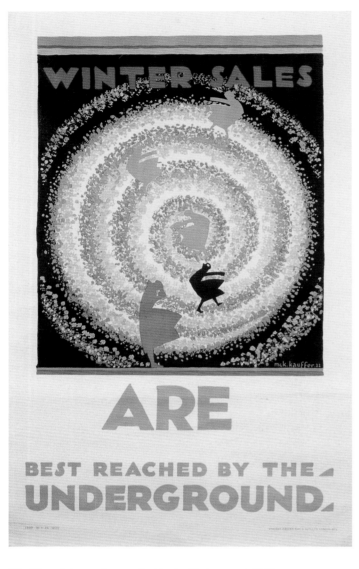

18. *Winter Sales are best reached by the Underground,* 1922
poster, London Underground
E.629-1923

frame of mind evidently slows the wits very perceptibly.' Fry wrote of Kauffer's design – a highly abstracted scene of elegant figures in a rainy London street – as a 'fascinating silhouette of dark forms to begin with, and out of these forms gradually disengage themselves hints of the flutter of mackintoshes blown by a gusty wind, of the straining forms pushing diagonally against the driving rain. In fact, all the familiar shapes of such a scene are taken as the bricks to build up a most intriguing pattern. But they demand a rather quick-witted recognition of slight indications for the design to become intelligible.'

The flat diagonal stripes which represent rain are taken direct from Japanese colour print conventions but so too is a great deal of the composition. A remarkably similar group of figures caught in a squall of rain, their umbrellas forming abstract patterns, was published by Utamaro in *Yehon Shikino Hana* in 1801. It seems likely that Kauffer once more fused Vorticism and a Japanese source. Writing of Toulouse-Lautrec's similar use of this source, Kauffer said that Lautrec 'did not, however, imitate. He emulated its simplicity, finding Western types in the Music Halls and Cafés, that, eccentric as they were, could be adapted to the Japanese atmosphere of his compositions.'[42] So Kauffer's design is, in fact, a three-way synthesis: Utamaro, Lautrec, Lewis. As such it is, paradoxically, pure Kauffer. Further remarkable *Winter Sales* posters followed in 1922 and 1924.

While X Group collapsed Kauffer found greater success as a poster designer. Pick followed up his earlier commissions by publishing 13 landscape posters in 1920, with more to follow in 1921. Kauffer's career as a painter finished in 1920 with his resignation from the London Group, the failure of X Group – and, perhaps, with the birth of his daughter Ann in October. Kauffer now found a hypocrisy in maintaining distinctions between 'pure' and commissioned work.[43] After the attempt to unite them in X Group had failed, Kauffer abandoned easel painting. There was one technical exception. In 1921 Kauffer provided a set of oil paintings illustrating oil refining processes and the originals were displayed on hoardings outside the Shell company headquarters in London while a new building was being constructed at 'Shell Corner' (Kingsway and Aldwych). Thereafter, as Lewis later put it, Kauffer 'disappeared as it were belowground, and the tunnels of the "Tube" became thenceforth his subterranean picture galleries'.[44]

19. *Winter Sales are best reached by Underground,* 1924
poster, London Underground
E.58-1926

3

THE EARLY
TWENTIES

In 1921 Kauffer was sufficiently in funds to attempt to establish himself as a designer in New York. On a visit to London in 1920 Robert Allerton Parker, director of the Arts and Decoration Gallery in New York, had sought out Kauffer. An exhibition of 100 works was subsequently arranged and shown at Parker's gallery at 48–50 West 47th Street from 17–30 October 1921. Leaving his wife and daughter in London, Kauffer went over for the show and stayed for several months trying to find commissions. Parker also contributed to *Arts and Decoration* magazine and he wrote up Kauffer in the November 1920 issue, drawing attention to something that was already of importance for Kauffer: 'He claims that personal contact with the men requiring advertising art in the exploitation of their products is an absolute necessity in obtaining good results.' The article was titled 'E. McKnight Kauffer: A Commercial Artist with Ideals'. Kauffer contributed an article to the same issue that reviewed his exhibition in November 1921. He moved straight on to the attack, his targets being know-nothing designers and complacent publicity men. He charged that ordinary designers presume to be specialists without ever having investigated the properties of their medium: 'Non-representative and geometrical pattern designs can in effect strike a sledge hammer blow if handled by a sensitive designer possessing a knowledge of the action of colour on the average man or woman. Knowledge of a similar nature is involved in the uses made of masses and line movements.'

This quasi-scientific point of view occurs on a number of occasions in Kauffer's writings in the early 1920s. There are good reasons for thinking that he was close at this period to the British Vorticist Edward Wadsworth. The source of Kauffer's analytical interest in colour and form may well derive from Wadsworth's

20. *E. McKnight Kauffer*, 1925
Vogue, May 1925
NAL PP1

translations, published in *Blast*, from Kandinsky's book *On the Spiritual in Art* – a title which would at once have aroused Kauffer's interest. It is also likely that Kauffer was well aware of the gift for formal analysis of his friend Roger Fry, whose approach was most widely disseminated in *Vision and Design* published in 1920. 'The Poster', Kauffer insisted in his article, 'has an interpretive vision, and is not imitative slavery … an intense realism may be more real than a photograph because of its power of suggestion.' And 'Posters are telegrams'. The last remark can be compared with A. M. Cassandre's formulation that a poster is a 'machine à annoncer'.[1]

Kauffer was struck by a contradiction between the pace of life in New York City, with its dynamic neon lighting, and the static prettiness of its posters. The business of advertising was to match actual urban pace, so that a poster could become an incident on the street as real as seeing a fire-engine at speed:

The fascination the public has for the race of fire apparatus is mainly colour and movement – the romance of fire is further back of the head. The swift flash of red, the glitter of the engine, the slender arrow of a hook and ladder, make the public feel differently for a few moments, long enough to have fixed a definite impression upon the mind.

Kauffer showed exactly what he meant in a poster designed directly he returned to England (see below). His exhibition received a friendly notice in the *New York Times* for 16 October 1921 and Kauffer was given a hero's welcome when he visited Evansville to see his parents the following February. A banquet in his honour was held in the Pompeiian Room of the Hotel McCurdy. A local paper records the occasion with some pride, detailing table decorations in pink, a basket of Columbia roses as a centrepiece and smaller baskets of winter lilacs and calendula at each end of the table. This was not all: 'Pink candles in crystal holders illuminated the table. The place cards were miniature palettes with brush and the favors were Columbia roses.' Kauffer's doings were regularly reported to readers of the *Evansville Courier* and *Evansville Journal*.[2] An exhibition was arranged in the studio of a professional photographer in the town, Neal Walden, and Walden's photograph of Kauffer taken on this visit is one of the earliest surviving photographs of him.

A press-cutting also records that Kauffer befriended a young painter called 'Birchfield', described as working in a factory in the Mid-West, and that Kauffer attempted to promote the artist on his return to London. This may well have been Charles Burchfield, who exhibited successfully at the Grosvenor Gallery in London in 1923 and became one of America's better-known painters in the 1930s. Either way, the story is typical of Kauffer's generosity towards other artists, which many of his friends stressed. Kauffer's visit to the United States was not, however, a success. Already in England his position was supported by a few innovators in publicity – but in the United States his work fell on less well-prepared ground. He did a small commission for the Manhattan Electrical Supply Co – a pack for radio headsets. And he did find one important client – Theatre Guild in New York. He designed large-scale posters for Theatre Guild's 1922 productions of Bernard Shaw's *Back to Methuselah* and Leonid Andreyev's *He Who Gets Slapped*. These must have been very large as they were described as too big to be shown in Kauffer's next major exhibition of posters, held in 1925. Their size may account for the fact that no surviving copies of them are known. The *Evansville Courier* described them as 'mammoth', which was probably correct (even though the possibility of confusion arises as the poster for *Back to Methuselah* is dominated by a mammoth!). Kauffer may have got the commission, a valuable one, too late in his stay to affect the outcome of his visit. He later said that, despite his favourable press, he 'did not go down' and 'experienced a great rebuff'.[3] He returned to London in the spring of 1922.

Kauffer in London: Early 1920s

Practically unknown in New York, Kauffer was by contrast almost a national figure in England by the early 1920s. His place in English cultural life is made beautifully clear in a passage from Evelyn Waugh's novel *Brideshead Revisited*. Waugh wrote the novel during the Second World War and confessed that war-time conditions had given him a craving for exotic luxuries. His description, therefore, of the rooms at Oxford decorated by the protagonist of the novel, Charles Ryder, on going up in the early 1920s, is a somewhat jaded one. Nonetheless, Charles Ryder's enthusiasms are not to be discounted by Waugh's mordant account:

I should like to think – indeed I sometimes do think – that I decorated those rooms with Morris stuffs and Arundel prints and that my shelves were filled with seventeenth century folios and French novels of the second empire in Russia-leather and watered silk. But this was not the truth. On my first afternoon I proudly hung a reproduction of van Gogh's *Sunflowers* over the fire and set up a screen, painted by Roger Fry with a Provençal landscape, which I had bought inexpensively when the Omega Workshops were sold up. I displayed also a poster by McKnight Kauffer and Rhyme Sheets from the Poetry Bookshop, and, most painful to recall, a porcelain figure of Polly Peachum which stood between black tapers on the chimney-piece. My books were meagre and commonplace – Roger Fry's *Vision and Design*, the Medici Press edition of *A Shropshire Lad*, *Eminent Victorians*, some volumes of *Georgian Poetry*, *Sinister Street* and *South Wind* …[4]

Admirers of Kauffer will forgive this disparaging passage on the strength of the ironic precision with which Waugh locates early twenties aestheticism in the process of discarding it for 1890s aestheticism. When Waugh designed the frontispiece for his novel *Vile Bodies* (1930) his design was definitely School of McKnight Kauffer.[5] The passage is richer in information on Kauffer's standing than might at first meet the eye. As well as the poster, which Ryder/Waugh could have bought from the Underground for a shilling or two, the copy of *Eminent Victorians* probably had the jacket designed by Kauffer just before he left for America. Among the Rhyme Sheets might have been Sacheverell Sitwell's poem 'The Parrot' – with decorations by Kauffer. The Rhyme Sheets and the volumes of *Georgian Verse* were published by Kauffer's friend Harold Monro of the Poetry Bookshop, who often went to another friend of Kauffer's, Gerard Meynell of the Westminster Press, for his printing. Roger Fry's *Vision and Design* completes the scene. Kauffer was already well on the way to becoming the dominant design influence in England of the inter-war period.

Some clients: Gerard Meynell

Kauffer did not minimize the importance of his clients. Writing of poster advertising he acknowledged that designers were no more important than 'the purchaser … who, seeing eye to eye with the designer, puts his convictions to the test of the hoarding itself'. With a retrospective glance he added, 'the hoardings of England today show more of this adventuresome spirit than do those of America, where new advances are supposed to be as welcome as central heating in winter'. In Gerard Meynell he found a pugnacious ally, as Frank Pick had done earlier. Gerard Tuke Meynell (1872–1944) came into printing from banking, and was a distant cousin of Francis Meynell. Gerard Meynell's work at the Westminster Press from 1900–31 was exemplary of the transition from the standards of 1890s private press printing into the mainstream of commercial work.[6] It was also Gerard Meynell who had persuaded a reluctant Edward Johnston to accept Pick's commission for the Underground's new alphabet in 1913; Gerard Meynell again who had persuaded members of the Senefelder Club, an association of artist-lithographers, to design

Underground posters for Pick in 1913. The Kauffers had known Gerard Meynell since 1917 when they went on a painting expedition to Ditchling, beside the South Downs in Sussex. This is the date of one of Kauffer's finest early water-colours, *Oldlands Mill, Ditchling*, which he inscribed to Meynell. It was on the same visit that the Kauffers met the sculptor and type designer Eric Gill, whose Gill Sans type-face Kauffer put to good use in the 1930s. Grace Kauffer was quietly impressed when she visited Gill's studio and noticed the little shrine to the Virgin where the sculptor always kept a lighted taper – only to be quietly shocked, in turn, when she saw Gill imperturbably lean over to the shrine to revive his pipe.

Meynell recognized that printing skills, especially in colour lithography, were being persistently wasted through poor creative talent. His magazine *The Imprint* (1913), a model of typographical clarity and elegance, charged that 'We see around us high technical skill, but almost no culture or taste. The artistic possibilities of lithography are scarcely realized by the public or the trade.' For example, the banal pantomime posters designed for Bovril by H.H. Harris or Septimus Scott misdirected lavish technical craftsmanship of great potential. Pleasant enough as Bovril posters were, they were also an abuse of six- or eight-colour lithography. Kauffer's simplifications were both aesthetically and practically an advance. Meynell took Kauffer on at the Westminster Press, after the American trip, as Director of Pictorial and Poster Advertising. Kauffer's poster for the Press used simple stripes in purple, red and orange – a scheme possibly derived from Ballet Russe designs – which set off the trade-mark of the Press, contributed by Gill. The mark includes a harrow – a neat reference to the address of the firm's works in the Harrow Road and presumably an indication of Meynell's reforming intentions. Kauffer also designed bright and economical publicity cards for the sister-company Sun Engraving.

An *ABC of Wines* published in 1924 is typical of Kauffer's association with Meynell. This was a rhyming wine list for Francis Downman of Dean Street ('whose wines are even better than his rhymes') –

A is for ABSINTHE: let it alone.
B is for big-bodied, blood-making BEAUNE.
COCKTAILS are nice: but I honestly think
Whoever takes cocktails is taking to drink (etc., etc.) –

but it was also a type specimen list for the Press and each line showed off a different type-face. Other productions were posters for 'Pomeroy Skin Food' and an inventive series of press advertisements with Kauffer drawings for Shell. Francis Meynell was also designing witty press advertisements for Shell and others at his Pelican Press. The Underground quickly commissioned layouts from the Francis Meynell-Kauffer team. These bristled with new, newly imported or newly revived typefaces, set off by Kauffer's hand-drawn ornaments.

22. *Pomeroy Day Cream*, 1923
poster
E.637-1923

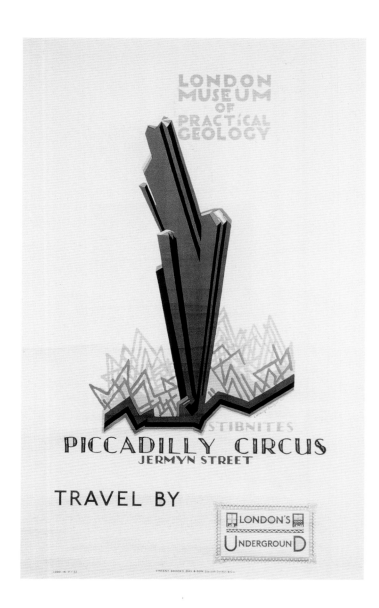

23. *London Museum of Practical Geology*, 1922
poster, London Underground
E.1088-1923

Posters for the Underground: The 'Museum' Set

On his return from New York Kauffer resumed work on a set of posters commissioned by Pick to advertise the principal museums in London. Some of these suggest a new range of influences that Kauffer began to channel into his work. A 1922 poster for the 'London Museum of Practical Geology' (now the Geology Museum), continues Kauffer's streamlined Vorticist style. To illustrate his poster for the London Museum (plate *right*) Kauffer chose the Great Fire of 1666. He may well have been turning this over in his mind when he wrote his article for *Arts and Decoration*, with its notes on colour and symbolic effect. Whether his ideas were influenced by Edward Wadsworth or not, his design for this poster seems to have been. The hint on which he based his poster may have been a few centimetres of curling flames in Wadsworth's woodcut *Black Country, Blast Furnace* (1918). The presumption is supported not only by a general similarity in the treatment of flames, but by the facts that – although usually printed only in black ink on white paper – Wadsworth also printed copies on orange paper (the predominant colour in Kauffer's poster), and finally that Kauffer himself owned a copy of the two-colour Wadsworth print. It is worth stressing such a derivation to give an idea of how Kauffer transformed slight hints into large-scale designs. This was also Kauffer's finale as a Vorticist.

A very different note is struck in his poster, dated 1923, for London's Science Museum. This illustrates 'Mr Stephenson and his Rocket' and was based on the museum's miniaturized push-button display of George Stephenson's prototype steam locomotive. A historicist general flavour to the design is compounded by a direct affinity with a precise historical source. Kauffer seems to have been looking at Georgian trade-cards. A scroll of curling engine smoke containing lettering might actually be a translation into twenties idiom of the elegant engraved cartouches common to trade cards of the eighteenth century. Kauffer also prepared an alternative design for the Science Museum poster which survives in the form of a gouache 'rough'. This continues his Vorticist ideas: but either he or Pick had had enough and the milder neo-Georgian scheme was the one printed.

24. *Museum of Natural History, South Kensington*, 1923
poster, London Underground
Circ.412-1971

MUSEUM OF
NATURAL
HISTORY
SOUTH KENSINGTON

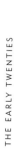

Eastman and Son Ltd

A series of posters commissioned by Cyril Eastman for his dry-cleaning firm was also characterized by a pastiche, period flavour, in which Kauffer drew on period costume design and open-faced Regency type designs and mixed them up with jazzy decorative borders. The series appeared on the walls of Underground stations from 1921 to 1927. Kauffer preserved all his life the gratifying sticker issued by Eastman's on an occasion when there was a production gap between two of his posters for their campaign. The sticker read: A NEW MCKNIGHT KAUFFER POSTER will be here shortly.[7] There is little hard information on Kauffer's commercial effectiveness in advertising, whatever his public acclaim. One poster for Eastman's was reported in a trade paper to have increased orders for glove-cleaning from 9000 to 15,000 pairs a week.[8]

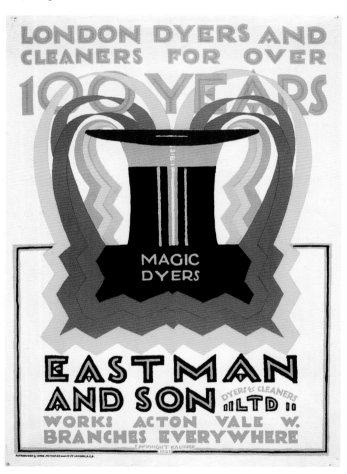

25. *London Dyers and Cleaners for over 100 Years,*
Eastman and Son: Magic Dyers, 1921
poster, Eastman and Son Ltd
E.624-1925

Some Responses to Kauffer's Work

A casual reference to the banality of posters issued by Pear's Soap, made in passing by a writer in the *London Mercury* in 1921, occasioned an angry and tautological reply:

Impossible ducks, futurist trees, vermilion grass, and such like absurdities may appeal to what, as I have no wish to be offensive, I will call the 'higher thought', but believe me, Sir, those people who live their lives in the ordinary, conventional way, as do the bulk of the general public, need nothing more subtle in a poster than a straightforward appeal to their sense of pleasure, duty, or whatever it may be. They don't understand, and have no wish to understand, the essentially unacademic.[9]

This riposte came from S. Bernard Smith, advertising manager of Pear's. The company's notorious *Bubbles* poster, the Millais painting doctored to include a bar of Pear's Soap, was still selling 10,000 copies a year. The Design and Industries Association arranged a meeting two years later to discuss quality in poster advertising.[10] Kauffer spoke and his statement follows the general lines of an article he published a year later as 'The Poster and Symbolism'. He described himself as designing for a fast-moving public and spoke of his use of symbols:

Daily new devices are invented which the designer can develop into a symbol. The aeroplane, for example, would, if we used signs as a means of communication, convey to us speed, travel, an engine of war and terror, as well as aspiration on the part of man to be as a bird.[11]

Bernard Smith replied at the meeting that the public was not interested in such things and even that 'there was an antipathy to new design and colour itself'. A report of the proceedings goes on: 'Mr Smith had only discovered that evening that Mr Kauffer's latest Eastman poster was not a lampshade, but a dress such as the wife of no member present would wear.' These humdrum sallies were followed up by the invention 'McKnightmare' in a trade journal. On the other hand, Kauffer was chosen to design nine of the posters for the different pavilions at the British Empire Exhibition at Wembley in 1924. He was unlucky not to have been given the commission to design the British lion which symbolized the event. This went to F. C. Herrick, whose

26. *First Thing Every Morning: Eno's Fruit Salt*, 1924
poster, J.C. Eno Ltd
E.338-1924

design is very close in stylization to that of one of Kauffer's most widely seen inventions. This was the crowing cock he designed for Eno's Fruit Salt ('The Effervescent Saline') in 1924. The company were pleased with the success of the poster, which was also used as a full-page colour advertisement, and sent Kauffer a cheque for £50 on top of his original fee.'[12] As a non-national Kauffer may have been thought an inappropriate choice for the British Empire symbol and he was not included in the British pavilion at the Paris Exhibition of decorative and industrial arts in 1925. As Britain's major graphic exponent of the style named from the exhibition, 'Art Deco', he was unlucky not to have been included. There was no American pavilion.

The official general report found the entry of British posters to be faulted by prolixity of detail and lack of clarity in presentation. The art critic of *The Times* patriotically stood up for British design and said that the British Section was simply not well chosen:

There is nothing in their respective kinds being better done anywhere on the Continent than the pottery of Mr W. Staite Murray and Mr Bernard Leach, the weaving of Mrs Mairet, the furniture of Mr Gordon Russell, and the posters of Mr E. McKnight Kauffer.[13]

This was good company for Kauffer to be in. French book illustration and theatre design, together with painting and poster design, became increasingly influential in his work in the mid-twenties. He also made a fateful visit to Paris in the summer of 1923. The Kauffers were about to leave for Paris when a quarrel broke out. Kauffer went on his own. In Paris he met Marion Dorn, a designer from California whom he had first encountered in New York in 1921. He returned to London with her and repeated the pattern of his own childhood by leaving his wife and young child. Kauffer and Marion Dorn lived together unmarried until 1950, when they were eventually married in City Hall, New York. Grace Kauffer brought up her daughter, Ann, with great hardship. She did not have the opportunity to continue her career as a concert pianist but over the years, as Grace McKnight, trained many young soloists.[14]

New Notes in Design: Jazz and Archaism

'What will become of those stern and grandly plastic glimpses of a novel universe, which first saw the light in the Western capitals immediately before the war, it is impossible to say', Wyndham Lewis wrote in 1937.[15] He recognized that, although 'one Kauffer does not make an Underground summer', Vorticism had had a general influence on design. By 1923 Kauffer had exhausted the immediate possibilities of the style and was adopting a new range of interests:

It seems at the moment that the designer must contemplate his 'modernism'. In itself it is an excellent accomplishment, and in the service of advertising psychologically of importance. It has, or should have, increased the scope of one's invention, so that the newer devices of mankind could be incorporated as symbols or motives for the designer's use. But like everything else, the 'new' spirit in design must grow to continue to be of use. Growth is more often a matter of going back to reconstruct from the past, which in itself stabilises the tentative suggestions coming from the designer. He is a link between old and new, and the results of his experiments can be analysed and found to be correct according to the traditional principles. In turning back the designer finds that the architecture of design has few 'ground plans', but many varieties of edifices have been and can be built upon these perhaps limited outlines. In the latter the designer displays his individuality, while in the former he can but use what is his by right of understanding.[16]

A second glance at Charles Ryder's Oxford rooms shows that Waugh had caught that retrospective note well too – in the Polly Peachum figure, the archaizing lyric poems of Housman, and the volumes of *Georgian Poetry* – one of which borrowed a puce colour for its cover from *Blast* but decorated its title-page with seventeenth-century printer's flowers. Kauffer himself noted that 'the tendency of press and periodical advertisement today is toward the sedate title page of years past, and because of this the designer should know the earlier forms, and should as well be familiar with the best type-founts'.[17] Forgotten type-faces were at that moment not only being revived in press layouts but more significantly being adapted for modern printing through Stanley Morison and the Monotype Corporation. Kauffer's typographer friends Francis Meynell and Gerard Meynell were also active in

this reclamation of traditional type designs.

Another immediate source for this mood in Kauffer's work was Harold Monro, poet, publisher of the Rhyme Sheets – based on traditional broadside ballad sheets and intended to find a new and wider audience for verse – and proprietor of the Poetry Bookshop. Kauffer contributed drawings to Monro's journal *The Chap-Book*, including a portrait of Monro and an illustration to T. S. Eliot's poem *Doris's Dream Songs*.[18] In 1926 Kauffer designed a painted sign-board for the Poetry Bookshop when it moved to new premises at 38 Great Russell Street, opposite the British Museum. Typically of Kauffer's mid-twenties style. The sign-board is a jazzy interpretation of traditional devices. Its dominant scarlet colouring would have been intended to pick up the red window surrounds and red interior of the shop. By this time, however, beige and cream were also part of Kauffer's range of colours and these began a further transition in his work which belongs to the next chapter.[19]

In 1924 Kauffer published his book *The Art of the Poster*, which he dedicated to Frank Pick. The title on the cover is set in Johnston Sans. Among friends Kauffer thanked for their help in making the book were Harold Monro and Gerard Meynell and the printers were Westminster Press. The book includes a historical note on posters by R. A. Stephens and theoretical notes by Phillips Russell. Kauffer provided passages of exemplary formal analysis of a number of the plates. The illustrations included the historical and ecumenical: Greek vase drawings, Byzantine mosaics, Chinese stone reliefs, medieval brass rubbings, Chinese and Japanese woodcuts, eighteenth-century trade cards, nineteenth-century broadsides, and historical and contemporary posters. Kauffer himself owned a number of posters illustrated in the book, including examples by Toulouse-Lautrec, Chéret, Beardsley, the Russians Stelletski and Soudekeine, and Picasso. Of these only the Picasso, a costume design of 1917 for *Parade*, which Kauffer captioned as having been used as a poster advertising the Russian Ballet 'when in England', seems to have a direct bearing on Kauffer's posters of this period. At the time he was active as a set and costume designer for the Arts League of Service Travelling Theatre.[20] Little evidence of his work for the ALS survives but the Picasso poster provides a clue to the major source of Kauffer's next important set of posters.

27. *The Poetry Bookshop*, 1926
painted sign
courtesy of Bertram Rota Ltd

28. *Whitsuntide in the Country*, 1925
poster, London Underground
E.1020-1925

In 1925 the Underground published three 'Whitsuntide' and 'Summertime' posters by Kauffer.[21] The trio resembled a triptych – a large central panel flanked by two smaller subjects. However, the large poster was shown in station vestibules and corridors, while the smaller ones flanked station entrances. The group together forms one of Kauffer's most splendid sets. The symmetry of the landscape of *Whitsuntide/Summertime in the Country* was said at the time to symbolize summer.[22] Kauffer might have seen symmetrical landscapes in Indian paintings when he designed a poster for the Indian Museum in 1924. A more obvious source, however, would be in theatre design. His poster suggests a proscenium arch and theatre backdrop.

One of the smaller posters represents Jack i' the Green, a fertility king from English folklore, who appears on May Day dressed in green leaves and persists as the 'somerkyng'. The crown he wears in Kauffer's poster is not dissimilar to the head-dress of the Chinese conjuror in Picasso's poster, and the sunburst behind it is suggestive of the sun which adorns another costume Picasso designed for *Parade*, this time for the Acrobat. Jack i' the Green's costume, on the other hand, derives – appropriately enough – from the 'folklorique' costumes of Bakst, Goncharova and Tchelitchew. These assimilate peasant motifs to a sophisticated geometric style. The third poster shows *Summertime* – a Pierrot playing a guitar among parked circus caravans. The background again suggests a theatrical *mise en scène* and the Pierrot is perhaps less a direct borrowing from Picasso's *Pulcinella* (1920) than the generalized figure of the Noel Coward lyric 'Parisian pierrot (what makes you so blue?)'. The Ballet Russe performed, during their 1924 London season, in a novel context – as part of a Variety programme at the Coliseum. This link between avant-garde and popular elements was furthered by Kauffer's posters, which gave a sparkling rendition of the style at street level.

29. *Summertime*
Pleasures by Underground
(Jack i' the Green), 1925
poster, London Underground
E.1020-1925

30. *Summertime*
Pleasures by Underground
(Pierrot), 1925
poster, London Underground
E.1021-1925

Work in the Theatre

Kauffer's early experience of travelling theatres was put to good use by the Arts League of Service, which regarded its travelling theatre as its most important activity. Kauffer designed a poster for the travelling theatre and sets and costumes for *The Man who Married a Dumb Wife* by Anatole France. The plays toured all over Britain in a converted Lancia van – venues included Borstal reformatories as well as theatres.[23] Kauffer also designed sets and costumes for productions of the Incorporated Stage Society – *The Rumour* by C. K. Munro at the Globe Theatre in 1922, *Progress* by C. K. Munro at the New Theatre in 1924, *The Colonnade* by Stark Young at the Aldwych Theatre in 1925. He seems to have had a little more success with a production by A. E. Filmer and Ernest Milton of Pirandello's *Henry IV* at the Everyman Theatre in Hampstead, for which he designed 'Stage Decorations' and Marion Dorn designed costumes. *Vogue* published a photograph of Ernest Milton as *Henry IV*, holding a length of silk printed by Marion Dorn with her own abstract design.[24] Such scarce records of Kauffer's early theatre work as survive suggest that the *Summertime* posters are a fair guide.

The Anatomy of Melancholy

At this period Kauffer was a close friend of Francis Meynell, from whom he rented a studio at 16 Great James Street in Bloomsbury. The office of Meynell's Nonesuch Press was next door and he recalled that Kauffer was 'a romantic theorist about art and there was more discussion between us than work. Admired as he was, his was not so lucrative a success as to make it easy for him always to pay his quarter's rent. No matter; for I had made a bargain with him that whenever he began a sentence with the words "The Artist" he was to pay me half-a-crown spot cash. This more than sufficed to clear the arrears.'[25] Kauffer was fond of quoting lavishly and often from Robert Burton's *The Anatomy of Melancholy*. Burton's remark that 'literature is high-born stealth' would, transposed to poster design, admirably describe Kauffer's adaptive-creative method. For Meynell, as he later wrote:

Kauffer was an example of the abandoned truth that art is indivisible: that the man with the root of the matter in him can paint or design rugs or make posters or illustrate books or decorate a room or parti-colour a motor-car or scheme an advertisement with the best of the over-specialists.[26]

Certainly in 1925 Kauffer designed an 'Art Deco' office for the advertising agent T. B. Lawrence,[27] turned to rug designing in 1929, had already 'schemed' press advertisements with Meynell, designed the jacket for Meynell's first edition of that typical twenties production *The Week-End Book* (Kauffer's motif picks up the title of Harold Monro's prefatory poem 'The Train') – and he did also parti-colour Meynell's car. Unfortunately no photograph was taken of this – but if, as seems likely, it was in Kauffer's 'jazz' style it must have been spectacular. Kauffer batiked a purple and puce silk evening dress for Esther Meynell in 1924.[28] Francis Meynell commissioned from Kauffer his first illustrated book – perhaps inevitably, Burton's *Anatomy*. Meynell recalled in 1955:

When last I saw him he told me that he still kept something like forty letters of mine, letters nagging, beseeching, criticizing and praising the drawings as they came singly or in batches, with long gaps, over many months, months during which his own art so changed that the early drawings and the late have little in common. What a pity that only the worthless end of our correspondence survives![29]

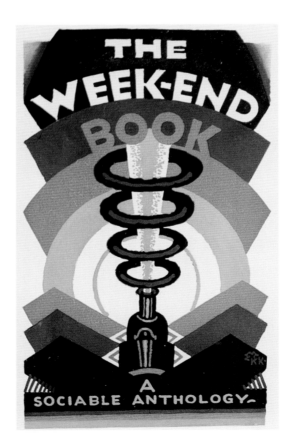

31. *The Weekend Book*, 1924
book jacket, Nonesuch Press
AAD 10/3-1979

The volumes of Burton suggest a close relationship between illustrator and typographer in the matching of text, image and format. The book is a good example of Kauffer's interest in erecting new edifices on 'old ground plans'. The title-page neatly updated Christof Le Blon's engraved title-page for the fifth edition published in 1638. The weight of the emphatically hatched line drawings is balanced by Meynell's choice of Plantin – robust as well as elegant – for the type-face. The weight and simplicity of stylization suggest an origin for Kauffer's style in Paris, possibly using hints from Derain, Georges Laboureur and perhaps distantly from the Neo-Classicism of Picasso. Roger Fry aptly defined the style as a 'cubistico-cabbalistic mixture'. (The mixture includes a dash of Surrealism.) Fry was alive to the qualities of the whole production:

The general effect of an ancient portfolio is preserved without any affected archaism, all is clear, lucid, well planned and admirably printed on very good paper. Mr Kauffer has clearly appreciated these qualities in his drawings. He has determined that in every way they should conform to the general effect of 'colour' of the printed page. This means that he has had to maintain a certain average density of tone in his drawings, nowhere allowing too heavy or too closely placed darks, and nowhere becoming so thin as to leave a 'hole' in the page.[30]

Fry also found Kauffer's illustrative commentary on Burton's allusive, rambling, pseudo-scientific prose entirely apt. Kauffer's playful use of Cubist devices combined 'pseudo-scientific witticism' and 'pseudo-archaistic pedantry'. Kauffer rarely designed a humorous poster: his 150 drawings for *The Anatomy of Melancholy* are the best graphic evidence for his genuine vein of whimsical wit. Fry exactly pinpointed Kauffer's spirit of 'affectionate raillery':

He must enjoy Burton's flavour to the full, but he is guilty of no ill manners if, after all these centuries, he now and then takes us, rather than the author, into his confidence; if he now and then whispers to us in a voice which the old man cannot overhear, 'Isn't he a delightful old buffer? Let's keep him at it!'

32–3 *The Anatomy of Melancholy* by Robert Burton
engraved title-page by Christian Le Blon, 1638
title page and illustration by E. McKnight Kauffer, Nonesuch Press, 1925

Retrospective Exhibition of Posters 1925

Almost comically, Burton closed his enormous and convoluted tome with a very plain final precept indeed: 'Be not solitary, be not idle.' It is clear that Kauffer's gifts included two that were important for his career: a gift for friendship and a gift for hard work. His crowded year, 1925, was crowned by a Retrospective Exhibition of his posters of the previous ten years. Fifty-six posters were shown at the exhibition, which was arranged by the Arts League of Service at 60 Gower Street, Bloomsbury, in May and June. In addition Kauffer showed original drawings, first drafts, colour schemes, a selection of calendars, show-cards, labels, book-jackets, drawings for newspaper advertisements, and ten stage-proofs showing the lithographic printing of his poster *Hadley Wood* by Vincent, Brooks, Day & Son. The ALS chose the occasion to announce the opening of a 'Poster Bureau', in collaboration with Kauffer. This was intended 'to secure the work of the younger artists for the advertising world by finding them an immediate outlet for their work'. A note in the catalogue of the exhibition states that Kauffer's larger posters could not be displayed because of lack of space – specifically, the *Back to Methuselah* and *He Who Gets Slapped* posters for the Theatre Guild, and the nine sectional posters for the British Empire Exhibition.

Roger Fry provided an introduction to the catalogue, reviewed the exhibition in *The Nation* on 23 May and, when the exhibition was afterwards shown at the Ashmolean Museum, Oxford, gave a lecture on *Commerce and Art*. The lecture was revised and subsequently published as a pamphlet by the Hogarth Press.[31] Fry spoke critically of the 'romantic' images built up through advertising by railway companies which 'give us progressively worse and worse accommodation', and induce the loyalty of a public they simply exploit. Was Kauffer's work, then, gilt on stale gingerbread? Clough Williams-Ellis, a critic no less astringent than Fry, wrote more favourably of at least one railway company in his 'Material Review' column in the *Spectator* in 1923:

When the old Metropolitan Railway exchanged steam and smoke for electricity and grimy brickwork for gleaming tiles, it also set up a new standard of civic decency and established a lead in commercial efficiency that it still maintains.[32]

Certainly for Frank Pick every detail was of importance. Fry continued:

What is interesting to me in this new business is that I see a possibility of commerce doing something to redress the balance in favour of art – that balance which it so ruthlessly upset in the other direction by driving all artists out of the business of designing for the textiles, pottery, etc., of ordinary use. For the poster is not a very expensive object. It is possible here for the industrialist to take risks which he would never take in setting up a textile design, or a design for linoleum, or for any of the objects of large-scale production.

The cost of a print-run of 1500 Underground posters at this date was about £25 – say, the price of one painting by a reasonably well-known artist. The designer's fee was probably at about the same level. In addition, Fry pointed out, poster art was 'a new medium without preconceptions', with 'no fixed and traditional notion of the kind of thing a poster ought to be':

There is as yet no pedantry, no culture, no lecturing, until tonight, to hamper and harness the man who happens to have a gift for expression in this medium. For all these reasons the art of poster design holds out opportunities of a kind that are all too rare in modern life. This exhibition tells me how far they have been realized.

Other critics agreed, from R. R. Tatlock in the *Burlington Magazine* to Raymond Mortimer who wrote an unsigned profile of Kauffer for *Vogue*'s 'Hall of Fame' page. The year 1925 marks the climax of Kauffer's early period as a designer. The second half of the decade saw his enthusiastic amateurism shade towards a new professionalism.

34. *Twickenham by Tram*, 1924
poster, London Underground
E.674-1924

TWICKENHAM
BY TRAM

4

THE LATE
TWENTIES

There are remarkably few stories or anecdotes about Kauffer.
Even the late Poet Laureate Sir John Betjeman, who must have
received many appeals for such information – and signed his
letter of reply 'Archivist to the late twenties' – admitted that

There is nothing that I can add to all that has been written about that
great and good man. He was one of those mild, gentle people on
whom everyone ambitious, such as I, imposed. I am sure that it was
out of the goodness of his heart that he did the dust-wrapper of
Continual Dew ...[1]

As well as that jacket for the Laureate's first book, Kauffer
provided the title-page for the first volume published by another
Oxford aesthete of the Betjeman-Waugh vintage – *Cornelian* by
Harold Acton. Acton's *Memoirs of an Aesthete* provides a rare close-
up view of Kauffer and Marion Dorn when they lived in a flat
in the Adelphi in the late twenties:

Ted's flat was all beige and aluminium, ultra-modern, austere yet
comfortable with discreet lighting and the latest gadgets ... Marion's
modernist rugs kept one's eyes riveted to the floor. Their work
detained them in town when they longed for the country, for they
were superstitious about physical fitness and fancied that the London
air was noxious. They should have been nudists, playing in the
sunshine, but some ingrained puritanism held them in check.[2]

Acton also noticed Kauffer's restless drive for work:

he had hitched his wagon to some unattainable star, for he was morose
and misanthropic. People sapped his energy, and the attractive, sociable
Marion had the irksome duty of keeping them away.

35. *E. McKnight Kauffer*, 1927
photograph by Howard Coster
© National Portrait Gallery

This is an interesting view of Kauffer, whom most people found gentle, generous and charming. Acton's description of the flat is a valuable document as Kauffer's living quarters were always fastidiously designed. It was probably this flat, according to Douglas Cleverdon (who had the distinction of initiating the prototype of Eric Gill's famous Gill Sans type-face) 'a masterpiece of modern interior design', which Kauffer was obliged by the landlord to restore to its original state when he left it. Photographs of one or another of Kauffer's flats of the twenties may survive but at present their whereabouts is unknown. The beige and aluminium recorded by Acton neatly suggests the style of the later twenties and Kauffer's role, supported by the 'gadgetry', less as 'artist in advertising' more as professional designer. The main theme of this chapter is a growing institutionalization of his role.

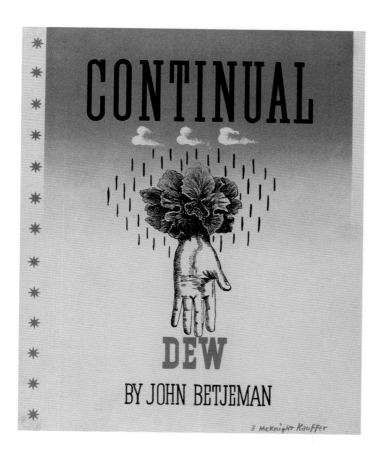

The Empire Marketing Board 1926–33

The Empire Marketing Board, the EMB, was an ambitious new departure into mass communications made by the British government. The purpose of the Board was to create favourable market conditions for Empire and Home produce. The electorate had in the 1923 general election rejected proposals to raise tariffs against foreign produce. The EMB was to be an exercise in persuasion, to establish a mass preference for Empire produce by appeals to loyalty, solidarity and interest. In a nutshell, the agency saw its task as 'to bring alive the idea of Empire'. The interpretation of the Board's function was very much influenced by its Secretary, and Civil Service head, Stephen Tallents. Presumably without any ironic intention, *The Times* titled his obituary simply 'An Imaginative Civil Servant'.[3] Tallents's colleague Gervas Huxley recalled meeting him when the EMB was founded:

He was in his early forties. a trim military figure, spare, balding, and moving briskly with a limp, the legacy of a severe wound at Festubert in 1915. Radiating confidence and energy, he spoke of his new job with contagious enthusiasm.[4]

Tallents's distinguished career had included the Governorship of the Baltic port of Riga during a period of emergency. He regarded the EMB as 'an early response to a demand more catholic and more penetrating than the need to promote the marketing of Empire products'.[5] He saw it as pioneering mass communications in a mass society, and recognized value in the way such a society explains itself to itself. The major and widely admired achievement of the Board was in documentary film. John Grierson's *Drifters* of 1929 is its classic. Grierson's documentary film fulfils his demand that 'the affairs of our time should be brought to the screen in any fashion which strikes the imagination, and makes observation a little richer than before'.[6] The poetics of realism in his work is defined by contrast with a film of much the same date. Anthony Asquith made *Underground* (1928) for British Instructional Films – but if they saw it neither Grierson nor Frank Pick can have been happy with the result. Instead of finding interest in the actual running of a complex mass transportation system, Asquith superimposed on the facts a banal love story and *crime passionel* involving scuffles in lifts and bloody clamberings over turbines in power stations. Sentimentality overlaid a complex subject which might itself have proved to have dramatic potential on film. In contrast to this Tallents quoted with approval some remarks of Walt Whitman's, from his *Backward Glance O'er Travel'd Roads*, which proved to be a widespread inspiration for the documentary movement: 'Whatever may have been the case in years gone by, the true use of the imaginative faculty of modern times is to give ultimate vivification to facts, to science, and to common lives, endowing them with the glows and glories and final illustriousness which belongs to every real thing and to real things only.'[7]

An international outlook at the EMB is registered in the influence from Russia in the film unit, while Tallents immediately recognized the German contribution to exhibition design. Of Mies van der Rohe's German pavilion at Barcelona in 1929 Tallents wrote:

One feels in this pavilion the expression of a lonely, powerful and forward-looking spirit – a gesture, incomplete in itself, which was fulfilled in the displays of German industry elsewhere in the Exhibition.[8]

Kauffer shared this internationalism of outlook, and it is appropriate to make a connection between him and the

documentary film-makers. With his friend Sidney Bernstein and others Kauffer founded the Film Society in London in 1925 – a principal channel through which England became aware of modern experimental film (and which premiered *Drifters* in 1929). Lord Bernstein recalls that Kauffer 'was persuaded to design the monogram for the Society – a much admired, bold FS with a tiny attenuated figure attached, deciphered variously as a Cupid and as a Red Indian'.[9] One of the ambitions of X Group had been to design for the film industry. In 1926 Kauffer made a poster design for the Fritz Lang film *Metropolis* – perhaps on speculation (it was never used).[10] Film continued to fascinate him and in the thirties he talked of making a series of films with Aldous Huxley on such subjects as dreams and 'Types' (presumably printing types).[11] His one graphic contribution to film history was his collaboration with Ivor Montagu, another Film Society associate, on the main title and inter-titles of Alfred Hitchcock's feature *The Lodger* (1926). Kauffer's designs came about in the following way, as Ivor Montagu explained:

The film had been more or less completed by Hitchcock, but, like the latter's two previous films was held up by the distributor who disliked or pretended to dislike it. M. E. Balcon (now Sir Michael), the producer (as Gainsborough Pictures) of the film asked me – who had never previously done any commercial work but whom he knew from

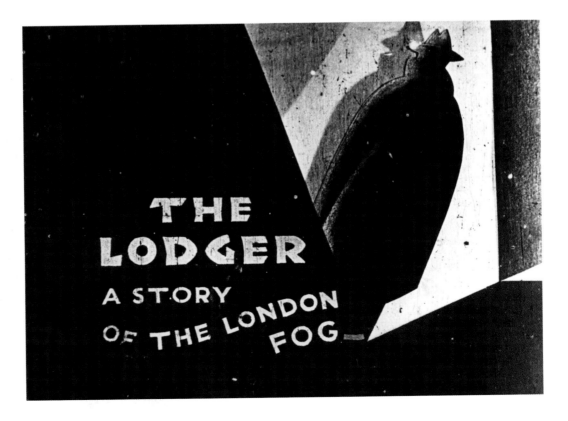

37. *The Lodger*, 1926
main title for film directed by Alfred Hitchcock

Empire Marketing Board Hoardings

the Film Society – if I would look at it with a view to re-editing it. His idea was: if the film was too highbrow for the distributor, perhaps it was spoiled by not being presented 'highbrow'. I undertook the job and because I admired Kauffer's graphic work so much, and partly, possibly, following out the same sequence of ideas, asked him to view the film and work out with me backgrounds for the titles (rewriting of which of course was part of the re-editing). This he did with readiness and enthusiasm, and no doubt contributed thereby, as we all had hoped, to the singularity of the treatment of the whole and so to its success.[12]

Kauffer's punchy titles, using the bold Neuland display type-face, sustain the strength and dramatic tension of the narrative. An introductory title sets the scene for Hitchcock's menacing 'tale of the London fog'. Kauffer's proposal for the film poster, however, was rejected by the distributor as being 'too artistic' – surprisingly in view of the film's adaptation 'upmarket'.[13]

Tallents formed a Poster Sub-Committee at the EMB and appointed to it Frank Pick and Sir William Crawford, head of Crawford's Advertising Agency. Tallents later described the committee meetings in his still unpublished book on the EMB, *Empire Experiment*:

A small group under Pick's chairmanship used to meet at night, week after week, when the ordinary office day was ended, to devise new themes, to choose the artist to which each should be entrusted, to talk over its treatment with the chosen artist and later to discuss and sometimes to criticize first his roughs and then his finished designs. Pick was accustomed to commission artists. Some of them, he knew, must be left to follow their own inspirations. But many, he knew also, gain by having definite subjects suggested to them, provided that those subjects are suited to their talents, and that each man is left free, once a theme and its general treatment had been agreed, to pursue the idea in his own manner and style. Sometimes we thought him a bit dogmatic in his handling of the men and women who would come in succession with their portfolios to sit with us at those evening meetings round the table of our modest board room in Queen Anne's Gate Buildings. Now and then, I felt, we damped a man's enthusiasm and lost something in the quality of his work. But in the main those late night meetings secured the delivery of the goods we wanted.[14]

This account suggests that Pick was no soft touch as a buyer of design and in the next decade even Kauffer had his disagreements with him. The poster campaign opened with a special one-day exhibition at the Royal Academy on 2 November 1926, which was held for the benefit of delegates from Empire countries, and for the press. A pair of tropical scenes by Kauffer, *Cocoa Pods* and *Banana Palms* – which successfully used an Art Deco style to represent exotic lands – were regarded as the outstanding designs.[15] They appeared on the hoardings in autumn 1927 under the title 'One Third of the Empire is in the Tropics'. The design of the hoardings themselves was considered (a typical Pick touch). They were to be special and used only for EMB posters. Hoardings were constructed in English oak and British Columbian pine and by the end of 1928 occupied nearly 1000 sites around the country which were given free or at peppercorn rents.[16] In design these hoardings were again distinct because they were divided into five panels: either two large ones below, three smaller ones above, or a horizontal sequence. Pictorial posters – like Kauffer's tropical set – were placed in the larger panels (40 x 60 inches in size). The central panel above was used for a main title and flanked by letterpress information at the

38. *One Third of the Empire is in the Tropics*, 1927
hoarding, Empire Marketing Board
Commercial Art, February 1928
NAL P.P.7.P

wings. The Publicity Committee at the EMB recommended that the Board restrict itself to posters of 'real artistic value. It is thought that such work makes a deeper and more arresting appeal to the public than ordinary commercial work while being more in consonance with the character of the Board's campaign.'[17]

The campaign opened with a world map by Macdonald Gill. Copies 10 x 20 feet in size were shown at Piccadilly Circus and Charing Cross. William Nicholson, half of the great 'Beggarstaff Brothers' poster partnership of the 1890s, contributed a five-section poster on Empire Children. Other commissions included a set on English orchards by John and Paul Nash, a modernist

industrial series by Clive Gardiner, a trio of still-life oil paintings by Mark Gertler (which proved too expensive in colour printing and were not used) and, more adventurously, a set of industrial scenes titled 'Peace' by Stanley Spencer. The Publicity Committee regarded Spencer's work as too provocative and his designs were never used – to Pick's fury, which abated to some extent when he sold them to a dealer at slight profit to the Board. The Board was, in fact, attacked for its policy by the British Poster Advertising Association, which issued *Some Arguments and Suggestions Submitted to the Empire Marketing Board* in 1929. The Association was nettled because the Board spurned conventional hoardings. It also charged the EMB with failure to 'appreciate the mass-mind':

39. *Cocoa Pods*, 1927
original design for poster, Empire Marketing Board
E.331-1934

Not only are the 'masses' – that is to say, the poorer 95% of the population – indifferent to good art, *but they do not understand it*. It is not that they fail to appreciate the merits of a good picture in the modernist style used by most of the Board's artists. *They don't know what these pictures are meant to represent!*

The pamphlet, for all its underlinings, cut no ice with the EMB. A series of 836 posters was completed in the Board's six years. Pick clearly dominated the campaign, which also utilized Johnston Sans. This remained the best sans serif display face until Eric Gill's Gill Sans became available from the Monotype Corporation in 1930. The EMB hoped at one point to secure the new face for its exclusive use. In addition to its hoardings the Board distributed class-room size versions of its posters to a list of 27,000 schools.[18]

Kauffer's contributions to the EMB included a lion symbol which was used on a large-scale 'message board' (16-sheet) in May 1927.[19] He also designed a 'National Mark' which identified British goods on packaging and in advertising. There were three versions of this National Mark – one for England and Wales, one for Scotland, one for Ireland. Kauffer used this design as the basis of a cover he designed for Tallents's major public statement on mass-communications, *The Projection of England* of 1932. Tallents published this pamphlet because by 1932 the future of the EMB was already uncertain. His arguments were intended to prevent the dissolution of the Board, or at least to redeploy it as a national propaganda machine. *The Times* published an article by Tallents under the same title on 16 April 1932. The authorities were not moved and the EMB, which had always been disliked by bureaucracy, was dissolved in 1933. *The Projection of England* called for a 'school of national projection' and it was clearly based on Tallents's admiration for Soviet film-making of the twenties. He argued that the Soviet classic *Storm over Asia* could be outmatched by a British-made *Dawn over Africa*. Tallents saw exhibition design as another under-developed resource. He argued for the creation of an organization which would operate with some of the authority of government and much of the freedom of free enterprise (anticipating the 'Quango' – quasi autonomous national government organization – of modern parlance). His team would be creative and experimental, entering fully 'into the ordinary life of their country, avoiding that instinct of withdrawal which has made the government services of the world the legitimate successors of the monastic orders'. Lord Clark suggests that Tallents never fully realized his talents, as he was obstructed by the Civil Service.[20] Another passage from his pamphlet is of interest because it shows the temper of one of Kauffer's key clients of the late twenties and the thirties:

Private art has become a luxury scarcely to be afforded and remote from our manner of living. Already the public patron is yearly superseding the private in the arts of architecture and decoration. The call is for the encouragement of a national rather than a private art, and the patron who gave that encouragement would know that he was not merely satisfying a noble taste but was fulfilling one of the great needs of his country.[21]

Tallents did not save the EMB, which was dissolved after the Ottawa Conference of Empire Nations in 1933. Tallents took some pleasure in being appointed the first 'Public Relations Officer' – a new phrase imported from America – appointed in the Civil Service when he joined the General Post Office in 1933. There he set about projecting England in spite of the Civil Service. His splendid ambitions match Kauffer's romantic idealism and their partnership continued in the next decade.

Kauffer at Crawford's 1927–9

The EMB poster campaign had been Pick's Underground policy expanded, and was a lesser achievement than was effected in film. It was probably a useful step for Kauffer to join Sir William Crawford's agency, which – through its Berlin office Dorland's – was alive to continental developments in graphic design. Kauffer's two years' association with the firm prompted or coincided with large changes in his style. Perhaps more valuable than that, his presence there so impressed his colleagues that, through their memories, we have our first glimpse of Kauffer at work. He was brought into the firm by its dashing Art Director Ashley Havinden.[22] Ashley, as he was known as a designer, pooled his memories with those of Mr W. Hellicar, Kauffer's assistant at Crawford's, 45 years later.[23]

Kauffer's arrival had a revolutionary effect on Crawford's designers. While they sat at cramped work tables, Kauffer stood up at an adjustable architect's desk imported from Germany. He worked with plenty of space around him so that he could study his design from different angles as he developed it. Expensive long-handled brushes stood in readiness in a huge stone jar. While the other designers used Clifford and Millburn's poster paints and shiny white hot-pressed boards like starched collars, Kauffer used artist's materials: Newton's gouache and Ingres paper. Working in a standing position as he did, Kauffer had tailored for himself a special waistcoat which omitted the untidy strap at the back. He would test colours against each other from a hoard of coloured papers, with which he also made experimental shapes. Novel letter forms were cut out in brown paper. To achieve colours which were rich but not glaring he always passed them through a proportion of black. When he found a colour which satisfied him he would mix up a good quantity of it and keep it with others in a nest of ceramic paint dishes. A junior would keep these colours fresh by adding a drop of moisture to them each day. On a rack was a series of white enamelled butcher's trays on which designs could be placed and slid into the rack to dry. Beside him Kauffer kept a battery of flexible rulers, French curves and hinged triangles. The walls of his studio were painted in different tones of grey to achieve a diffused light.

His studio was high up in the building at 233 High Holborn designed for Crawford by Frederick Etchells, itself a confident and elegant structure in the style of Le Corbusier. Kauffer's studio was off the part called 'The Palace of Beauty', an old Victorian edifice encased in Etchells's streamlined new one. Here Kauffer worked under an arrangement which was probably for three days a week. He was always happier as a freelance but often took part-time positions such as this to provide the basis of his income. A designer of Kauffer's calibre would at this period have earned in the region of £3000 a year, averaging £50 for an individual poster design (at twenties monetary value).

The two years at Crawford's saw an end to the 'Jazz and Archaism' flavour of Kauffer's style. Professionally and stylistically he became an arch-modernist. Photo-montage appears in his work for the first time, adapted from Russian and German examples. Rectangular layouts replace the dynamic diagonal movement of the earlier twenties. The sobriety of blue and brown colour schemes displaces Ballet Russe exuberance. Defying traditional typographic good taste, aluminium ink makes its appearance, and blocks of type-matter – no longer emulating

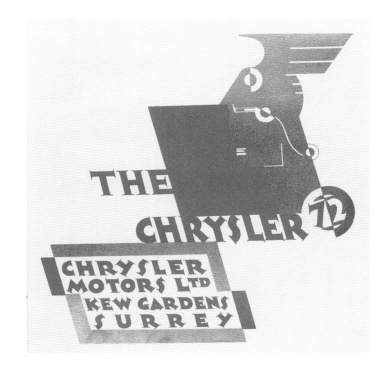

'the sedate title-page of years past' – are cavalierly crushed into parallelograms.

Typical of these developments is a brochure designed by Kauffer to promote the Chrysler 62 and 72 cars about 1928. A bronze-coloured ink was used for the cover, with lettering in terracotta and a symbol in dark blue. Each page opening is a variation of squares and circles printed in aluminium and royal blue, with text and diagrams in chocolate brown. The trick of using positive and negative lettering, which Kauffer first tried out in the Film Society symbol of 1925, became a favourite device. This habit of reversing lettering into light and dark as a word 'crosses over' broad rectangles of colour was a hallmark of Russian experimental graphics in the early twenties. The style reached Paris at least by 1923, when performances by the Moscow Chamber Theatre were advertised by a poster designed by Vladimir A. Stenberg which shows off the full repertoire of the style.[24] Photo-montage was in use at Crawford's at this period, and the agency produced a series of posters for Worthington's Beer which are entirely in this technique. Kauffer himself chose to counterpoint photographic quotation with areas of flat painted colour.

A new discipline also occurs in Kauffer's lettering, which was often the weakest part of his earlier designs, and all too obviously hand-made. To complete his conversion to a machine-made look to his work Kauffer took up the air-brush. In his early work Kauffer had mastered the art of 'feathering' paint so that one hue shades from full saturation to a diluted, paler, variant. The air-brush allowed such shadings to reach a mechanical exactness impossible to achieve by hand. Kauffer used it to suggest the softness of Kayser stockings and the smoothness of Bass ales. His interest in continental, particularly German, typography and graphics was reciprocated in May 1929 when his work was featured in *Gebrauchsgraphik* magazine. Published in this context Kauffer's work up to 1925 looks decidedly old-fashioned. His jazz style was over – by the time he designed a photo-montage emblem for the year 1929 reproduced in the *Gebrauchsgraphik* feature he could include a jazz element simply by 'quoting' a photo of a line of dance-band saxophone players.[25] When a bird motif appeared once more in 1930 it had also passed through a radical revision. When Sidney Bernstein's Phoenix Theatre opened in 1930 (Noel Coward and Gertie Lawrence in the hit *Private Lives*) its symbol was Kauffer's – a silver phoenix among bronze flames.

Book Illustrations

The Nonesuch Press followed up the two-volume Burton with another commission – illustrations for Herman Melville's story *Benito Cereno* (1926). This time the illustrations were in colour – in fact, in real watercolour. A line drawing provided the key for each of the nine illustrations. Two colours were then added through stencils. This was a new speciality at the Curwen Press. then presided over by two very distinguished typographers, Harold Curwen and Oliver Simon. This stencil or 'pochoir' process was popular in Paris in the early twenties and was very successfully transplanted to England by the Curwen Press. A team of young women was trained and the department flourished for six years. Kauffer's partnership with Curwen was one of the outstanding successes in book production between the wars. The historian of this relationship, Dr Desmond Flower, wrote that Kauffer 'made enormous demands of the Curwen Press department and they were met triumphantly'. Flower singled out the frontispiece for *Benito Cereno* as 'one of the most brilliant

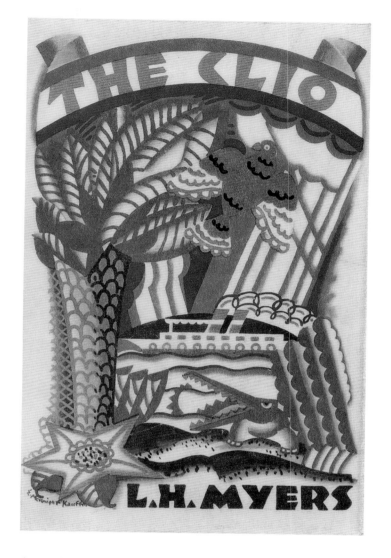

designs he ever conceived; with the pen and two tints – grey and mauve – he built up a shimmering design of a ship becalmed at last light which has an intricate beauty of which the eye can never tire'. The special style Kauffer created for the process stands quite outside his other work.

Three further commissions followed at once: a two-volume *Don Quixote* with 21 illustrations for the Nonesuch Press (1930); *Robinson Crusoe* with seven illustrations and a vignette for Etchells and Macdonald (1929); nine illustrations and a vignette for Arnold Bennett's story *Elsie and the Child* published by Cassell (1929). Dr Flower described the swift evolution in Kauffer's use

41. *The Clio* by L.H. Myers, 1926
book jacket, Putnam
NAL GG.58.C

of the process. For *Robinson Crusoe* and *Elsie and the Child* gouache was used rather than water-colour: the illustrations are literally as fresh as paint. But Kauffer also began to experiment with his 'key'. As Flower explained:

Illustrations which are going to be reproduced by stencil are usually made up of a drawing in pen or pencil on to which the artist adds his colour to taste; the basic drawing is called the key because, in addition to its primary purpose as part of the design, it serves also as a guide to the skilled girl who is applying the colour through the stencils. But in *Robinson Crusoe* the black key is used as an extra colour. There are large parts of the design in which no black occurs at all, but there are still enough patches for the operative to set her stencils by them. Another innovation was the use of spots of colour to break up a solid area of another colour or to reduce the brilliance of a patch of white … Either while he was working on *Robinson Crusoe* or immediately thereafter, Kauffer tackled *Elsie and the Child*. He now had complete confidence in the stencil department of the Curwen Press and felt that he could afford to let himself go. He dispensed – for the first time in book illustration – with a key altogether; in other words, the girl who had to do the stencilling started with a blank sheet of paper and had to key all her stencils to one corner of it.[26]

Elsie and the Child remains the triumph of this collaboration, which was also characterized by typography of the greatest distinction in the books designed by Francis Meynell and Oliver Simon. Bennett produced another story for illustration by Kauffer, *Venus Rising from the Sea* (Cassell, 1931). Kauffer discarded two sets of drawings – the second set had been passed at stencil stage – before deciding on a third and final set. In these there is a key once more but colour is applied completely independently of it. The series of books closes on this experimental note. As Dr Desmond Flower put it: 'two things had happened: the gifted girls who had superbly stencilled thousands of designs had got married, and the cold wind of the slump had begun to blow'.[27]

42. *Elsie and the Child* by Arnold Bennett, 1929
illustration, Cassell & Co
NAL 60.AA.76

Illustrations to T. S. Eliot

Although they were both members of the Council of the Arts
League of Service, the acquaintance of Kauffer and T. S. Eliot did
not ripen until the late twenties. In 1927 Eliot's publishing house
Faber and Gwyer (later Faber and Faber) inaugurated their series
of 'Ariel Poems'. These were well-printed (Curwen Press again)
little folders – each containing one poem, with a line or colour
woodcut frontispiece, and a design on the cover. Kauffer provided
the illustration and cover design for the first issue in the series,
Eliot's *The Journey of the Magi*. Other examples of Eliot's new
work appeared in the series with Kauffer's illustrations – *A Song
for Simeon* (1928), *Marina* (1930) and *Triumphal March*, a fragment
from the uncompleted *Coriolan*, appeared in similar format in
1931. It is unlikely that Eliot had much relish for any illustrations
of his work. He once wrote to Kauffer: 'Yours is the only kind
of decoration I can endure.'[28] Kauffer provided designs which at
least avoid the prosaic, and open rather than block avenues of
interpretation.[29] Eliot's poetry impressed him deeply. After a
reading by Eliot in the autumn of 1928 he wrote to the poet:
'Your work awakens in me memories beyond myself and before
myself … I am conscious too that I belong to something that
I can't find here.'[30]

When Kauffer wrote to congratulate Eliot on *For Lancelot
Andrewes* (1928) the author gracefully responded with 'You
seem to be the first person to look inside the book!'[31] In the
following year Kauffer wrote, 'I count it a genuine personal loss
not to see you more often', and inquired whether Eliot would
be interested in attempting a special edition of *The Waste Land*:
'I would like to do it – not illustrated – for that would be
impossible – but perhaps suggestions arising from some of its
sources.'[32] Nothing came of this idea, and although they discussed
sets and costumes for *Sweeney Agonistes* Eliot never finished the
play. Kauffer's first illustration-idea for *Marina* included, he wrote
to Eliot, 'the words "give, sympathise, control" as you have them
in the "Waste Land" and indeed is there not in these three words
the whole of equilibrium? They and the "freeing of the waters"
run in my thoughts constantly. My admiration for what you do

43. *Marina*, Ariel poem no. 29, by
T. S. Eliot, 1930
illustration, Faber & Faber
NAL 95.A.47(n)

is one of the important things in my life.'[33] (Understandably Eliot did not want *The Waste Land* 'stamped upon' *Marina*, and Kauffer prepared a second design without the words.)[34] Kauffer was present at a dinner party after which Eliot read *Ash Wednesday* aloud and invited criticism (in the event, Eliot only took seriously the suggestions offered by Virginia Woolf).[35] On 24 April 1930 Kauffer wrote to Eliot: 'I count this day one for which I am grateful for I believe it is publishing day for "Ash Wednesday". I am moved by the power of these magnificent poems. And I thank you for an experience that will become an influence.'[36]

Kauffer, always a great giver of gifts, presented Eliot with copies of his books – of *Robinson Crusoe* Eliot wrote: 'I like the illustrations immensely, and some of them have a quality which reminds me of Chirico, and which reminds me that it is my duty to finish the play [*Sweeney Agonistes*], so that the world may have the benefit of your scenery for it.'[37] Of Kauffer's *Don Quixote* Eliot wrote: 'I should not have thought anything possible after Doré, but you have done it.'[38] There was a touching bond between the two men – Eliot was even taken for Kauffer's brother by successive hall porters at Kauffer's apartment building – which became a close friendship over the next two decades.[39]

Eliot later gave an interesting account of the reasons for his friend's success, 'for such success as his needs a concurrence of causes':

First, of course, his great gifts. and I am thinking not only of his powers as an artist, but of the gift of sympathy and understanding which made him a good illustrator. I am grateful for his illustrations to my own 'Ariel' poems. *Second*, he found enlightened patrons to commission him. But perhaps one reason why he found such patrons was his personality: he had the kind of personality that attracts nice people. I daresay its attraction was still wider than that. But I mean that he had something deeper than is ordinarily implied by the word 'charm'. I mean that Ted Kauffer was an exceptionally loveable man.[40]

Interior Design

By the late 1920s modernism was not only in the air but entering avant-garde interiors. Kauffer's invitation card launched the interior design business of his fellow-American Curtis Moffat in 1929. Kauffer and Marion Dorn held a joint exhibition of rugs made to their designs at Arthur Tooth & Sons Gallery in January and February 1929. The collection was woven by the Royal Wilton Carpet Company. The rugs were intended to complement the change in taste: a preference for bare walls and

44. *Curtis Moffat opening*, 1929 invitation card, Curtis Moffat Ltd AAD 10/223

plain furniture. Decoration, banned from the walls, reasserted itself on the floor. Indeed the rugs could also serve as hangings. Kauffer explained the idea behind the designs in an article:

The modern window is definitely wide and horizontal in form. The modern rug should, therefore, by its pattern, suggest the horizontal (which is also the restful) … Another effort was made to keep the rugs *concentric* rather than *eccentric*. Our idea, in other words, was that the pattern should be self-contained. Many of the old designs were of the all-over type that was to be imagined as repeating itself infinitely and extending invisibly into space beyond the actual boundaries of the rug. We consider that pattern is much more restful and dignified when it is a definite decoration within a fixed area and has a distinct relation to the limits of the room.[41]

There are relationships between Kauffer's rugs and his colour schemes and geometrical patterns in his graphic work – favoured colours were chocolate brown, beige, royal blue, navy blue. Colours were used in 'flat' areas in circles and squares. There are also, as in the graphics, reversal patterns of light and dark/figure and ground. The rugs are exemplary of good materials used with a simplicity that displays their richness without becoming showy; the colours were chosen with Kauffer's habitual refinement. A more sumptuous carpet was commissioned from Kauffer by his friend Madge Garland (later Lady Ashton), who was one of *Vogue's* lively team of editors in the twenties. This 5 x 11 foot carpet has a pattern of leopard spots and rectangles on an off-white ground. Further colours completed the design – pale shades of blue, yellow and green, and no less than three shades

45. *Rug, 1930*
woven by Wilton Royal Carpet Co Ltd
T.440-1971

of brown. The colours were chosen to harmonize with the Bruton Street flat designed by Madge Garland for herself in 1930. The interior was predominantly white and dark brown: white walls, bookshelves and curtains (the latter made of white surgical rubber); a dark brown carpet and divan relieved by natural silk cushions of pale yellow and blue. Also to be taken into consideration were a square-armed chair by John Duncan Miller and a table with a thick blue-green glass top designed by Ronald Duncan.[42]

'We are very glad about the success of the rugs', Arnold Bennett wrote to Kauffer on 14 March 1929.[43] As a result of his work on *Elsie and the Child*, the novelist had every confidence in Kauffer's abilities. He commissioned Kauffer and Marion Dorn to design a study for him in his flat in the newly constructed apartment building Chiltern Court, Baker Street, where T. S. Eliot had a flat and into which the Bennetts moved in the autumn of 1929. For a short time Kauffer and Marion Dorn also took a flat there. The scheme included walls painted in 'delicate shades of pale beige, silver grey, yellow and grey-brown', with Kauffer rugs on the floor, a great range of steel shelving, and some square-ish but comfortable-looking furniture by E. A. Brown (probably designed under Kauffer's supervision).[44] Unfortunately, although some of the furniture survives, there is no record of the overall scheme, which, although more colours were used than in most present-day interiors, would have been intended by Kauffer to be not only lively but fundamentally 'restful'. Bennett resisted Kauffer's desire to arm his desk with a battery of gadgets: 'I have suppressed the dash-board gadget at the left of the desk, for bells, clock, lights, etc., as I don't need it. The leading idea of my desk is that it should be an *expanse*.'[45]

Bennett seems to have observed Kauffer with much of his novelist's shrewdness. Twenty years later Kauffer recalled, in an interview, that Arnold Bennett had compared him to 'a bird, forever in flight, forever searching for a place to come to rest'.[46]

THE THIRTIES (1)

In the thirties Kauffer became a very public figure in Britain, while remaining a very private man. The glimpses of him to be found in published recollections by friends and colleagues are few and precious. Remembrance imparted enchantment to Osbert Sitwell's passing reference to a boating trip 'on a golden Syracusan morning' with Kauffer, Marion Dorn and Adrian Stokes, 'in search of the Nymph Cyane in her fountain'.[1]

We learn about his utter seriousness in professional matters, and in everything else, from some brief remarks by Dr Desmond Flower:

He was an aloof person not because he meant to be, but because so much of his time was spent in his private world. He took everything seriously, most of all himself. I had entered Cassells by the time *Venus Rising from the Sea* was in production, and it was over these illustrations that I first got to know him. His reason for tearing up a complete set of stencils already passed for press and beginning to work again at his own expense was that he did not think that he had quite caught what Bennett had in mind.[2]

Kauffer was fortunate in often finding clients who became close friends. In the thirties he struck up a new set of relationships in which professional and personal loyalties were intimately mixed. This gave him a valuable basis of trust between private and public worlds. The letters and recollections that have survived from the thirties allow a fuller picture of Kauffer's working methods, and himself, to come into view.

46. *E. McKnight Kauffer*, 1939
photographed in his Swan Court studio, *The Artist*, March 1939
NAL PP.6.K

Swan Court

Kauffer and Marion Dorn moved into a newly built apartment block, Swan Court, Manor Street, Chelsea, when the first tenancies became available in 1931. A range of studio flats on the eighth floor was a special feature of the building. They took Nos. 139 and 141, which had the advantage of a balcony running around two sides of what was a double flat. It was a smart, stimulating and expensive place to live. Their neighbours included the novelist L. H. Myers, Eliot's friend John Hayward, the American photographer and film-maker Francis Bruguière

was just downstairs, the writer Bryan Guinness (later Lord Moyne) lived next door, and another close friend, Peter Gregory, was just across the passage. Kauffer's flat was always of impeccable orderliness. On the (then dashing) white linoleum and at the windows were Marion Dorn's rugs and curtains. The furniture was of natural wood finish and mostly built-in. There were important works of art: an African sculptured head, blown-up photographs by Man Ray, Jean Arp's painted relief *Constellation selon les lois du hasard* (now in Tate), *Four Forms, Drawings for Sculpture* by Henry Moore (also now in Tate), and one of the

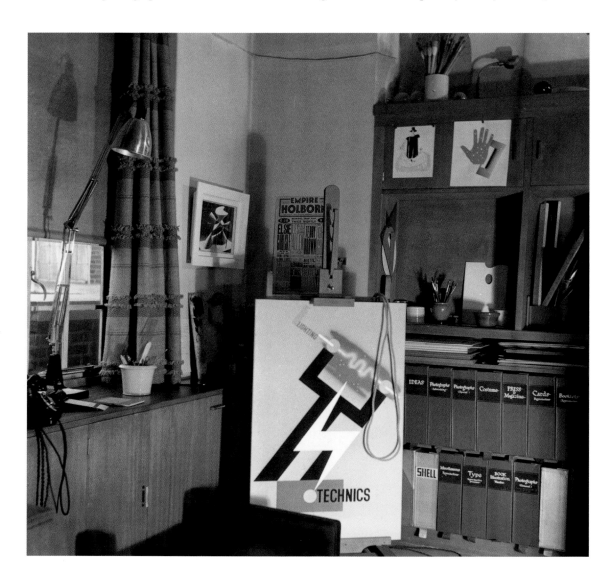

47. *Corner of Swan Court studio, c.1937*
photograph by E. McKnight Kauffer
The late Sir Paul Getty, KBE, Wormsley Library

white painted reliefs of Ben Nicholson.[3] Kauffer was also the first man in England to buy a painting by the German experimental painter Willi Baumeister. This he bought from Freddie Mayor about 1930–32. Mayor used to lend Kauffer paintings from time to time – say a Klee water-colour which was beyond his means.[4] There were many books and the latest issues of magazines such as *Cahiers d'Art*.

Kauffer also had a collection of over 1000 gramophone records. These included many by Sibelius, of whose music he was very fond, but also 24 discs by Bing Crosby. A new friend of the early thirties, Kenneth Clark, Director of the National Gallery 1934–45, recalled the typical 'gadgetry' of Kauffer's studio: 'it was full of things that went up and down and in and out and had all the gadgetry of a surgery'.[5] Lord Clark regarded the best description of Kauffer at this period as that written much later, in 1955, by Sir Colin Anderson:

Like a slim, russet eagle in appearance, and garbed in things which were at once slightly more *dégagés*, yet at the same time more elegantly combined than any garments one could have arranged upon one's own person, Ted Kauffer was a pleasure to the eye even without bringing into play his other pleasing characteristics. Cultured, intelligent and hypersensitive, his fastidiousness eternally governed his surroundings, his comings and goings, and his choice of company. One cannot remember anything he produced which hadn't the quality of orderliness and it was this, added to the brilliance of his basic conceptions, which made the impact of his work so dynamic. Neatness showed itself even in the arrangement of his work-bench and I well remember the astonishment of one of our children at the clinical order imposed upon it. His dazzling array of crayons, pens and pencils lay in regiments according to length (or so I seem to remember) so that one couldn't see how, having arranged them, he could bear to start work by breaking their ranks … He was easy with children, like so many people who are less so with grown-ups.[6]

Kauffer was able to take on an assistant at this time, the young Sidney Garrad, who joined him direct from school. Sidney's first task every morning was to dust the studio from top to bottom – but the maid Betty had already dusted it once and Kauffer himself dusted it afterwards. Kauffer carried orderliness to an extreme, even laying out in sequence silk handkerchiefs, each in its separate cellophane, for each day of the week. Francis Bruguière, with the film-maker Oswell Blakeston as accomplice, once amused themselves by muddling them all up – to Kauffer's vexation. Lord Clark remembered Kauffer as 'the least Bohemian of men'.[7] Lady Mosley remembered Kauffer and Marion Dorn as 'Henry Jamesian Americans, the "innocent" sort James so often describes, who make Europeans appear to be devious. Whenever I gave a party [when she was married to Bryan Guinness] they always came and looked very tall and distinguished, and were I'm sure as good as gold. Although they were not married they were far more "respectable" than most of their London friends, and in a trivial way that was probably rather typical.'[8]

Thirties Modernism

In an article in the *Architectural Review* in November 1934 Wyndham Lewis gave an account of the success and failure of 'modernism' in England, and neatly places Kauffer's position in this development:

A very small number of 'highbrow' men and women meanwhile – a very small number – have supported these 'extreme' expressions of cubist, surréaliste, expressionist art. A handful of modernist villas have been run up; a few factories have gone cubist. Women's dress has been affected more than most things, but Victorian modes have always routed the 'robot' fashion, whenever it came to a stand-up fight. One shop in a hundred has acquired a chromium-plated modernist façade, but only in the very large cities. Yet one swallower of the new forms of expression does not make a summer – for the artist! And for one who was a swallower there have been a thousand who were non-swallowers – who with teeth set have violently rejected the medicine. For a *bitter pill* it is – why deny it? – this art of the most 'modern' schools. In this country architects like Etchells, Holden, Connell & Ward, Tecton, Emberton, Tait, Wells Coates, Chermayeff, McGrath, Fry, painters and sculptors like Henry Moore, Epstein, Kauffer and the Nashes are in the nature of paregoric or codliver oil to the over-sweet Anglo-Saxon palate; about that there is no question.

Like the passage from Evelyn Waugh's *Brideshead Revisited*, this quotation provides a useful context for Kauffer's work. 'Robot' fashion, for example, is a noticeable ingredient in the set of illustrations Kauffer drew for a book published at the beginning

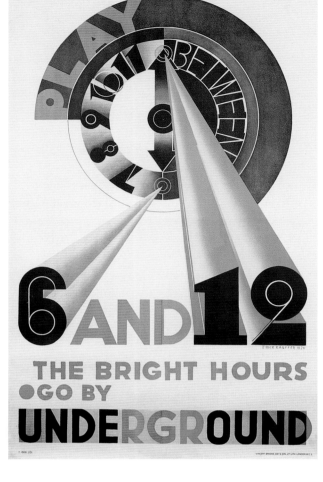

of the new decade. This was Lord Birkenhead's *The World in 2030* published in 1930. Kauffer provided one illustration for each of the book's nine chapters of prognostication. He evidently used the air-brush to arrive at a cold, metallic surface for the robot figures of his science-fiction fantasies. A robot-like figure was invented by Kauffer for his major new patron of the thirties, Shell, and occurs in a more heraldic mood in the costumes he designed for the ballet *Checkmate* in 1937. Of the architects listed by Lewis, Etchells was a former X Group colleague of Kauffer's and commissioned the illustrations for *Robinson Crusoe*. Charles Holden achieved a lasting reputation for the Underground stations he designed for Pick in the thirties – and the Underground continued to be a major client for Kauffer.

Joseph Emberton's career as an architect offers parallels to that of Kauffer. Emberton designed fanciful exhibition pavilions in the early twenties that are not remote from Kauffer's style at the same period; he strikes a more emphatic geometric note on

the façade of his Olympia building in 1929 – again, not distant from Kauffer at the same date; and reaches a much more assured International Style vocabulary in his Simpson's building in Piccadilly in 1936. Kauffer's work follows a similar evolution (and Simpson's came to him for designs at the same date).[9] Of the other architects, Chermayeff's designs for rugs are close to Kauffer's in style and Raymond McGrath won an *Architectural Review* competition for interior design in May 1930 with a scheme that included Kauffer rugs. Lewis was not overstating the case when he described what avant-garde artists were up against: Kauffer's daughter Ann visited Epstein's *Rima* monument to W. H. Hudson in Hyde Park with the sculptor's daughter, early in the thirties, only to find that Epstein's figure had been smeared with paint (presumably by a non-swallower of art of the most modern school).[10] Of the architects in Lewis's list the most remarkable was Wells Coates. He and Kauffer also worked together in the thirties and in a particularly interesting medium.

48. *The Amenities of 2030*, 1930
illustration from *The World in 2030* by The Earl of Birkenhead,
Hodder & Stoughton, NAL 95.LL.89

49. *Play Between 6 and 12 – The Bright Hours*, 1931
poster, London Underground
E.1238-1931

50. *Power – the Nerve Centre of London's Underground*, 1931
poster, London Underground
E.3338-1932

Cresta, Wells Coates and the Photo-mural

Cresta Silk was owned and directed by T. M. Heron, earlier an associate of Alec Walker – a client of Kauffer's Vorticist period. In 1930 Heron went to Kauffer for letter-headings, brand-labels and dress-boxes for his new firm. The letter-headings make excellent use of Eric Gill's newly available Sans Serif letter, use simple rules and circles as decoration and are embellished by a 'CS' monogram also designed by Kauffer. The same monogram, printed in chocolate brown on buff cardboard, was used for the dress-boxes in which the firm despatched its goods through the mails. Through an economical design requiring only one printing Kauffer gave the firm an abstract, witty and memorable trade-mark. The dresses themselves were distinguished – designers included the painters Paul Nash and Cedric Morris (and, in the forties, Heron's schoolboy son, Patrick). Perhaps even more important than these beautiful designs was the series of shop fronts which Cresta commissioned from Wells Coates. Coates's façade for Cresta's Bournemouth branch (1929)[11] has many of the qualities Stephen Tallents found in Mies van der Rohe's German pavilion in Barcelona in the same year. It might be claimed as the first modern shop front in England. The 'hygienic' shop had appeared in 1921 when MacFisheries transformed their premises in Old Bond Street, using only non-absorbent materials and eliminating mouldings.

By comparison with this, however, Coates's design is sublime. The company name became an integral part of his design: tall, elegant chrome letters, slim from the frontal plane but actually three-dimensional, receding grandly in depth to about 12 inches. The letters, and a series of circular light-fittings, are in carefully adjusted proportion to the main window – a wide oblong of plate-glass. The simplicity, spaciousness and elegance of this façade rebuke the bare, geometrical modernism of Emberton's Olympia building of the same year. Coates's position, at least by his own account, was not purely formalist – he described himself as less concerned with 'formal problems of style as with an *architectural* solution of the social and economic problems of today … the response that leads to freedom and fullness of life'.[12]

Pursuing this aim led Coates to enlist Kauffer's co-operation when he designed Embassy Court, on the sea-front at Brighton, in 1935. To establish a buoyant, cosmopolitan atmosphere for the building Kauffer was invited to design a mural in the entrance hall. Kauffer's design was an elaborate montage which combined photographic and painted elements – and the complete mural was in fact transferred to the walls by photographic means.[13] This was done by a process which had only recently been perfected by a firm of architectural decorators, Mollo and Egan. This firm was responsible for realizing Kauffer's Embassy Court photo-mural. First the wall was sprayed with photo-sensitive emulsion. Then, in dark-room conditions, the design was projected on to this. The image was developed, fixed and washed *in situ*. As in true fresco, image and wall are effectively one. The inventor of the process, Mr Eugene Mollo, experimented with different textured surfaces and once made a weird image by projecting a negative image of a sculpture back on to the sculpture itself. Needless to say, Kauffer was fascinated by the process. His design is a free assemblage – a sectional view of the Royal Pavilion, which stands half a mile down the road from Embassy Court, various Surrealist marine motifs (borrowed from the paintings of Edward Wadsworth), a baroque trumpeting angel in photo-montage with painted stars for musical notes, painted fishes and underwater plants, a nereid from the Étoile fountain in Paris (probably photographed by Kauffer himself, who was one of the first in England to acquire a Leica camera).

Kauffer wrote about the possibilities of the photo-mural at some length:

From my point of view this amazing invention is not revolutionary but a very natural extension of the camera as experience. Mural decoration, as we know, has come to a dead end both in subject matter and in surface texture. If the heroic is desirable in decoration we can now project the documentary evidence to any scale required. Hardly any surface can resist photo-mural technique. Rippled, fluted, convex, concave, plaster, wood, metal, glass can be impregnated with this technique, applied so directly to the material that surface and picture become part of each other. Pictorial 'reporting' with the camera has now developed a wide interest in the various activities occurring in daily life. News reporting, scientific and microscopic photography, have revealed new and astonishing experience for the eye and imagination, and all the easy and quick registration that the camera can give should be used as part of modern decoration. It is the world we live in.

The designer should in no way be subordinated by the mass of material now under his eye. In fact, much more is now demanded of

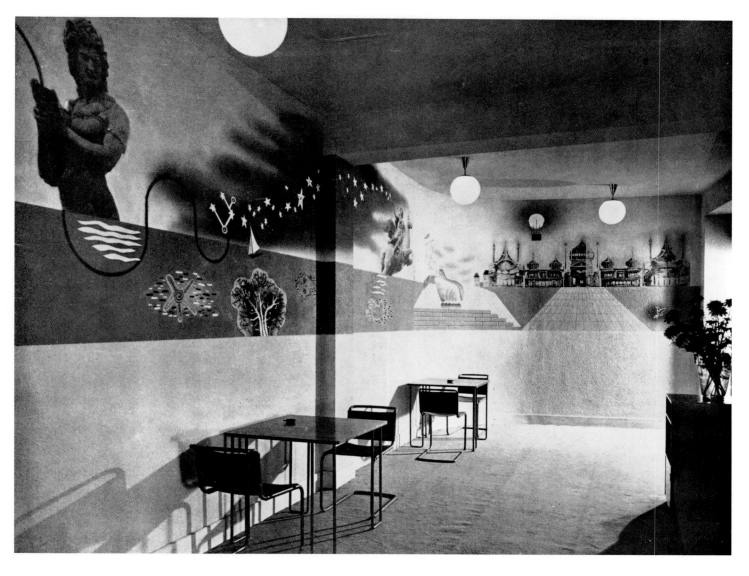

51. *Embassy Court mural*, 1935
photo-mural for Embassy Court, Brighton, architect Wells Coates

his talent; since it is for him to select and combine his material from a wide range of subject matter, surface textures, colour and colour treatment, exaggeration of scale, conflicts in pictorial interest dynamic and subtle, all depending upon the project. The range is wide, extending between the effects of splash headline dramatics to the quiet ease of a flight of birds or a classic head.

Surprise as an element in decoration is a factor which keeps the space alive, and in photo-mural technique the contrast between the painted line, pattern or symbol and the documentary photograph enlarged to fantastic scale and again designed for different materials, offers unlimited prospects to the imagination.

This medium now so ably handled by its inventors is the mural decoration of our time, and through this process we can extend our experience into new worlds of pleasure, surprise and wonder.[14]

Kauffer was not alone in taking to the new technique. With Francis Bruguière as photographer/designer Mollo and Egan made a giant photo-mural for the British Pavilion at the Paris Exhibition in 1937. They had decorated over 400 cinemas in Britain by the war, which brought the process to an end. (Mollo moved on to new interests after the war.) Kauffer employed the process again in 1936 as the main feature of an exhibition about 'London's New Entertainment Centre', Earl's Court. Pick had begun to use part of the Charing Cross Underground station as an exhibition hall. Here the model for the Earl's Court building was shown. Behind it was a huge photo-mural by Kauffer. The ubiquitous and industrious Kauffer was already involved with the new building, as designer of an emblematic knight in armour which still decorates its east façade. Pick also commissioned him to design posters and car-cards publicizing the new exhibition centre. The photo-mural uses 'splash headline dramatics', counterpointed by an abstract space-frame. Splendid divers float like birds, giant ice-hockey players jostle, street-crowds mill, within an elastic framework of lines and colours. Kauffer got the building off to a good start.[15]

52. *Earl's Court mural*, 1936
original (alternative) design
E.3288-1980

Friends and associates:
Peter Gregory and Lund Humpries

Peter Gregory lived opposite Kauffer in Swan Court and their flats offered a rich contrast in style. Gregory's was all untidy confusion, overflowing with books and pictures; Kauffer's was grand and immaculate. And yet Gregory was in a sense Kauffer's patron. Eric Craven Gregory (1887–1959), Peter among his friends, was one of two sheet-anchors for Kauffer's career in the thirties (the other, Jack Beddington of Shell, will be described in the next chapter). Sir Philip Hendy described Gregory as 'a handsome embodiment of the bluff and kindly Yorkshireman of fiction'.[16] Another friend, Sir Herbert Read, said that Peter Gregory was 'a man of perfect natural goodness'.[17] He was a tall, bear-like man whose kindliness was blended with shrewdness – 'an intuition for the balance sheet' – from which organizations with which he concerned himself, from the *Burlington Magazine* to the Institute of Contemporary Arts (and including several struggling art schools), were handsome beneficiaries. Hendy went so far as to say (writing in 1959) 'Peter Gregory perhaps played a larger part in the art history of the past forty years than any man who was not an artist'. Although his name is remembered in the generous endowments he left for artists and poets, such achievements as his are often lost to view.

Gregory became a director of the Bradford printing firm Percy, Lund, Humphries in 1919. He knew Kauffer from 1919 or 1920. The firm published a set of artist's Christmas cards in 1920 and one of these was illustrated by Kauffer. Gregory became a joint managing director of the firm in 1930 with Eric Humphries. Humphries was a master printer whose expertise was called upon in 1939–40 during an early stage in the development of atomic power. His outstanding knowledge of engraving techniques put him in a position to advise on the possibilities of making an ultra-fine copper membrane. Humphries ran the Bradford works, while Gregory controlled the business end in London. Kauffer's close association with the firm during the thirties began when Lund Humphries moved their offices from Amen Corner to 12 Bedford Square in 1932. Kauffer designed the change of address card, using a technique related to Man Ray's 'Rayographs' – burned-out whites and solid blacks. The Bedford Square building had enough space for an exhibition gallery to be constructed on the ground floor. This was designed

by the architects Hall, Easton and Robertson, with a specially designed floor by Marion Dorn – who also contributed one of her finest hand-woven rugs – and opened in December 1933.[18]

The first exhibition was shared by Kauffer with Francis Bruguière. Artist and photographer also worked together on schemes for Charnaux, makers of patent latex corsets. Bruguière photographed models standing in front of nude figures drawn by Kauffer. They also worked with a paper-model maker called Dronsfield on projects advertising Spey Royal whisky (Kauffer again providing the background illustrations).[19] Lund Humphries gave Man Ray his first London exhibition in the following year – which drew the august presence of Marcel Duchamp to Bloomsbury. A dark-room had been set up at 12 Bedford Square, as well as a studio for Kauffer, and Man Ray used both in 1935. It was probably through Kauffer that Man Ray's experimental films were shown in London (at the Film Society), and he was certainly responsible for the introductions which resulted in Man Ray's portraits of T.S. Eliot, Virginia Woolf and Aldous Huxley. It seems likely that Kauffer also got the Underground to commission a pair of posters from Man Ray – a mysterious set which eventually appeared in 1939. One collaboration between the two is known – again a brochure for Charnaux, which has a Man Ray photograph of a Venus de Milo cast and layout by Kauffer.

53. Change of address card, 1932
Lund Humphries
AAD 10/224

Man Ray recalled that Kauffer was a regular visitor to Paris in the thirties, that he seemed restless and driven, and that on these visits he experimented with opium – not a rare or unknown quantity in Paris in artistic circles at the time.[20] Man Ray photographed Kauffer, probably in 1936, and his portrait brings out the aquiline quality noticed by Sir Colin Anderson – it is a crystalline, aristocratic, Cocteau-like head. (No reproducible print survives and the negative is lost.)[21] Bruguière also made a portrait of Kauffer – this time a more intimate and relaxed study. A third portrait was made by the London studio photographer and portrait specialist Howard Coster. In this Kauffer seems to be entirely in his private world; the delicacy of the lighting and subtlety of the facial modelling recall a remark from Madge Garland, that Kauffer was 'a man born without a skin'.

Another important exhibition at Lund Humphries was shown in 1935 – the first in England of the great typographical innovator Jan Tschichold. It is hard to assess the influence of these exhibitions but it is at least likely that this one prepared the ground for Tschichold's post-war appointment at Penguin Books – which broadcast his standards very widely indeed. Kauffer also introduced the immigrant German graphic designer Hans Schleger, professionally known as Zero, to British design circles with an exhibition in 1934. This skilled designer made many contributions to the visual environment in Britain – from London bus stop signs to trade-marks for MacFisheries and the John Lewis Partnership, colophons for Allen Lane and Penguin Educational Books, and a whole series of distinguished Edinburgh Festival posters – including the familiar castle and dove motif. Perhaps some credit for this string of achievements goes to the exhibition with which an emigré from Nazi Germany, struggling to adapt to a new country, was set on his feet.

The gallery also introduced the poster partnership of Lewitt-Him, described by Kauffer in the catalogue in these terms: 'They are comic, they are amusing, they are thoughtful, they are serious, and they are good advertising.' They were, in fact, just the designers for the home-front campaigns of the Second World War, when they made their most important contribution. *Eight Commercial Artists* were shown in 1934 which included two of Kauffer's growing number of imitator-disciples, Peter Morgan and Theyre Lee-Elliott.

In the same year the gallery showed the first seven years' production of the Cresset Press. The Press was founded by Dennis Cohen in 1927 and began with typical private press luxury items such as an edition of – *The Shepheard's Calendar,* printed by George W. Jones ('At the Sign of the Dolphin') – a now obscure typographer, but one much admired by Tschichold. Cohen soon became an arch-Modernist, notably as the man who commissioned houses from both Mendelsohn and Chermayeff and Gropius and Fry, which stand side by side in Old Church Street, a stone's throw from Swan Court. Cresset Press moved into the contemporary field with illustrations by Edward Burra, D. H. Lawrence's *Birds, Beasts and Flowers,* the English edition of *Tobacco Road* and H. G. Wells's *Things to Come,* for which Kauffer provided the jacket in 1935. Kauffer's jacket draws on Sir Alexander Korda's film version of H. G. Wells's futuristic text, *The Shape of Things to Come.* In the twenties Kauffer had often used new type-faces produced by the Klingspor type-foundry in Germany, notably the Narcissus and Neuland display faces. Lund Humphries staged an exhibition of the foundry's work.

Kauffer himself showed a full range of his work at the gallery in 1935. It was widely reviewed. For the *Scotsman* Kauffer was 'the Picasso of advertising design'. The *Guardian* found a very different likeness: 'His strict and exciting personality has entered into the accepted life of our time as sharply as Noel Coward has through the bias of his characters and songs.'[22] D. S. MacColl, however ('The Iniquity of Fashion', *London Mercury*, May 1935), complained that Kauffer had been 'too easily contented by his flatterers and his own readiness, and has missed the difficult track'. MacColl, who did not like Cézanne either, did not say where that track might lie and was perhaps guilty of mere spleen.

The most thoughtful and perceptive review came from a young art historian called Anthony Blunt (later Surveyor of the Queen's Pictures and Director of the Courtauld Institute of Art). Blunt's review provides the best account of Kauffer's standing at mid-decade. His words also make a companion-piece to Roger Fry's assessment in the mid-twenties. The whole article is reprinted here:

Mr McKnight Kauffer is an artist who makes me resent the division of the arts into major and minor. Since he is not a pure painter or sculptor or architect, but an illustrator and a designer of book-covers

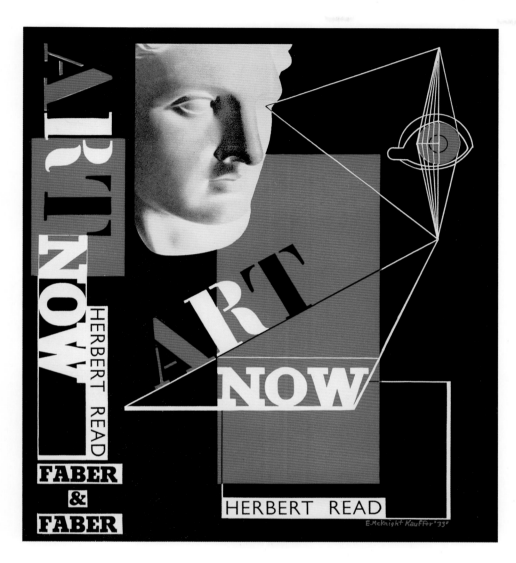

54. *Art Now* by Herbert Read, 1933
book jacket, Faber & Faber
E.508-1980

55. *Quack, Quack!* by Leonard Woolf, 1935
book jacket, Hogarth Press
AAD 10/29

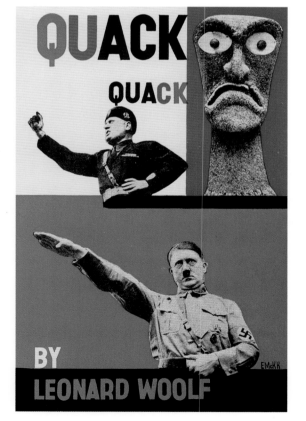

and posters, he must, technically, be classed as minor, but as I looked round the exhibition of his work at Messrs Lund Humphries's galleries in Bedford Square I was led to think: 'If he is minor, who then is major – at any rate among his English contemporaries?' For Mr Kauffer does to perfection everything to which he sets his hand, and it is only our inherited prejudice that somehow a poster is always a frivolity that prevents us from fully acknowledging his brilliance.

I hope that Mr Kauffer will not take offence if I suggest that his achievement is really parallel with that of a very good translator of literature. (He will, I think, forgive me if he recollects that this puts him aesthetically parallel with the Anglican divines who composed the Authorized Version of the Bible.) He has not himself invented any of the important styles such as Cubism or Superrealism which have appeared in the last thirty years, nor has he even taken a direct part in their inception. What he has done is rather to take from these styles as soon as they appeared exactly those elements which were relevant to his particular purposes and has translated these elements into terms of illustration or poster art. It is remarkable how quick off the mark Mr Kauffer has always been. In 1919 he was using the methods of the later kinds of Cubism, and by 1926 he had already spotted the possibilities of Superrealism and used its methods in a poster of the British Museum representing a large statue of Socrates. Superrealism, with its direct reliance on appeal to the subconscious, ought to be the art perfectly adapted to the poster, and Mr Kauffer has fully exploited it. His adaptation of the deliberate distortion of perspective practised by the Superrealists and his play with certain repeated motifs, such as the raised hand, all produce posters which arrest and slightly puzzle the passerby. But, apart from producing admirable posters, Mr Kauffer has rendered another important service to modern art. By using the methods of the more advanced schools and by putting them before the men in the street in such a way as to catch them off their guard, so that they are lured into liking the poster before they realize that it is just the kind of thing which they loathe in the exhibition gallery, by this means he has familiarized a very wide public with the conventions of modern painting and has greatly increased the chances which modern painters, who are not involved in publicity, have of being appreciated and widely enjoyed.[23]

Kauffer's wonderful landscape posters for the Great Western Railway (1933) exemplify this ability.

The last idea in Blunt's review was also expressed, in a

characteristically neat turn of phrase, by T. S. Eliot: 'He did something for modern art with the public as well as doing something for the public with modern art.'[24] Lord Clark regarded Blunt's comparison of Kauffer to a good translator as the most apt definition of his talent, and suggested that it was 'mediumistic, something that came up from inside him'.[25] His free use of available styles is probably not unconnected with his generosity to other artists, which Gregory described as 'a totally unselfish respect for style in others'.[26]

56. *Great Western to Cornwall*, 1933
poster, GWR
E.479-1953

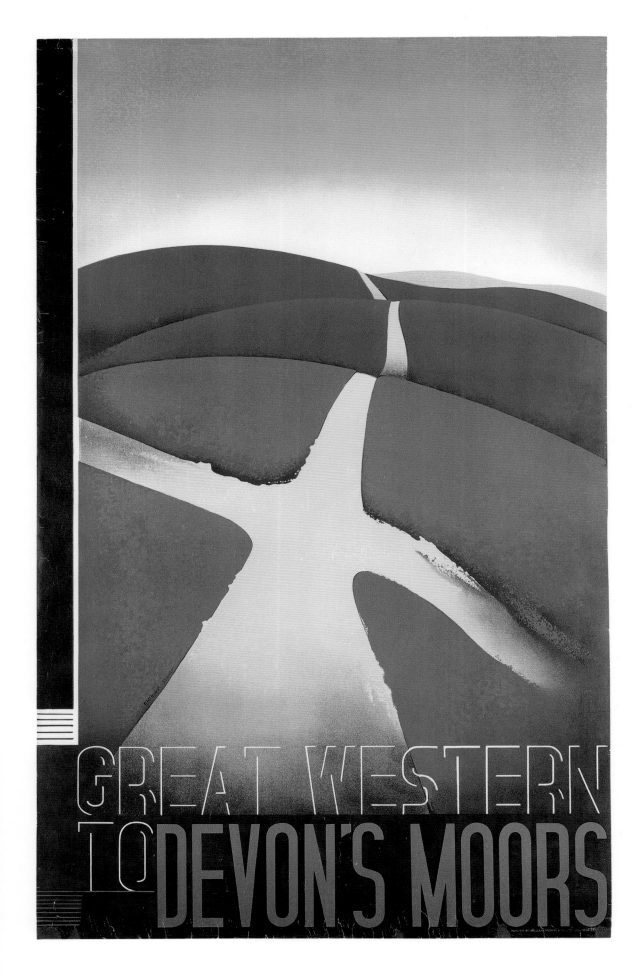

57. *Great Western
to Devon's Moors*, 1933
poster, GWR
E.544-1933

Marion Dorn Ltd

Marion Dorn founded her own company in 1934. Her output is so extensive and distinguished that it needs a separate study,[27] but the recollections of her assistant in the thirties, Elizabeth Edwards (Lady Robinson), afford a glimpse of her show-room and studio which should be recorded.[28] Her premises were at 10 Lancashire Court, off Bond Street, and were one of the exciting places to visit in thirties London. A stable was converted into a ground-floor stock-room and office, while the upper floor was show-room and studio combined. The upper floor was white and airy, 'communicating a sense of quality and detail, a Bauhaus feeling', Lady Robinson remembered. Lengths of fabric were thrown through chromium rings attached high up on the wall – now a standard display method. Marion Dorn collected objects which exhibited colours or textures she liked – so there would be neatly laid out pieces of emerald bottle glass, reels of bright copper wire.

Work in progress was indicated by a drawing-board, poster colours in pots, renderings of different colourways of a design being carried out as time allowed. She had a strong preference for sparkling white as a ground for bright patterns derived from floral forms. For upholstery she liked hand-woven Welsh tweeds in shades of green; for curtains, yellow – especially in small rooms. Sometimes she used very expensive materials – for example, curtains figured with vines and grapes for a Cambridge Combinations Room ran to £6 a yard. On the other hand she showed that simple materials could be used with distinction – for example a pair of screen curtains for the Paris Cinema: terracotta hessian with two enormous stripes of white cotton rag at the meeting edges. Clearly Kauffer and Dorn's relationship included shared professional opportunities – among these was the work they did for the Orient Line, flagship of the interior design of modern British ocean liners.

The Orient Line

Ocean liners became part of the scrapbook of functionalist design for young architects in the twenties and thirties, along with grain elevators and tobacco pipes. The sweeping lines and no-nonsense engineering of the superstructure of these modernist paragons tended, on the other hand, to house Scottish baronial ballrooms and other schizophrenic aberrations. Colin

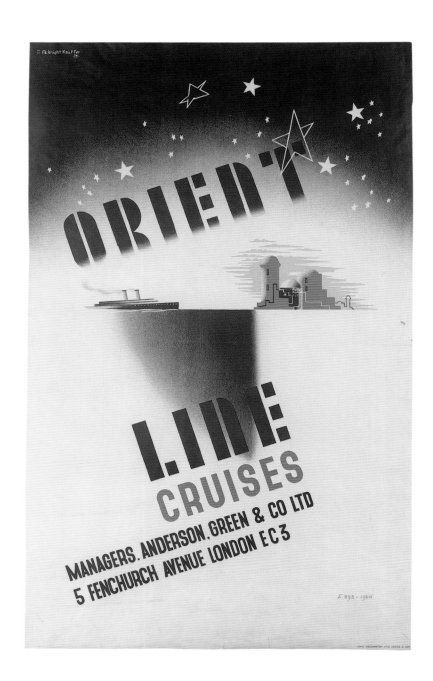

58. *Orient Line Cruises*, 1934
poster, Orient Line
E.393-1935

damask patterns, all the floral patterns, the cut velvet, plush and chintz, the 'galon', the bobbles and the vaguely Louis cutlery.[29]

What Anderson and O'Rorke were after was not actually on the market, and they found some difficulty in 'persuading proud and successful industries that not a single object in their entire output was acceptable for a modern ship interior'. Anderson makes the significant remark that these firms had no staff designers who understood what was wanted, and 'there were no such people as industrial designers. There were a few artist designers, if one knew where to look for them.' Anderson, who had Tommy Tallents (brother of Stephen) on his board of directors, knew where to look. Among the artist designers involved in the *Orion*, Kauffer gave general advice and encouragement, draughtsmanship, design know-how and typographic advice. Marion Dorn designed her first 'sea-going' rugs. They also contributed to the sister-ship *Orcades* (1937). Kauffer designed posters for the Orient Line, invitations and brochures for the new ships, and for the *Orion* he designed an engraved glass mirror.[30] At 9 x 13 feet this must have been impressive. Kauffer's design showed Orion the Giant in constellation form. The mirror was ripped out when the ship was converted for war use.

Kauffer also designed some of the minutiae of ocean travel – luggage labels. There are tie-on ones in stylish combinations such as raspberry and pink or lime and black, and there is a set of circular adhesive ones. These belong to a different era from his bright little pictures for Steinthal & Co. They fulfil the Functionalist aesthetic of the line. Kauffer divided the label into two halves, printed the lower half black with the words Orient Line 'reversed-out'. The upper half is also divided, the right side printed in primary red, the left printed with the letter which designated the part of the ship for which the luggage was destined. The alphabet was a slab-serifed Rockwell face, which Kauffer liked to use at this period like slabs of paint. It is a satisfyingly balanced and immediately recognizable design. A formal ambiguity of pattern occurs with some letters, surely intentionally (considering Kauffer's Cresta monogram) – for example in the confronted arrow-head shapes in the 'X' label. This minute little visual nuance is worth mentioning only because it is characteristic of Kauffer's interest in the last detail of any design.

Anderson decided to cure this by building an integrated ocean liner – the *Orion* (1935). The architect Brian O'Rorke was given the overall commission for the interior design. Sir Colin Anderson later wrote of this radical revision:

The sheer struggle represented by the creation of the Orion was immense, for almost all the components that made up her appearance had to be specially designed and made for her. For instance, we were setting out to escape not only from the shape of every handle but from the dominance of brass as a material. We were a spearhead of the use of white metal at sea, though aluminium was not itself yet freely available and anodyzing was a new word. We were fighting the baroque figuration of veneered panelling and insisting that straight and uneventful grain was what we must have. We were rejecting all the

59. *Orient Line* symbol, luggage label, Orcades brochure, 1936–7
Orient Line
AAD 10/143, 10/146, 10/152, 10/160

Institutionalization of Industrial Art

Aubrey Beardsley once wittily remarked that the poster artist was 'déclassé – on the street'. For Ashley Havinden and others, part of Kauffer's importance was as a leader of a new profession: 'Before his time, most people working in advertising design were disappointed "fine" artists. Kauffer, through his posters, helped to establish the career of designing for advertising as a worthwhile vocation.' The Society of Industrial Artists was founded in 1930: Kauffer served on its Council and was one of the first Honorary Fellows appointed. Frank Pick chaired the Council for Art and Industry set up in 1934 and brought in Kauffer as a Council member. In 1935 Kauffer joined the Advisory Council of the Victoria and Albert Museum. In 1936 he became the first Honorary Designer for Industry, chosen by the Royal Society of Arts. This title was intended to provide designers with professional recognition comparable to the Royal Academicians. The faculty soon received permission to add Royal to the title. In the late thirties Kauffer often signed his posters 'Hon RDI'. (The honorary nature of the award in Kauffer's case was because he was not a British subject.)

The Design and Industries Association, founded in 1915, of which Kauffer was an early member, had prepared the ground for these developments but had soon run out of steam. In 1936 Kauffer explained why the DIA was unsuccessful: 'It has been very gentlemanly in its habits, it has had too much good taste and it has concentrated on the hand-made rather than the machine made.'[31] Welcoming a new magazine in that year, Kauffer wrote to its editors:

If your magazine really intends to find out why industrial design is on the whole so characterless in England then your research will have to begin with the art teaching now going on in the various schools, with the buyers in the multiple shops and then with the manufacturers and finally with the public.[32]

This was very much the approach adopted by the young emigré design historian Nikolaus Pevsner, whose book *An Inquiry into Industrial Art in England* was published in the following year.

With the Empire Marketing Board government had acknowledged the role of designers. When Stephen Tallents left the EMB to become first Public Relations Officer at the General Post Office, he promised former colleagues at a farewell dinner that he was going to 'sing the EMB's song in a strange land'.[33] Tallents took the Film Unit with him and another masterpiece of documentary resulted in 1936, *Night Mail* (embellished by the Auden poem and Benjamin Britten's music). For Tallents Kauffer designed posters, publicity cards, and an exhibition stand. Institutional agencies in publicity developed in pace with the new profession of industrial designers.

Typical of the many design initiatives of the decade was a large exhibition of modern British industrial art arranged by the Royal Society of Arts at the Royal Academy in 1935. The exhibition had this lofty intention: 'To encourage British artists to give to industry the benefit of their talent and training, so that the objects with which we are surrounded in our daily lives may have an appearance which is not only attractive, but is based on genuinely artistic principles.' Herbert Read condemned the exhibition as mere 'novelism' – neither functional nor specifically modern. In particular the poster section was 'an outrageous misrepresentation of what is actually being done by artists in this country'.[34] Kauffer was not represented in the section; when Read inquired why he was told that Kauffer had been excluded because he was not British. 'Nothing', Read concluded, 'could so openly reveal the abject futility of the exhibition.' The Royal Society of Arts made amends with its award to Kauffer the following year. The episode does underline, however, that official initiatives were of far less consequence for designers like Kauffer than the patronage of clients in the commercial sector. One of the most important of these, Jack Beddington of Shell-Mex BP Ltd, forms much of the subject of the next chapter.

60. *Cheaper Empire Telegrams*, 1938
preliminary design for poster, GPO
E.3276-1980

CHEAPER

EMPIRE

TELEGRAMS

BY *CABLE & WIRELESS*

ORDINARY RATE XXXXXXX PER WORD

LETTER TELEGRAMS XNOPTSUABWORD

HAND IN YOUR TELEGRAM

HERE

B.

THE THIRTIES (2)

Peter Gregory was one sheet-anchor for Kauffer in the thirties, Jack Beddington was another. Jack Beddington (1893–1959) was a son of one of seven brothers called Cohen who were all members of the London Stock Exchange in the 1890s. The brothers collectively and simultaneously changed their name to Beddington (the name of a Surrey village). A story is told of the newly named brothers arriving for work one morning to find emblazoned across the main hall of the Stock Exchange 'And the Lord said unto Moses – Good Morning Mr Beddington!' Jack Beddington read Classical Moderations at Oxford and, like Tallents, survived the First World War only by being almost killed in it. He was severely wounded at Ypres in 1915 and invalided home. After the war he joined Shell and was posted to China for eight years. A short spell in the Oxford office was followed by his appointment as Publicity Manager in 1928 or 1929. In 1932 Shell and British Petroleum decided to combine their publicity and trading operations in the United Kingdom by setting up a separate company – Shell-Mex BP Ltd. Beddington became director responsible for publicity in the new company, answerable only to the General Manager, W. Halford.

Beddington made the most of his new opportunities. Lord Clark remembered him as looking like 'an amiable Levantine pirate'.[1] Professor Richard Guyatt described him as 'a wizard, albeit a suave and worldly wizard'.[2] Beddington was fond of quoting Wilde's remark 'Enough is

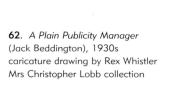

62. *A Plain Publicity Manager* (Jack Beddington), 1930s
caricature drawing by Rex Whistler
Mrs Christopher Lobb collection

61. *E. McKnight Kauffer, c.1933*
photograph by Francis Bruguière
Simon Rendall collection

63. *International Aero
Exhibition* – Shell, 1929
poster, Shell-Mex
E.418-1981

never as good as a feast.' He was a warm, buoyant and practical man. On taking over publicity he did one seemingly trivial, but typical, thing. He arranged for designers' fees to be paid directly from his own department. In this way payments did not have to be churned through an elaborate and lengthy accounting procedure which dealt in very large sums of money. Designers were paid as soon as final art-work was approved. Beddington knew what the Design and Industries Association was doing but Pick's concrete example impressed him more. He also recognized the possibilities of film and recruited two of Grierson's young directors, Stuart Legg and Arthur Elton. In 1932 he sponsored Paul Rotha's first film, *Contact*. He brought in promising literary men like Peter Quennell and John Betjeman, the illustrator Nicholas Bentley, established a studio under Tom Gentleman, and hired the photographer Maurice Beck. Betjeman began the lively and idiosyncratic series of Shell County Guides, a celebrated series which included Paul Nash's Dorset volume (and inspired Nash to a set of fine photographs).

Beddington had a serious interest in the art of his own time. He was a nephew of Sidney and Violet Schiff, who were among the very few who had commissioned work from the short-lived sculptor Henri Gaudier-Brzeska. Six de Chirico paintings hung in their drawing-room in Ilchester Place. Beddington's cousin Sir Edward Beddington-Behrens commissioned Stanley Spencer's Burghclere murals and maintained Oskar Kokoschka during the Second World War. Bryan Robertson has described Beddington as 'a man who really understood artists and continually sought new means of patronage without ever becoming patronizing in his own manner' – which was, Robertson added, 'unfailingly warm-hearted and full of fun'.[3] His collection included many works by artists who are not famous or even well-known – a sure sign of collecting for the love not the prestige of art – and he bought from artists who genuinely needed support. On occasion he bought paintings which he thought the artist might have difficulty in selling elsewhere. He was a familiar figure, rushing out at lunchtimes to see new shows and follow up artists who interested him. His collection included works by Wyndham Lewis, Sickert, David Bomberg, Merlyn Evans, L.S. Lowry and Bernard Cohen – also two water-colours by Kauffer, who resumed painting in 1931.[4]

and Albert Museum in 1931, presumptively the date of its use) has dramatically receding telegraph poles which are derived from Cassandre's *La Route Bleue* of 1929.

Kauffer's relations with Pick were those of an enthusiastic professional who liked to discuss art with his client. With Beddington the relationship was social, and they and Olivia and Marion were often together at the Café Royal, the Gargoyle Club, the Ivy Restaurant or the Savoy Grill. Kauffer's letters to Beddington are the only surviving clues to his inner life at this period. They are often uninformative in themselves but are worth recording as evidence of the kind is so rare. Without such letters Kauffer might seem a mere designing machine. Kauffer wrote to Beddington – away on a business trip to America in 1935 – of the excitement of having his posters on the streets. 'My new posters have all been printed now and I am longing to see them up.' He goes on:

I have kept so close to my studio that I've seen no one. Man Ray is over – sends his best to you. Eric [Gregory?] has gone to Spain until Boxing Day. I've not seen Grierson or Philip [?]. I'm doing some new Underground things – there is a great wave of pro-Chinese ideas – and the weather is sad – and I wonder often and often what it is all about! I would like to do great things with my designing – but I never seem to get there. I wish you were here – I need to talk to you.[7]

In 1936 Kauffer and Marion separated temporarily with the aim of discovering each other afresh. Kauffer went alone to Aix-en-Provence in April on a painting expedition and wrote back to the Beddingtons. Writing on the notepaper of the Café des Deux Garçons he explained that 'the name of this café does not signify that I have changed my morals':

I am starting to paint in dead earnest. Up to now I have with weather permitting made attempts – but the results have been discouraging. Hoping and working towards being a good artist requires courage – for when one sees how miserable results can be – to face the problem again and again and still with failure – does I say require a courage which most people do not understand. I wish I could stay on until about August. I could I feel get a really good show for the autumn … I like the quiet life I lead here. I am early to bed – and up early in the morning. I see Matthew Smith at least once a day and we have

Shows of Kauffer's water-colours and gouaches were held at Tooth's in 1931 and 1933. A stay at Clive Bell's villa behind Cassis in the South of France resulted in enough work for the 1931 show (which included original designs for book illustrations) and a second trip produced the landscapes shown at Tooth's in 1933. Some individual works are far above 'holiday painting' and achieve real distinction: suitably 'posterized', the style of his paintings appears in the series of landscape posters for the Great Western Railway published in 1932. The Beddingtons acquired a Kauffer rug for the house in Lansdowne Road which they took in June 1929. It is one of Kauffer's most successful rugs, in navy blue, black, off-white and beige.[5]

Later in the same year Kauffer wrote to Beddington and his wife Olivia to thank them for offering him a stay in the country. Kauffer says that he has too much work on but hopes to get over to Paris soon:

This will be a change for me – which is all that I need. And it will be a stimulus as well – also all I need – for Paris thrills me with its constant surprises, its continual surprises, its continual experiment – all the painting – all the designing – all the new ideas.[6]

On this visit he felt the influence of his great French counterpart, A. M. Cassandre. Kauffer's 16-sheet poster for *Pratt's High Test Motor Spirit* (of which a copy was given to the Victoria

64. *Aldous Huxley's Garden, Provence,* c.1932
gouache
Helen Rendall collection

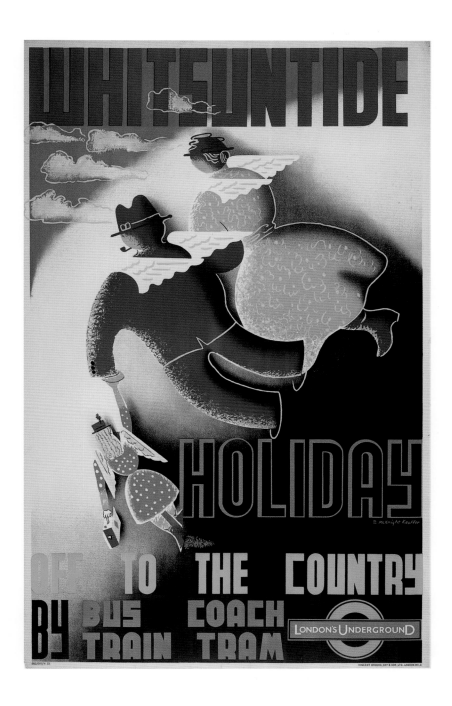

65. *Whitsuntide Holiday*, 1933
poster, London Transport
E.552-1980

become quite intimate friends. He is very interesting and has the greatest of charm. He and I are in very similar situations oddly enough. Our conversation however is not confined to our problem. I think he is England's finest painter as perhaps you know …[8]

It is interesting that Kauffer should have preferred the sensuous, even luscious, work of the painterly Smith over the austere abstractions of Ben Nicholson or the Surrealism of Wadsworth (although Francis Bacon shared the preference). Of the trio, Smith represented the most traditional kind of painting in his exuberant renditions of nudes, landscapes and still-life. Kauffer wrote again a week or two later:

Matthew Smith has gone now and I find that I had grown very fond of him – because I miss him. Vague and never knowing what he is going to do next – full of anxieties – nervous – shy – yet so very charming. He wrote me a note when he left – began 'cher ami' and there is something touching about this …

I get bored to death with a man by name E.McK.K. so much so that I could easily kill the b——d (ask Jack). I have done two watercolours that I am willing to take my hat off to and when the rain stops again I feel I am now on the track of big business. Jack – you must not worry about my gambling – playing with francs does not amuse me and since I can play with no higher stakes – I don't play because I don't wish to be bored with petty winnings or petty losses. So the old paternal spirit can park its hips!

… A young Scotsman whom I did not meet stayed here two days – told the proprietor I was a big shot in England and the proprietor came rushing up to me so out of breath that I thought the place had caught on fire – but just to say 'I now know who you are' to which I replied 'Achille, you're telling tales out of school.' He is a funny little man and I have always joked with him and by doing this kept getting my pension cheaper. But he had the first laugh on me because I tried to tell him when I first arrived that I was an artist – But what I evidently said was 'I am a painting' – sounds pretty conceited to me.[9]

Kauffer also wrote to Beddington when both were in England, sometimes asking for payment at the 'rough' stage of a design. On 1 April 1937 he wrote:

You are always so sympathetic and good to me – I hesitate to ask any special consideration – but I thought the Aeroplane job would be well complete by now and I promised to pay my income tax on Monday. I have other things finished for which payment is due – but these are not yet turning up! I have been passing through a strange – slow period which always precedes a new development in my work – but which is painful and often very impractical. As I get older these periods become more insistent – I suppose the years behind and the years coming wedge one in between – experience past and hope for the future. My domestic life is completely happy – and Marion's sweet devotion strengthens me – but there is this persistent desire to go further and further with my work which if I allowed to take possession of me would be disastrous from an economic standpoint. This is my problem, my mal de coeur – only this.

Kauffer's phrase the 'Aeroplane job' might give rise to speculation, given his status as a design all-rounder. In fact he did design the exterior colour scheme, or livery, of an aeroplane. This was the Handy-Heck plane developed for Whitney Straight in 1932–3. Only one was produced. A water-colour records Kauffer's stylish livery for it in chocolate brown and black.[10] He also designed other items for Straight's Aluminum Ltd, such as desk sets which were apparently used at Claridge's and the Savoy Hotel. The 1937 job was probably an 'Aero-Shell' poster incorporating a photograph of the Miles-Whitney Straight aeroplane. The poster uses the 'space-frame' device which Kauffer tried out in his photo-mural for the Earl's Court exhibition at Charing Cross Station, a simple spatial illusion in which the aeroplane takes off. The device is of great consequence for Kauffer's last and finest work in the theatre, in this same year, which will be discussed below.

The poster was one of a whole series of 'lorry bills' Kauffer designed for Shell in the thirties. The series ranks as one of Kauffer's more grand achievements. The bills were printed to a size of 30 x 45 inches. Beddington had seen to it in 1929, when he first began his publicity work, that Shell advertising was

67. *Stonehenge – See Britain First on Shell*, 1931
lorry bill, Shell-Mex
Circ.168-1968

66. *Lubrication by Shell – Miles-Whitney Straight*, 1937
lorry bill, Shell-Mex & BP
Circ.577-1971

disciplined.[11] Instead of disfiguring rural areas, posters were shown on the sides of the company's lorries. The lorries were painted green and red and even in the early thirties the drivers sat up exposed to the weather in cabs without windscreens. In the back was a large tank and a set of oil-drums kept in by cattle-truck sides. On each side and across the tailboard were special panels for the bills, which framed them with a trim black margin. This was how Kauffer's Shell posters were usually seen in the 1930s, although some of the lorry bills were also printed at '48 sheet' size, 10 x 20 feet. An example is the 1933 BP Ethyl poster, which is altered when one imagines it at the size of a hoarding: so too is one's appreciation of the audacity of Beddington's campaign. He was a bold client but perhaps not as advanced in taste as his principal designer. Kauffer designed three

68. *BP Ethyl Controls Horse-power*, 1933
lorry bill, Shell-Mex & BP
Circ.317-1971

extraordinarily advanced petrol pump tops for Shell–Mex in 1934 – simple but revolutionary abstract designs in primary red, yellow, and other bold colours, which were never used.

The letter to Beddington suggests an anxious period of preparation for change. A few months later Kauffer designed a poster which embodies this change. It is the one poster which Kauffer described his working methods for, and it is an account reinforced in interest by some recollections from his assistant Sidney Garrad.

69. *Magicians Prefer Shell*, 1935
lorry bill, Shell-Mex & BP
Circ.156-1968

70. *Shell Mex*, 1934
design for Shell petrol pump top, Shell-Mex
E.3767-2004

New Shell Lubricating Oils 1937

The starting-point is a discussion with the client (Beddington) which releases a swarm of first impressions of the product – and some internal questions like 'Will my client understand what I propose to do? Will he trust an intuitive solution to the problem?'[12] Back in his studio Kauffer settles down to experiment with different weights of lettering, different ways of presenting the actual product – a conical oil-can, with a red robot symbol on it (based on an artist's lay-figure) which Kauffer had designed some years earlier. He looks for some way of balancing lettering and product, and reaches a point where the two ingredients establish 'a direction which seems to suit the character of the product. If this is so a new *stimulus* is set up.' At this point he remembers that when the client gave him the name of the product 'a ribbon came into my mind'. 'Now why did I associate the movement of a ribbon with the product at the time of our interview? A ribbon, so I think, suggests smoothness. softness – yes … I accept the ribbon as a symbol – so now I have three parts to my design. The framework, as it were, is complete.' With relief he can now put the client out of his mind. What about the public? is his next consideration. A suggestion of speed is discounted – 'only a few specialists are allowed this extravagance'. But 'the design nevertheless should express movement – smooth curvilinear movement – a suggestion that everything is working well.' He devises a scheme to convey this idea. A contrast between an oily black ground, purple ribbon, yellow lettering and red and yellow oil-can establish an attention-getting colour scheme. The ribbon provides the co-ordinating link and implies the reading order of the words.

Kauffer went on to speak of the 'latent symbolism' of his ribbon. The poster was intended to satisfy client, public and also himself. The ribbon, in a sense, represents 'Kauffer-as-Artist'. He thought it was related to an act of spontaneous, intensified vision when 'a strip of cardboard fell from one of my shirts as I took it out of a drawer. I started to pick it up off the floor and suddenly became aware of something unusual in the shapes of light and dark.' The fascination was genuine, if inexplicable, and he began to draw the card from different angles. Sidney Garrad remembered that the poster was designed during another bout of separation from Marion Dorn. Kauffer took a room at the Mount Royal Hotel in Oxford Street. He repeatedly drew

lengths of ribbon – throwing actual pieces over his shoulder and then drawing them in poster colours as they lay. As was often the case Sidney was entrusted with the task of enlarging the design for lithographic printing. Kauffer saw a minute flaw in his assistant's copy and flew into a rage – a most unusual occurrence. In a fury he tore up not the enlargement but his own original. The poster was lithographed from the assistant's copy. (Kauffer also used the ribbon motif in the poster *Ford Approves Shell*, 1936.)

Surely to take poster design so seriously, to get into such a state about pieces of ribbon and invisible errors, surely all this seems faintly ludicrous? Perhaps it is, but perhaps it is best understood as an expression of Kauffer's frustration as a private man working in a very public medium. The importance he attached to work in the public sector is made clear in the address he gave to the Royal Society of Arts in 1938. Nothing much had changed technically, he thought, since the time of Lautrec, compared to another kind of change:

Our social background … has changed within thirty years almost beyond recognition. This has had its effect upon the artist, and a profound one, too. With the world as it is, and social values what they are, there is an almost inevitable tendency for thoughtful and creative people to seek sanctuary in a private world. I cannot help feeling myself that external reality has to some extent lost something of its collective significance, or perhaps it is that its significance seems less valuable and less immediate in its appeal, contrasted with the distress that social disruption on such a colossal scale as we have witnessed in our time, has created.[13]

In these circumstances – as Europe moved closer towards another war – Kauffer saw his work as a healing art, the more effective as it was part and parcel of ordinary business transactions. He even saw the enlightening commerce between artist and public as obstructed only by conscience-less, badly directed, commerce; and he went so far as to suggest that artists who did not work in advertising were – in the face of massive social dislocation – contributing nothing. (Presumably this was said in the heat of the moment – he would surely not have preferred Matthew Smith to flounder among problems of design which he himself handled with mastery – and yet his friend

71. *New Shell Lubricating Oils*, 1937
lorry bill, Shell-Mex & BP
Circ.576-1971

Kenneth Clark said almost as much in 1939: 'To be a pure painter
seems almost immoral.')[14] Kauffer's words may seem 'extreme'
but they may simply be visionary: undoubtedly they are utterly
genuine.

The artist in advertising is a new kind of being ... it is his business
constantly to correct values, to establish new ones, to stimulate
advertising and help to make it worthy of the civilisation that needs it.[15]

A Note on Technique

Kauffer published a short note on technique in the catalogue of an exhibition of his work held at the Museum of Modern Art, New York, in 1937 (about which more will be said in the next chapter):

… I have used all kinds of instruments common to most contemporary painters, such as tooth brushes, cheese cloth, wire netting, etc. – in fact anything that suggests interesting textures. The air-brush I seldom use now, but when I did use it a few years ago I realized that it was a tricky instrument and that its use required an exceedingly disciplined technique. At the moment I prefer methods less exacting and with more direct contact between my idea and the medium.

A sponge-brush was a favourite tool, used for the illustrations to *Elsie and the Child*, for example. Tooth brushes were used to achieve a 'splatter' effect through a wire grid – this resembles air-brush technique at first glance but has a rougher, less machine-like, texture.

Kauffer usually provided clients with two 'rough' designs for posters, often quite similar treatments. The one chosen was then enlarged in scale for printing. In the thirties Sidney Garrad was responsible for much of the work of enlargement, including the lettering. Kauffer's use of lettering has not won favour with typographers. He would not allow his assistant to adjust letter spacing, for example, to compensate for the inequalities of spacing inherent in letter forms. He also insisted on a number of incongruous distortions of letter forms in keeping with his own ideas of consistency – so that, for example, the horizontal bars of Ps and Rs defy good typographic usage. His early posters were Double Crown size (20 x 30 inches, or One Sheet). For these he provided same-size originals. After 1921 the Underground used the Double Royal size (25 x 40 inches), for which Kauffer made half-size scale originals. The Shell lorry bills, at 30 x 45 inches, were a special variation on the standard Quad Crown (30 x 40 inches) size. Kauffer's expertise included photography – he himself took the night photograph of the Horse Tamers in the Place de la Concorde, which he used in montage on *BP Ethyl Controls Horse-Power* (plate 68). His albums of photographs are now in the late Sir Paul Getty Library and the Cooper-Hewitt National Design Museum.

THE OPENING OF THE NEW SPRING

COLLECTION ON TUESDAY MARCH 15TH

3 P.M. AND THEREAFTER SHOWN DAILY

ON THE FIRST FLOOR

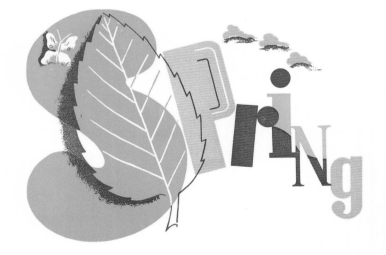

72. *Spring*, c.1936
invitation, Fortnum & Mason
AAD 10/238

73. *Our new Colours for Spring 1933*
outside cover of invitation, Fortnum & Mason
AAD 10/239

74. *Checkmate*, 1937
costumes and stage set, Sadler's Wells Theatre
The Bystander, 15 December 1937

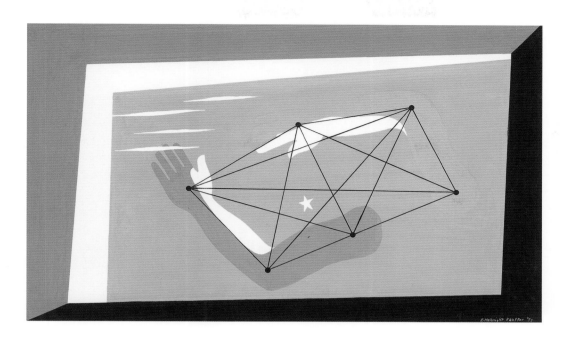

75. *Checkmate*, 1937
original design for prologue curtain,
Sadler's Wells Theatre
E.6-1957

Checkmate 1937

Kauffer's designs for *Checkmate* form the climax of his work in the theatre. He had maintained contact with this medium by designing the stage settings and principal dresses for Ernest Milton's production of *Othello*, which opened at the St James's Theatre on 4 April 1932. Milton himself played the title role but was generally thought to have miscast himself – he lacked physical stature and presence and the play was soon taken off. Flora Robson's Bianca and Henry Oscar's Iago drew praise from James Agate, who felt that the production had been 'run away with by Miss Robson and Mr Oscar pounding neck and neck, with Mr McKnight Kauffer's beautiful scenery half a length behind'.[16] In the *Observer* Ivor Brown praised Kauffer's designs for their distinction and lack of 'selfconscious fuss'.[17] Little evidence survives to give a good idea of Kauffer's work for the play, although the sets were naturalistic, rather geometrical and low-key in colour.[18]

His next theatre work was for John Gielgud's production of a new play by Gordon Daviot, *Queen of Scots*, which opened at the New Theatre in St Martin's Lane on 8 June 1934. Gwen Ffrangcon-Davies played Mary Stuart, Laurence Olivier was the Earl of Bothwell and James Mason played a minor part. Kauffer contributed the scenery – which is austere in design and calculatedly crude in painted finish – and the principal men's costumes. Motley designed the dresses of the principal women. There was no relationship between the conventionally sumptuous historical costumes and the archaic austerity of the

sets. The *Morning Post* critic found nothing to complain of in the contradiction of styles and described the production as 'a joy to the eye at every point, simple in stagery, gorgeous in costume'.[19] The *Sunday Times*, surprisingly, found the play 'too pretty. The fault is magnified by Mr McKnight Kauffer's smart scenery which is like the shop window of some ultra-modish decorator. The dresses are handsomer still, and one feels that the entire company might be going on to the costliest and most charitable ball.'[20] The play was widely noticed and generally well received but failed – unfortunately for Kauffer, whose fee of £20 was to have been augmented by a percentage of box-office receipts.

76. *Marion V. Dorn*, c.1937
photograph by E. McKnight Kauffer
The late Sir Paul Getty, KBE, Wormsley Library

Kauffer's collaboration with Ninette de Valois and Arthur Bliss to create *Checkmate* in 1937 was his first and last triumph in the theatre. He had first worked with de Valois when he provided a special curtain used for a musical interlude (Walton's *Portsmouth Point* overture) in an evening of ballet arranged by the Camargo Society at the Savoy Theatre in 1932. Ninette de Valois, once a soloist in the Ballet Russe, filled a vacuum in ballet after Diaghilev's death in 1929. Her Vic-Wells Ballet company was founded in 1931, later taking the name of its home theatre as the Sadler's Wells Ballet. *Checkmate* was the production which marked the company's arrival at international stature. Bliss provided the book and score, de Valois the choreography, McKnight Kauffer the costumes and the two stage curtains required. The ballet was first given, as *Echec et Mat*, at the Théâtre des Champs Elysées in Paris on 15 June 1937. It was the first night of the season and the Vic-Wells Ballet had been taken to Paris by the British Council as part of the national contingent for the International Exhibition of that year. The cast for the first performance included June Brae as the Black Queen, Harold Turner as the First Red Knight, Robert Helpmann as the Red King, Pamela May as the Red Queen, William Chappell as the Second Red Knight, and Richard Ellis and Michael Somes as the Black Knights. The two chess players, Love and Death, who form a prologue to the ballet, were given by Frederick Ashton and Alan Carter. The *corps de ballet* included Margot Fonteyn (as a pawn).

Kauffer's curtain for the prologue was blue-grey in colour and decorated with a giant arm and hand, suggestive of an artificial limb operated by wires and pulleys. The isolated hand was a typical quasi-Surrealist feature of Kauffer's design repertoire in the thirties. Here it is aptly used to focus on the crucial moment about to be enacted in the game of chess between Love and Death. It is a visual magnification of the moment and a dramatization of the geometry of chess – but also perhaps implies an impersonally operating destiny. The curtain rises to reveal a giant chess board on which the dance of Love and Death is enacted. Kauffer's block-like costumes echo the geometry of the squares: red for the forces of love, grey-blue and black for the

side of death. The dancing – Bliss said that de Valois 'moved the pieces like an Alekhine' – takes place before Kauffer's second curtain. This again made use of items from his basic stock of devices. He chose to adapt his space-frame convention – sets of parallel lines angled to imply sharp backward recession (or abrupt forward movement). These are linked with a sequence of four large-scale triangles, which are again tilted to imply movement. The shapes shift on different visual readings and in scale, angularity and colour provide a symbolic setting for the action: heroic, restless and intense. The Black Queen first seduces, then treacherously kills the Red Knight, and finally forces the Red King to submit to her will. The ballet critic Clive Barnes singled out as the most striking visual images the entrance of the Red King and Queen, the funeral cortège of the Red Knight and 'the sudden twist of the body given by the Red King as he sees himself trapped by the inexorable Black forces'.[21]

The ballet was well received in Paris and in London, where it opened at the Sadler's Wells Theatre on 5 October 1937. Barnes perceptively suggested that the theme must, in 1937, have carried with it 'political overtones (of which possibly even the composer and choreographer were unaware) greatly adding to the poignancy for contemporary audiences. Abyssinia, Austria, and later Czechoslovakia, all forced to their knees by the aggressive forces in Europe, probably gave a particular truthfulness to the Red King's tragedy.' This would have been much enhanced by Robert Helpmann's dancing, which an eye-witness of the performances in 1937 described as 'a tremendous performance of nervous terror that has never been approached by any of his successors'.[22] The ballet drew very large audiences and earned the admiration of Toscanini. All the sets and costumes were lost in Holland in May 1940 when the Vic-Wells Ballet was caught in The Hague by the German invasion. The company was able to make its way back to England in safety, but was obliged to leave behind the scenery, costumes and music for six ballets. Kauffer redesigned *Checkmate* – effectively streamlining his original conception – for its post-war revival at Covent Garden on 18 November 1947.[23]

The White House at Northend

'We have the cottage – Field can leave mid-May – we are so excited – too good to be true sort of feeling – so now we shall be neighbours,' wrote Kauffer to Olivia Beddington on 14 April 1938. They had the lease of a charming, small Regency house in Buckinghamshire – the White House, Northend – not far from the Beddingtons' country retreat at Turville Heath. The village of Northend was a scatter of houses with a shop or two, some farms and a duck pond, eight miles from Henley-on-Thames in the Chiltern hills. The White House has a large garden with a wood behind it. This swoops down to a valley with cornfields laid out among gentle knolls. They were pleased to discover that the

proprietor of the village store was Harold Curwen. One thing still marked out the reformer of printing in his retirement job: the big drawers of flour, brown sugar and tapioca were labelled in a neat calligraphic hand learned from Edward Johnston thirty years before.[24] Kauffer took great interest in the house and extended the sitting-room and panelled it. He also converted an out-house into a studio. French windows looked out on to newly planted shrubs, apple trees from an old orchard, and a handsome walnut tree. Away to the left was a paddock, a farm-house beyond that. Grass plots were laid out and bordered with bricks, vegetables put in, hedges planted.

77. *The White House, Northend,*
c.1938
photograph by E. McKnight Kauffer
The late Sir Paul Getty, KBE,
Wormsley Library

The surrounding Buckinghamshire landscape made a great impression on Kauffer. Despite the growing certainty of war and scarcer commissions, the next two years were among Kauffer's happiest. He made many photographs down in the cornfields at harvest-time. It was in the valley below the wood that he saw a 'Phoenix' one day – at least that is what one of his photographs makes out of the simple ingredients of a corn-stook, a jacket and a stick. Something of this scene appears in his posters – *TVO–Draw Bar Pull*, an agricultural theme no doubt specially commissioned by Beddington in 1938, and two landscape posters for the Underground in the same year which are lyrical Buckinghamshire fields and woods (*right*). At every opportunity Kauffer and Marion would jump into their Packard car – with their silver cairn terrier Timsy – and make the quick journey from Chelsea to Northend.

No sooner had Kauffer put down roots in the English countryside than war threatened to remove him from England altogether. On 5 June 1939 he sent his daughter Ann the present of Rimbaud's *Poesies* and wrote: 'Since the September crisis my work and work like mine has been very much cut down but I

78. *May to October – Summer Shell*, 1939
lorry bill, Shell-Mex & BP
Circ.159-1968

79. *Autumn Woods*, 1939
poster, London Transport
E.1453-1959

expect business will pick up again.'[25] A little later he wrote again. War had already been declared. 'My usual work has been stopped of course and unless I can get some other kind of work I shall be forced to go to America. In the meantime I am doing the tasks of an ordinary country labourer – and not minding it.' On 5 October he wrote: 'My work is dead for the moment, but here I work in the fields and vegetables and saw and chop wood.' They took an evacuee, a boy of 11.

On Christmas Day 1939 he reported to his daughter that he had been invited to New York, where a retrospective exhibition of his work at the Museum of Modern Art had brought him some reputation in 1937. He had an agent there eager to promote him and had already designed a series of covers for *Harper's Bazaar*. 'Work here is practically nonexistent and I find when I do see heads of propaganda departments for the Government – I am appalled and disheartened by the triumph of the second-rate intelligence. All the jobs are occupied with inferior advertising "professionals" except one. I have seen Robert Bevan [son of the painter] at the Ministry of Information – I knew him as a young boy. He is the only one I have met who tries and will try to get something above the commonplace.'

Kauffer occupied himself reading Kierkegaard and Dante and tried his hand at illustrating the *Inferno*. He encouraged his daughter to think of the future. 'The war is awful and wasteful – yet if your generation can see it through – there will be a new world – a really new one this time for there is a new and strong desire of the people for spiritual values – such as was not apparent during and after the last war. No dear, it's going to be a fine world – Truly.' He was given part-time employment at the Ministry of Information – poorly paid, but worse, a hack job which he felt wasted his talents. He wrote to Ann from the Ministry of Information on 19 June 1940: 'I understand from the U.S. Embassy that all American citizens will be considered liabilities if conditions become bad. I have made inquiries about work for your mother – no Americans can get work unless they do it voluntarily for American organizations. Whether I wish to leave England or not I more than likely will have to do so because of a means to earn a living which can not be expected to be obtained here.' His position was aggravated by a strange bureaucratic necessity which obliged him to obtain a travelling

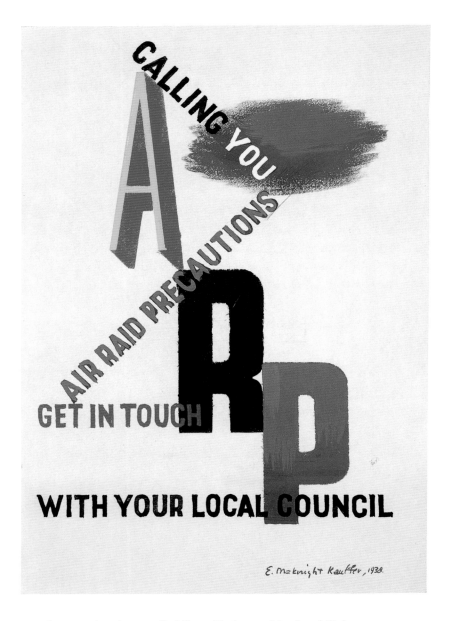

permit every time he travelled from Chelsea to Northend. 'I do hope in any case', Eliot wrote to him on 5 June 1940, 'that the position will be dealt with sensibly, so that you do not need to get special permission to move between Chelsea and Northend on each occasion'.[26]

The two men were on intimate terms by this time. On Easter Monday 1940 Kauffer wrote to congratulate Eliot on a newly published poem: 'Your greatness of spirit and humility have never been set down better than in "East Coker". It is difficult not to write to you without reverence – but it is a reverence of appreciation and thankfulness that you live and that you write

80. *Air Raid Precautions – Calling You*, 1938
original design for poster, ARP
E.3266-1980

and that we can read what you write.'[27] 'Now about the White House', Eliot replied, 'nothing would give me more anticipation of content than the prospect of another visit to Mr and Mrs Roosevelt … May I come down after the middle of June?'[28] A little later he acknowledged the gift of a water-colour from Kauffer and confessed: 'I have imitated you and bought a pair of fawn corduroy trousers: but mine are only Daks.'[29] He came to Northend for the weekend of 7–10 June 1940. At Kauffer's request he wrote a poem for use as a 'broadside' at a British photographic exhibition to be held later that year in New York, 'Britain at War'. Under the walnut tree Eliot composed 'Defence of the Islands'. He inscribed the original pencilled draft, now in the Pierpont Morgan Library: 'For Marion Dorn in remembrance of June 7–10 1940'. When he later collected the poem Eliot dedicated it to Kauffer's memory.

Already German raiders had appeared over Buckinghamshire and the Dunkirk evacuation had occurred. Eliot's moving poem is one long sentence which is almost of prose plainness, closing with the words:

… to say, to the past and future generations
of our kin and of our speech, that we took up
our positions, in obedience to instructions.

Within a very short time of its completion, however, on 1 July 1940, Kauffer and Marion Dorn had left the country. The next day Peter Gregory began a diary:

On July 1st I suffered a great loss in the departure of Ted and Marion Kauffer: they returned to America on SS *Washington*, which sailed from Galway: they went at almost a moment's notice. The American Ambassador issued an intimation that the *Washington* would probably be the last boat to take back American citizens and that those who remained would become liabilities: so there was practically no alternative but for them to go. They only knew a few days beforehand and then they had to make hurried preparations … they could only take such personal belongings as clothes and twenty-five pounds each.[30]

In retrospect the decision to leave seems to have been a mistake – a mistake serious enough in its consequences to be called tragic. Eliot had taken British citizenship, Kauffer had not – as an 'alien' he was not only subject to petty, misapplied regulations governing his movements, but also, it seems, not quite accepted at the Ministry of Information. As an alien he was paid on a fee rather than salary basis – at £3 3s a day.[31] This level of payment was not ungenerous. What disheartened Kauffer was the lack of intelligence and awareness at the Ministry. He felt that his assistant could do all the tasks which he himself was assigned – and when Kauffer left his assistant did take over the post. Marion was worried about family affairs in California. Kauffer felt that they were already – giving no real return in work for the valuable food and supplies they consumed – liabilities. New York seemed to want him. The decision was made. Hans Schleger rang the Swan Court flat by chance to be told by the maid that Kauffer and Marion Dorn were already on their way to the railway station en route for Ireland. Schleger hurried to the station. After Kauffer's death he wrote this account of the departure, which was also his final tribute to him:

On a dismal afternoon in 1940, I said goodbye to Ted Kauffer and Marion in a railway carriage – made smaller by Marion's harpsichord. We had been friends since we met.

Ted was an infinitely complex person. Known to the world by his austere and masculine work, friends knew his frail and sensitive inner being – clients loved his great charm and courage, feared his unwillingness to make concessions. He liked to smile and to tease his friends – yet he was an intense and serious man; he rarely designed a humorous poster. He was tender but remote … among designers: the 'First Gentleman'.

He loved England but remained American in fact and in feeling. As Laver said of Whistler, he had something of the potted plant, transferred but never transplanted.

Ted wanted to serve public rather than commercial interests – that is why he liked Jack Beddington's Shell and Frank Pick's and Christian Barman's Underground.

We lost his leadership during the war. He left because – impatiently mistaken – he believed himself suddenly unwanted. The shock felled him.

In America he did not find contact with his home soil – the plant had grown unaccustomed to the now foreign climate. He was a great and generous friend.[32]

7

NEW YORK
1940 – 54

Kauffer and Marion Dorn left nearly everything behind in England, down to the sheets on the beds. Peter Gregory took on their flat at Swan Court and the painter Hubert Wellington and his wife Irene (the distinguished calligrapher) took over the lease of the White House. It was not until 23 February 1941 that Kauffer wrote his first full letter back to Jack Beddington:

My dear Jack –

I should have written to you long ago though I did write you a letter thanking you for the notes to Resor and Cecil but it was a note and not a real letter. I have not seen either of the above yet! And I won't explain because it is too long and irrelevant.

I need not tell you that New York on extremely short rations (money) is no joke. By infinite scraping and working like hell on small jobs, anything that comes along, we have between us been able to eat (modestly and our own preparing) and to pay the rent. I have seen the winter through with a raincoat and one pair of shoes. I brought two pair suedes with me but these are like paper in the cold and snow so I bought a pair $10.49. You see I have a swell reputation but I have a 'European point of view' and the English point of view interesting as it is is not the American point of view. So I have to 'build up' slowly again. I *will* do it, my teeth are set but it can't be done in a hurry.

Shortly after we arrived I did a job for N.W. Ayer for the Lincoln Continental car. Ayers were just losing the Ford account and the catalogue was so badly printed that as a job for getting others it was a washout and poorly paid to boot. During the last fortnight I have landed (again Ayer) some colour pages for The American Container Corporation, Fortune and Life ads – but this is a prestige job and not a money maker! So what! Bread and butter thin at times has been obtained by my doing bookjackets principally for Donald Klopfer

81. *E. McKnight Kauffer and T.S. Eliot in New York*, 1948
Photograph by George Platt Lynes
Simon Rendall collection

[of Random House] and Knopf.

Marion has been wonderful about the situation. She has worked every minute, peddled Seventh Avenue and made scarves. She too will come out on top but it's slow and we have no resources and honestly I would hate to try and borrow money in N.Y. at the present moment.

We see Marjorie quite frequently. She is beginning a new venture for designers and manufacturers. It opens in a fortnight. Marion is one of her headliners – no money yet! She is well and I like Mr Moss – we always speak lovingly of you – wonder what you are up to! She sends her love.

I have heard much about your films [Beddington was appointed director of the Ministry of Information films division in April 1940]. I must be frank and tell you that we have not been to a movie but once since we arrived. You see England is a touchy spot with us – we break down on the slightest provocation – we can't bear to think of her heroic spirit being put to such long and constant endurance. Any actual picture – God Save the King – or a voice on the air – Marion and I are reduced to sobs and despair, because we are not there – this is the reason. We live hermit lives because we feel that while England is in trial and suffering we can by being ourselves be closer to the country and people we love so deeply and dearly.

The White House is sold. I don't know all the reasons why but finances I daresay are the main reasons and it was for these difficulties which were mounting higher and higher we thought it best to try our luck here and not get beyond recovery staying on in England. Had I felt myself to be indispensable at the Ministry I would most certainly have stayed on – but I could not honestly rationalize myself into believing that I was doing anything that my assistant who now fills the job could not do as well. With the sale of the White House went our most precious belonging. We loved this place – it was our first real home. Our other belongings, even my books, affected us not so deeply. In my sleep and in quiet moments of the day I walk the lovely lanes of Buckinghamshire and I see the beechwoods and now the tiny wild flowers and soon the lanes will be busy with nesting.

England will have a beautiful spring again, of this we are all certain, maybe not this one but again for a certainty. It will be renewed in greatness and it will shine again as it did in Queen Elizabeth's day and we here in this new country will envy the growth that has been made through suffering, and endurance such as the world has never seen. We admire Mr Churchill – his is the voice of England both in meaning and in beauty. He is the real statue of liberty which the

people of Britain have made. England is truly the light of the civilised world. God bless England.

I have tears in my eyes, I have a longing to be with you all, a longing that will *never* die.

I love America too but in a different way. It is an objective attachment perhaps and I would have to live here for a long time to feel any intimacy such as I felt so much in England. I love our concept of liberty, I love the clear light and the vast sense of space. I admire our history and our fight for some of the essential rights of man. Our figures in history such as Washington, Jefferson, Lincoln, our men of letters like Franklin, Emerson, Whitman, Poe and many others inspire me with hope and ambition, but I am very sad.

New York streets are lonely I think and I have seen so many people with a homeless kind of expression. This is new to me for you never see that in London.

Dearest Jack. It is now March 2nd! I must get this off to you – quickly – on the next 'Clipper'. There is so much to tell you, yet it all seems so remote from the real thing that is going on in the world. So much stupidity in America: people literally do not know – do not take the trouble or have the interest in finding out *what* the world that loves freedom is up against. I hear their remarks and I beat my head with anguish. If suffering brings understanding – then America must suffer to gain greater capacity to understand.

No day goes by – hardly an hour – the last thing at night – the first thing in the morning – our thoughts are of England.

March 6th

Time passes – another few days since I last tried to finish this letter. It must go – now even though I have left so much unsaid. But I will write soon again and fill the gap.

Have you built the brick wall in the garden? I can see it all and now so many things will be showing their green faces. We give Olivia our devoted love and to the children too. Marion sends love – my affection and love to you – I miss not seeing you – but all our lives are now different so very different – England – beloved England – Devotedly,
Ted

P.S. Joe [Blumenthal? of Spiral Press] sends most affectionate greetings – I will write to you about the 'big shots' in New York designing and tell you how they do not design at all! Its a wonderful racket. I look on in rapt amazement. I now know what's wrong with U.S. design. – Ted

'21' is out of my class, so I can give you no news of your favourite haunt. My best wishes, please, to Miss Spendlove, Vernon Nye and John B. Oh dear, why am I exiled *now!*

Write soon.

Tell Sidney, I shall send a $5 note when the war is over this summer – and give him fondest good wishes from us both – Ted.[1]

Kauffer unburdened himself to his close friend Beddington but he wrote in better order to Colin Anderson a little earlier (10 February 1941):

What seems so strange is that I am here at all. I never imagined myself anywhere except in England – yet I would not become naturalized – a strange conflict. But I think I do know why – simply told it is this – I am an American from the West – no matter how strongly I feel about England, how much I should like to belong to England I could only do so so far. In other words I could not become English because it isn't in my bone and heritage and as I would only be part instead of whole as I should like to have been …

Except for a visit to the Planetarium, the Metropolitan Museum and the Natural History Museum I have hardly moved out of the radius between 46th Street and 60th and across a matter of six American 'blocks' and they are very short. I work every minute – I have none of my work here, either originals or reproductions. So I've had to make a portfolio of work. My European reputation which preceded me by a few years has definitely stamped me as English. This is not a criticism with material inference – but a difference of 'advertising thinking'. The American advertiser respects the European achievement but in no way will he admit it in American practice – so I've got to wear that off! I've got to show them. Shall I be able to do it? My American youth may now be useful at last!

Our winter light is clear, cold and bright. The towering buildings stand out so solid against an infinite blue sky with puffs of white clouds passing on to other frontiers – perhaps to the South where it is warm or perhaps to the West where they will float slowly across deserts and finally rest on the peaks of the Rockies. Wherever you are in America there is always a beyond – the seas are too far from each other and the Mississippi is too long for one to ever stop.

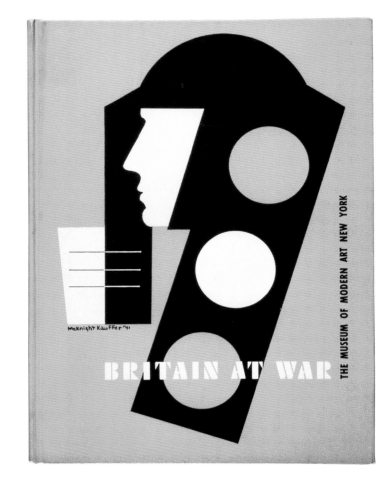

82. *Britain at War*, 1941
catalogue cover, Museum of Modern Art, New York
Simon Rendall collection

The Museum of Modern Art have just opened a very comprehensive exhibition of American Indian Art – sculpture, pottery, some painting, costume and implements. Here is a rich, virile background for Americans to take stock of. It is very Picasso, it is very Chinese, it is even Brancusi – it is not violent like Aztec art. It is in most cases highly sensitive to texture, purpose and use. It is the most stimulating evidence I have seen of an American art …[2]

Kauffer was on very friendly terms with Alfred H. Barr Jr and Monroe Wheeler of the Museum of Modern Art. His 'Britain at War' exhibition was first shown in the British Pavilion at the New York World Fair in the autumn of 1940. The following year it became a Museum of Modern Art exhibition and book – with a cover designed by Kauffer. In 1941 he also designed the cover of the Museum's exhibition catalogue *Organic Design*. Barr had introduced Kauffer's work to the American public in 1937 with an exhibition of 85 posters, which later travelled to other museums in the United States. This was only the second one-man exhibition the Museum had given a poster artist (Cassandre was the first to be so honoured), and the occasion was given added distinction by Aldous Huxley's introduction to the exhibition catalogue. Huxley defined the kind of advertising with which Kauffer was embattled in London and then New York:

Most advertising artists spend their time elaborating symbols that stand for something different from the commodity they are advertising. Soap and refrigerators, scent and automobiles, stockings, holiday resorts,

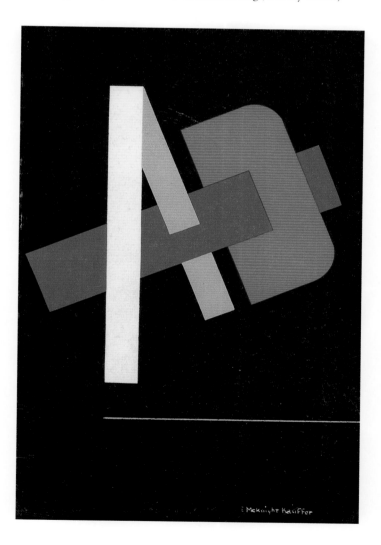

sanitary plumbing and a thousand other articles are advertised by means of representations of young females disporting themselves in opulent surroundings. Sex and money – these would seem to be the two main interests of civilized human beings.

For Huxley, Kauffer's value lay in his use of a rather different type of symbolism – 'the symbols with which he deals are not symbols of something else; they stand for the particular things which are under consideration.'

Eliot wrote on 29 August 1941 giving news of mutual friends, mentioning in passing his fire-watching duties at Faber and Faber, and apologizing for the long silence:

I wish I might have some direct news from you or Marion, but so far I have not deserved it. It must have been very difficult for you to make the decision to leave, but I can well understand and sympathise with the reasons, and I think it was the best thing to do. I have no doubt that the problem of adaptation to New York has been very trying too.[3]

There was no reply to the letter until Marion Dorn wrote back to Eliot on 14 December. Kauffer had had a breakdown during the summer. Marion wrote:

The doctors can talk all they want about germs and viruses, but I knew he wasn't tough enough to meet New York. He dreamed about Lincoln's America and the pioneers, and I remember telling Eric once all about Ted's vision of America, and how the thought of his coming here frightened me.[4]

Kauffer momentarily lost his nerve. In the extreme competitiveness of New York advertising he found it difficult to sell work because, Marion wrote, he was no longer confident enough to sell himself. Fortunately, Marion came into some family money, and they were able to establish themselves in a grand flat overlooking Central Park at 40 Central Park South. The apartment was more opulent than their previous quarters, but bare of decoration except for lots of house plants and a Quattrocento angel in a painted blue robe.[5]

In October 1941 Kauffer was represented in an exhibition at the Katharine Kuh Gallery, Chicago, called 'The Advance Guard of Advertising Artists' – with Frank Barr, Lester Beall, Gyorgy

83. *A-D*, 1941
journal cover, A-D Publishing Co
Graham Twemlow collection

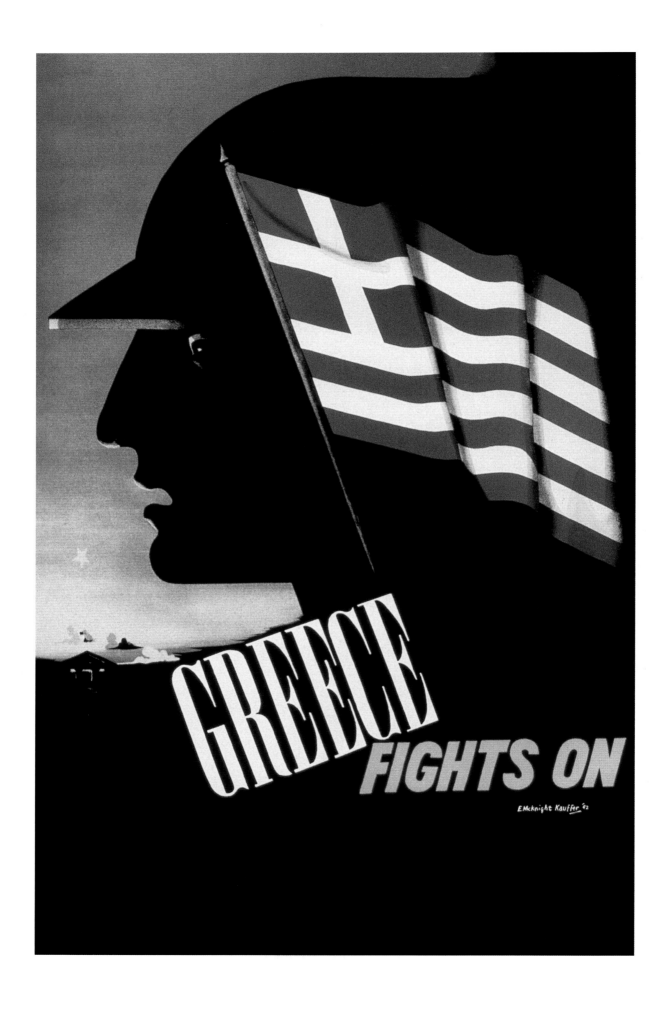

Kepes, Herbert Matter, Moholy-Nagy, Paul Rand, and Ladislav Sutnar. The exhibition was also shown at the A–D Gallery, New York, in the following March. On 26 November 1941 he addressed the Art Directors' Club of New York.[6] He opened with a quotation from C.H.Waddington's book *The Scientific Attitude*: 'The true, or at least the most important, task of the cultural worker is to reveal to man the spiritual riches which result from the full exploitation of the immediate, practical possibilities.' He went on to make two points which he was to make on many future occasions. The first was that American businessmen were, in general, remote from contact with their designers compared to their English counterparts. He later wrote of the 'in-between world of research, rationalization and sales-talk' which divided client and designer.[7] His second point was that American advertising was not ambitious enough in relation to its political and literary heritage and the grandeur of its natural environment: 'Does it compete or throw into relief anything of this big scene?'

Perhaps inevitably, Kauffer's reputation remained a rather esoteric one and his commissions for posters came mainly from institutions. He designed institutional magazine advertisements for the Container Corporation and American Silk Mills, war posters for Asuntos Interamericanos, the Greek War Relief Association, Friends of Greece, Inc., American Friends of Norway, the Office of Civilian Defense, the CAA War Training Service, the United Committee of South Slavic Americans, the United CIO War Relief Committee and the American Red Cross. Of his poster *Steel! Not Bread* (a bayoneted hand) Kauffer said: 'America has been trying to sell the war to the public with pretty legs and bosoms. War is grim and you have to be grim to win.' The poster was designed for the US War Bond Drive and in 1943 Kauffer was honoured by the US Treasury Department for 'distinguished service in the War Savings Program'.

The 1945 Red Cross contribution campaign was heralded by Kauffer's *Give* poster. The design featured a blue-black background with a white arrow pointing diagonally downward to the simple one-word message GIVE. The small red cross in the white arrow was the focal colour spot. Millions of copies of this poster were printed in a variety of different sizes, down to postcards. They were distributed for posting on wall panels, sides of lorries, bulletin boards in schools, churches and public

buildings, in the interiors of trains, buses and stores, as well as on giant outdoor hoardings on highways and city streets. The design was no doubt a potent factor in the highly successful Red Cross appeal.[8] Kauffer received a 'Certificate of Honor' from the American Red Cross in 1945.

Other clients included Barnum and Bailey's Circus, and the New York Subways Advertising Co Inc. For the New York Subway Kauffer produced a design on a theme dear to his heart – a minimal indication of a clown's face with the text *Subway Posters Perform Daily Before Five Million Pairs of Eyes*, devised for a campaign in 1947–8. The design won the Art Director of the job, Jefferson Tester, an Award for Distinctive Merit from the Art Directors' Club of New York. It appeared as poster, mailing piece and magazine advertisement and was shown in exhibitions of contemporary American poster art in Vienna and Japan. In 1947 Kauffer became Honorary Advisor to the Department of Public Information of the United Nations. A commission from the Container Corporation gave him especial pleasure. He was asked to contribute an image of Montana for a series of full-colour magazine pages depicting every state in the Union, commissioned by the Corporation in 1945–6. When contact with Eliot was resumed after the war Kauffer liked to call him Missouri (Eliot was born in St Louis) and to be called 'Montana' in return.[9]

In addition to these institutional commissions Kauffer was busy with the designs of scores of book jackets – for his old friend Alfred Knopf, the Modern Library, Harcourt Brace, Random House, Pantheon Books and other companies. For Knopf he illustrated Langston Hughes's book *Shakespeare in Harlem*, a congenial task as he was fond of Harlem and its Negro population.[10] At a public meeting of the Committee on Art Education of the Museum of Modern Art in April 1948 Kauffer spoke as follows:

New forms of education, social problems of adjustment, racial discrimination and the Negro problem for which there is now an urgent necessity for intelligent and human cooperation, the activities of municipal public services, state problems and finally national problems, all of these need the services of intelligent thinkers, capable writers and the best designers.[11]

84. *Greece Fights On*, 1942
poster, Greek Office of Information
E.2907-1980

Books and their illustration were, however, to take up more of his time than his typical milieu of poster art (apart from one significant exception which we shall come to). The illustrations for *Shakespeare in Harlem* are unhatched line drawings which were reversed to make white drawings on a black ground – by this means they relate well in visual 'weight' to the letterpress of Hughes's poetry.

Bennett Cerf of Random House invited Kauffer to illustrate W. H. Hudson's pantheistic story *Green Mansions*, which Kauffer had admired since first reading Hudson in the early twenties. The charm of Kauffer's illustrations is not fully suggested by the printing of the published book (1945). A more satisfactory result was achieved in the two-volume illustrated edition of Edgar Allan Poe published by Knopf in 1946. Kauffer contributed

85. *Edgar Allen Poe portrait*, 1946
book illustration, Alfred A. Knopf

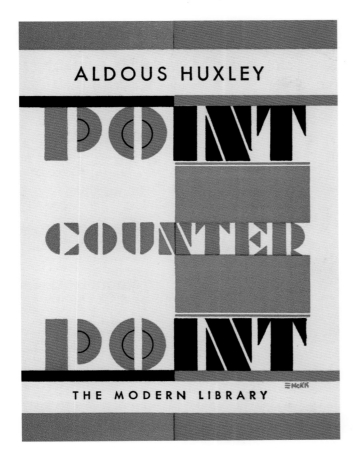

86. *Point Counter Point* by Aldous Huxley, c.1951
book jacket, Modern Library
AAD 10/24

10 illustrations which were reproduced by colour offset lithography, and a number of line vignettes. He had wanted to illustrate Poe since Eliot had introduced him to the story *The Assignation* in 1929.[12] Dr Desmond Flower singled out Kauffer's portrait of Poe as the finest of the illustrations: 'Poe's hopelessness and slow disintegration are wonderfully suggested, and it is an unhappy thought that the poignancy of this design may have sprung from Kauffer's own bewildered state at that time.'[13] The work on Poe may even have contributed to Kauffer's feeling of isolation in New York. This was professional isolation rather than personal – but Kauffer had become used to a happy mixture of client/friends.

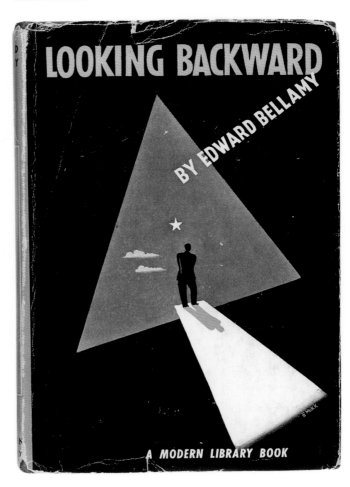

87. *Looking Backward* by Edward Bellamy, 1949
book jacket, Modern Library
NAL 801.AE.0030

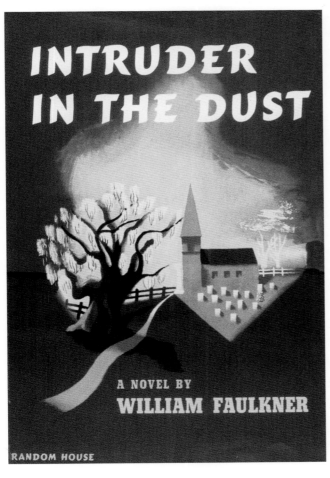

88. *Intruder in the Dust* by William Faulkner, 1948
book jacket, Random House
AAD 10/31

Early in 1943 Kauffer became acquainted with a young man who fulfilled his hopes of what advertising might be in America, and also provided him with the same intimate professional friendship he had enjoyed with Peter Gregory and Jack Beddington. Bernard Waldman remembers looking up from his desk one day to receive his first impression of a new designer who had come to see him. Waldman was used to hearing the quick rattle of self-promotion and seeing a portfolio persuasively opened. He saw an exceedingly tall, very thin man, with a book under his arm. Craning forward, Waldman could hardly hear the man's soft voice. Here was someone who was decidedly not of Madison Avenue, hardly – the young man thought – of this world.

Waldman commissioned a poster, *Fashions in Flight*. Bold, determined and convinced of Kauffer's ability, in autumn 1945 he took a calculated risk:

After Ted made the poster for 'Fashions in Flight' I tried to interest American Airlines in having him do some of their posters. I was so sure that they would be well received that I suggested to American Airlines that I go on a trip with Ted and then submit the posters on speculation. In other words, if American Airlines did not like them they would not have to accept them – but I was so sure they would.

Our first visit was to Los Angeles, where the local sales manager recommended what he called the 'sun countries' – California, Nevada, Arizona, New Mexico.

Ted and I went to Las Vegas and as soon as we got there it was a completely changed man that I saw. Here was the America he loved and felt a part of. We did not stay too long in the city but travelled to the desert and to the mountains. We then went to Arizona – Phoenix, Tombstone, etc.

Ted was rejuvenated, revitalized and happy as I had never seen him before.

I had to return to New York and he stayed on a couple of weeks longer. Two or three months later he made the posters and American Airlines accepted them enthusiastically.

Ted was in his proper environment. For weeks, months and years he talked about the West, which to him was America rather than New York City which he called a depressing canyon of mortar, steel, bricks and glass.[14]

The series of posters is Kauffer's finest and most extensive from his New York period and continued until 1953. Here his lyrical landscape gift and his subtle colour sense reasserted themselves. In 1947 he also redesigned the curtains and costumes for *Checkmate* which was revived at Covent Garden on 18 November 1947. The new designs follow the originals in general character but improve upon them by removing unnecessary mannerisms of Kauffer's earlier style (such as the cloud wisps he transferred directly from his posters to the costumes).[15] The main act curtain was also effectively simplified. The 1947 designs are those still used in this often revived ballet, which continues to be a popular item in the repertory of the Royal Ballet Company at Covent Garden.

Kauffer's influence continued to be felt by British designers after the war, perhaps partly because of *Checkmate*. The Festival of Britain symbol designed in 1950–51 by one of his most enthusiastic admirers, Abram Games, is perhaps the last notable echo of Kauffer's style in England. *Checkmate* was given its New York première at the Metropolitan Opera House on 2 November 1949. Kauffer held a concurrent exhibition of his original designs for the ballet and his illustrations for Edgar Allan Poe at the American British Art Galleries in New York. His personal distinction had soon won him a circle of friends in America, including the humorist S. J. Perelman and the poets St John Perse and Marianne Moore. The latter wrote an introduction to Kauffer's exhibition which is as eloquent as any he ever received and exemplary of its author's prose style:

E. McKnight Kauffer is a very great artist. Instinctiveness, imagination, and the 'sense of artistic difficulty' with him, have interacted till now we have an objectified logic of sensibility as inescapable as the colours refracted from a prism. Mr Kauffer's posters, book-jackets, and illustrations, partake of one attitude which is affirmative in all directions, so that here if nowhere else in the world, 'street art' is art. Shadows are as arresting as objects; numerals and letters are so rare in themselves that opposing angles, contrasting sizes, and basic parallels, are of consummate elegance – the only kind of eloquence not intrusive. This language of blacks and greys is colour in the sense that Chinese brush masterpieces are colour. Literal colour, moreover, rivals the acetylene blue of the cotinga and the tones in the beak of a toucan. We have here a poetry of synonyms like 'the immediate

89. *American Airlines – Chicago*, 1950
poster, American Airlines
E.1896-1952

American Airlines to Chicago

E. McKnight Kauffer

meaning and possible meaning' of poetry, as where a Mexican hat has the form of a plane, the heroism of helplessness is symbolized by a Greek child, and 'the medieval tower is half castle and half castle in the air'.

E. McKnight Kauffer is a parable of uncompromise – a master of illusion, focussing scrutiny upon the crease and curl of a Stetson, or on the firm solidity of a winter apple, verifying Democritus's axiom, 'Compression is the first grace of style.'

'What is to be more feared than death?' the man asked; the sage replied 'Disillusion'. Here, actually, we have a product in which unfalsified impulse safeguards illusion!

Marianne Moore also caught and preserved – embedded in one of her own poems – the precision, delicacy and deliberation of Kauffer's speaking voice. She used a passage remembered from his conversation to open her poem *The Icosasphere*, which was presumably written in or soon after 1950:

'In Buckinghamshire hedgerows
  the birds nesting in the merged green density
    weave little bits of string and moths and feathers and thistledown,
      in parabolic concentric curves …'

On one occasion Marianne Moore sent Kauffer a $10 bill and strict instructions to go out and buy himself a good dinner. Her tender, sisterly concern for him is also expressed in a note found inside his copy of Valéry's *Selected Writings* (which he lent to her in 1950): 'You really are safe; I am not disturbed about you and enviable of your height if only you could just realize it.' On another occasion she pronounced that 'Edward's jaws should be pryed open like the jaws of an elderly mule – and a great big pill called "Joy" should be forced down his throat.' Kauffer marked two passages in his copy of Valéry: 'Page 93: [I am] "in sum, the effect of an incalculable dis-order".' 'Page 97: "We are deceived by what is definite".' On the back of this note there is a sketch for a poster with a drawing of the globe and the words WORLD TRAVEL and Fly.[16]

Kauffer took great pleasure in the literary aspirations of Bernard Waldman's young daughter Grace, who became a poet of international reputation and remained mindful of his kindness to her, and loyal to his memory:

He introduced me to the best books I read, such as Paul Valéry's poems and essays, *The Cantos*, Lu Chi's *Wen Fu* in translation, Stendhal's *On Love*. He loved those books, and shared the things he loved generously with me and my parents. I remember that he was very wise, but with humour in every gesture as when I asked him to recommend a book that would help me to be a better writer and he presented me with a good dictionary (which I still have).[17]

In 1968 she received a letter from Marianne Moore saying 'I wish Edward Kauffer could see that his ambition for you was not misplaced.'

Kauffer continued to take pleasure in the American classics, in the landscape of the South-West, and in solving interesting problems of design. In Emerson he found the remark 'We eat and drink and wear perjury and fraud in a hundred commodities' and wondered: could Emerson have been thinking prophetically of what was to come? He continued to insist that advertising could be a healing, not a destructive, art:

The daily life of a citizen is punctuated with slogans, pictures, stops and go's. It is logical to assume that the mind welcomes and responds to any symbol or interpretation that expresses a sense of order, and good design is exactly concerned with this elementary and always compelling fact.[18]

He revisited the South-West in 1950 and called it 'a good kind of reality' – 'robust, uncomplicated, direct', with brilliant light and great spaces. Quixotically he bought a horse and left it in Arizona in the care of a cowboy called Jesse Crick. He carried a photograph of Crick and the horse in his wallet and liked the link he had established with that spectacular and inspiring country.[19] Eliot wrote to him that his friends were alarmed by the effect that New York had on him: 'Your friends here would like you back … I should feel happier about you in Chelsea – or in Arizona.'[20] Returning to New York in the war, as Kauffer had done, Man Ray said 'it meant joining the ranks of those whose greatest thrill consisted of buying and selling, if I wished to survive.'[21] He escaped to California to teach.

Friends have spoken of a sense of guilt which kept Kauffer from returning to England, as if he had betrayed his adopted country.[22] His feelings on the subject were deep and complex.

In 1950, cheered by his visit to the South-West, he spoke enthusiastically of his return and its great possibilities:

America has a profuse variety of cultural and racial backgrounds. The people, despite our traditions of Puritanism and pragmatism, are romantic and imaginative, responsive to the drama of presentation. Those qualities find little satisfaction in the safe, literal forms advertising has adopted. It is a country of intense light and dark contrasts, a wide, rich canvas against which to work. The possibilities for broadening communication through the graphic arts, in this country, are limitless.[23]

In the very same year, however, he wrote to Jack Beddington that 'Some kind of buried masochism drove me insanely back [to America] – and now I am reaping the "pay-off".' He dwells in the letter on his favourite Buckinghamshire lanes and breaks off with: 'Oh, my dear Jack – I must not think of it – Do you see what I mean?'[24] To Christian Barman, in the same year, Kauffer wrote:

Advertising is 'streamlined' according to the dictates of high-powered agencies and the lack of adventure to say nothing of imagination is deplorable. I am disillusioned and really sick of it all. Apart from the practical side i.e. making a living the whole thing has had a devastating effect on the psychological side and my bewilderment so often experienced has at times alarmed me. I have to say the least been driven into a corner and my talent for whatever it is worth thrown into the ash can.[25]

Kauffer's friends have sometimes insisted that his work never had any correlation with his day-to-day life, and this is no doubt true. On the other hand, there are occasions when his most imaginative inventions seem to correspond with what is known of him biographically. *Flight*, for example, remained a special talisman for Kauffer, and in the forties he illustrated it in a pamphlet which expressed his views on the potential of advertising art.[26] It is not difficult to find a connection between his most famous design and the characteristic movement of his mind – ardent, forward-looking, aspiring and even visionary in his flights of fancy for what might be. Perhaps the most original and compelling design of his American period is a jacket he

designed for a book of poems by St John Perse, *Exile* (1949). The illustration is light on dark and consists of a simple graphic treatment of the 'X' in Exile. The crossed arms roam free of the island of the word, one hard, straight and rapid in movement, the other leisurely, hand-drawn, exploring beyond the border of the sheet. To the opposition of light and dark is added the simple opposition of the lines. There is possibly a suggestive link with a passage in Eliot's *Burnt Norton*, which Kauffer would have known well:

Words strain,
Crack and sometimes break, under the burden,
Under the tension, slip, slide, perish,
Decay with imprecision, will not stay in place,
Will not stay still …

90. *Exile* by St John Perse, 1949
book jacket, Pantheon
Private collection

No subject could have roused Kauffer's deepest feelings so much as the idea of exile. He was exiled not only from England but also from the America he cherished as an ideal and for which he had found the physical evidence in the South-West. He was exiled from his wife Grace and daughter Ann in England. It is only one of many reflections that the *Exile* design inspires, that the arms of the X correspond in detail to the two country roads which meet at the White House at Northend – an observation which came from Ann's husband Peter Rendall as soon as he saw the design. With Kauffer, whose best work is a subtle and layered synthesis, such an ingredient is by no means to be ruled out.

A daybook kept by Kauffer at this period records favourite memories of Northend – the wild flowers along the hedgerows, the cat coming in the evening to sip milk from its saucer – and unhappy reflections on his real environment:

If it is true that our teeth are whiter – our breath sweeter – our smoking cooler and our drinking more 'high class' – the gain is of doubtful value compared to what we lose in civilizing values – so far as the eye and mind are traduced. After the rest brought by sleep we awaken fresh – but only for a moment and then the day brings its fearful anxieties.[27]

As Kauffer began to lose interest in the New York advertising scene, Marion Dorn – on the other hand – was achieving success. Her important commissions included an interior scheme for Lockheed Airport, Los Angeles, and she contributed to a White House carpet which featured emblems of all of the States in the Union. She adapted better to the demands of New York City and continued to produce high-quality work. Unfortunately the disparity between her success and Kauffer's exacerbated difficulties between the couple – and although they married at City Hall in 1950 they lived increasingly separate lives.[28]

Kauffer's loyal friend and most effective partner in the New York years, Bernard Waldman, said that Kauffer chose to kill himself with drink, that it was a form of suicide. He continued to work to the end, almost obsessively, spending weeks on lettering that could have been left to an assistant. 'Poor Ted', wrote Mrs Waldman to her daughter, 'he has emptied his life of everything but his work and when that fails him he is lost.' His old friends Frank and Mary Dobson visited him in 1953 and found him 'still

his old sweet self, but already a very sick man'. On 10 July 1954 Kauffer was admitted to hospital, made a recovery, but then had a final relapse. On 13 October Aldous Huxley wrote to Ann that her father was in Lenox Hill Hospital, 'desperately ill and in great pain, kidneys and liver being affected. Emaciation is extreme and it will take him a long time to get back to anything like normal health – if he *does* get back; for I judge that he is still in danger. I saw him last spring for the first time in several years and was shocked by his appearance even then. He was evidently working up for the crisis of this summer.'

Kauffer died on 22 October 1954. Huxley wrote to Ann on 10 November: 'Poor Ted – his last years were dreadfully unhappy, and he had reached a point where it seemed psychologically impossible for him to do anything that would in any way lessen his unhappiness. I think of him with affection and a kind of helpless pity – for there seemed to be nothing one could do to help him.'

Marion Dorn wrote to Eliot on 31 October. She told him how Kauffer's past life had seemed to fall away until he was simply 'Edward Kauffer' and of his intense fear at the end. 'I felt that he didn't want us – not any of us – that only his fear was real.' Eliot wrote back on 7 November with all the fine-grained sympathy one would expect of him. He also made this penetrating observation:

I think the fear has some obscure connection with not loving life, paradoxical as it may seem. I believe that something had left him, some years ago; and that all the external troubles, physical and spiritual, were perhaps merely attempts to find an objective reason for something for which no reason can be found, because it is simply the Void …[29]

Eliot had, perhaps, constructed his life and his healing art of poetry over just such a void. Evidence of it appears in his plays as well as his poems. He once compared the role of an artist in advertising with that of a poet in the theatre who must 'aim to write a play that will please theatregoers who neither know nor care about poetry, and he must try to write it in verse that will win the approval of poetry lovers who care nothing for the theatre'.[30] From *The Family Reunion:*

Now I know that all my life has been a flight
And phantoms fed upon me while I fled.

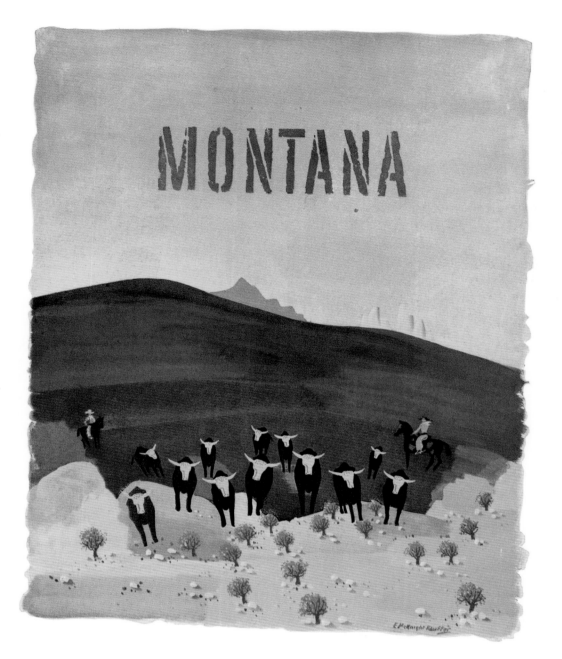

Marion Dorn asked Marianne Moore to write to Eliot about everything that had happened in the last weeks. She wrote on 27 October:

I can *not*, Tom; but can say this – I was aware above everything, of the love Edward had inspired – of the wondering reverence for him ... Service so touchingly, so privately, rendered Edward day by day.

Unselfative Nancy [Nancy Reid, who chose the music for the funeral service]. Bernard Waldman let nothing keep him from supplying certain necessities Edward would scarcely ask for; said

'I assure you, Miss Moore, he lacked for nothing'; was with him daily, a silent self-effacing man like Nancy.[31]

The service was held at the Campbell Chapel, at 81st Street and Madison Avenue, and Kauffer was buried in Woodlawn cemetery. His friend Sabro Hasigawa, a teacher at the New School of Social Research, had brought to the hospital a large white square of paper inscribed in Japanese brush characters: 'May the sun be in your heart.' To the grave Hasigawa brought a folded paper bird, bearer of the soul.

91. *Montana*, 1946
advertisement, Container Corporation of America
Graham Twemlow collection

APPENDIX

The role of the lithographic artist in poster production
By Graham Twemlow

In a note on technique published in the catalogue accompanying the retrospective exhibition of his posters held at the Museum of Modern Art in 1937 Kauffer wrote, 'Lithography still tends to be commercially practical for reproduction and most of my posters are done by an old firm still using in most cases actual lithographic stone.'

Chromolithography continued as the favoured medium for large-scale printing until the Second World War and beyond. Although some artists, namely those belonging to the Senefelder Club, were active in drawing their own poster designs directly onto stones, it was uncommon to do so and certainly Kauffer drew none of his own in this way. However there is evidence that he became familiar with the autolithographic medium as early as 1917 when two prints were listed as lithographs in the catalogue of his one-man exhibition held at the Mansard Gallery.[1] Over the ensuing years his knowledge of and feeling for the lithographic medium played a large part in his success as a poster artist.

The normal procedure for translating an original design into a printed artefact began with a printing company's representative visiting the client to view the full-colour artwork and formulate a price quotation. This calculation was based upon the number of separate colour printings it required and the degree of complexity that might be encountered by the craftsman at the printing company assigned to the job.

The task for an artisan at the printing works was to recreate the original design as accurately as possible using traditional lithographic methods. The craftsman, known as a lithographic artist (or litho artist), achieved this by scaling up the artwork (if necessary), tracing it off to make a key-line drawing of every shape and separating it into the requisite number of colours that had formed the basis of the price quotation. The design might be presented in media ranging from oil paint, gouache or watercolour. It often included specialist techniques such as paint applied by sponge, airbrush, spatter, or a combination of these. The litho artist then drew each colour (in black), recreating the original media by use of chalk, pen or brush with additional tints and tones achieved by stippling, airbrushing or mechanical Ben Day tints.

Much of what is known about the role played by litho artists in the first half of the twentieth century emanates from the published works of Thomas Edgar Griffits (1883–1957), the most influential exponent of his trade.[2] Griffits completed his apprenticeship as a litho artist in 1903. He soon gained a reputation as an experienced journeyman and by the early 1920s his knowledge of the craft of commercial lithography was unsurpassed. During the 36-year period he worked for Vincent Brooks, Day and Son, one of London's foremost printing companies (and probably the one referred to by Kauffer in his statement quoted above), it is certain that he must have overseen the translation of many of Kauffer's poster designs – but which ones are not recorded.

Near Waltham Cross by Tram, 1924
The Baynard Press, another of London's major lithographic printing companies, printed Kauffer's 1924 poster for London Underground, NEAR WALTHAMCROSS BY TRAM.[3] The artwork for the poster reveals that Kauffer presented the printer with patches of the ten colours he had used on his design. This acted as a useful guide for the litho artist but adding colour samples was, surprisingly, not common practice amongst poster artists and not evident on other original designs by Kauffer. The lettering conforms to a sans serif style that he had used contemporaneously on a number of posters (see *Winter Sales*, 1924), with unusually long cross-bars to the 'T's which often resulted in uneven letter spacing – especially noticeable on this poster is the gap created between 'L' and 'T'. Litho artists were copyists and in the translation process the craftsman responsible has faithfully followed the original lettering by replicating Kauffer's errors in letter-spacing (note that 'BY TRAM' is not centred) and, unfortunately, not dividing 'WALTHAMCROSS' into WALTHAM CROSS . The reproduction has been achieved by using nine colours and the richness of colour of the artwork is most expertly retained, although the translucent watery effect in the foreground has been simplified in the printing process.

Original design for *Near Waltham Cross by Tram*, 1924
58.6 x 39.7cm
Circ.618-1924

Near Waltham Cross by Tram, 1924,
poster, London Underground
E.673-1924

NOTES

Chapter 1: The Californian

1. Kauffer's mother wrote down the history of the family for her son and the manuscript is among the Grace Shulman papers divided between the Cooper-Hewitt National Design Museum and Yale University.

2. Information given to the author by the late Maria Zimmern Petrie in 1970. Further information is to be found in her unpublished autobiography *Yesterday*, a copy of which is with her grandson Mr Brian Petrie, London.

3. 'E. McKnight Kauffer, Poster Designer', *Portfolio*, vol. 1, 1950, pp. 20–35.

4. The City Directory lists Ed. L. Kauffer as painter in 1907, scenic artist in 1908, and artist in 1909. Although his name was recorded at birth in the Cascade County records as Edward Kauffer the artist later added the family name Leland. I am grateful to Mr William A. Gumberts of Evansville Museum of Arts and Science for checking the Directory listings.

5. Article in *Portfolio*, op. cit.

6. The painting is in a private collection, London. A head and shoulders portrait of Kauffer, also by Armfield, is in the National Portrait Gallery, London – although Kauffer never adopted British citizenship. Both paintings are dated 1915.

7. 'Montana artist upsets another British tradition', by R. Gram Swing, *Evening Post* (New York), 12 June 1926.

8. See Harvey L. Smith, *Mathews: Masterpieces of the California Decorative Style* (Oakland Museum, 1972) for an account of San Francisco art circles during Kauffer's period there.

9. The letter is with the Grace Shulman papers – see n.1.

10. Undated press cutting, Cooper-Hewitt National Design Museum, New York.

11. Records of the Art Institute of Chicago.

12. Article in *Portfolio*, op. cit.

13. Milton W. Brown, *The Story of the Armory Show* (New York, 1963), p. 178.

14. Article in *Portfolio*, op. cit.

15. Dated pastel of Venice by Kauffer in the Sidney Garrad collection, V&A, London; Maria Zimmern Petrie states in a letter to the author, 1970, that Kauffer attended an art school in Munich.

16. Ed. Felix Klee, *The Diaries of Paul Klee, 1898–1918* (London, 1965), p. 276.

17. *The Studio*, vol. LV, 1912, pp. 245–8.

18. *Art et Décoration*, vol. xxx, 1911, pp. 257–64. The poster is illustrated in *Das Plakat*, vol. 4, 1913, no. 3, p. 106

19. Letter to the author, 1970.

20. Collection of Mr Brian Petrie, London: dated to spring 1914 by Maria Zimmern Petrie in a letter to the author, 1970.

21. Letter to the author, 1970.

Chapter 2: Painter into Designer

1. 'An Appreciation' by Sir Francis Meynell, E. McKnight Kauffer memorial exhibition catalogue, Victoria and Albert Museum, October 1955.

2. 'E. McKnight Kauffer, Poster Designer', *Portfolio*, vol. 1, 1950, pp. 20–35.

3. 'Brief Biography' in exhibition catalogue of E. McKnight Kauffer posters at the Museum of Modern Art, New York, 1937.

4. From Maria Zimmern Petrie's unpublished autobiography *Yesterday*. Collection of Brian Petrie, London.

5. Collection of Brian Petrie, London.

6. See n. 4.

7. Hassall's advice is recorded in Adolphe Armand Braun's article on Kauffer, *Commercial Art*, December 1923, pp. 324–6.

8. For a biography of Pick see Christian Barman, *The Man Who Made London Transport* (Newton Abbot, 1979). For a synoptic view of the posters see Michael F. Levey, *London Transport Posters* (London, 1976).

9. 'Architecture and Advertisements', an address to the Society of Arts on 1 December 1893 by Richardson Evans. *Journal of the Society of Arts*, vol. XLII, 1893, p. 39. Evans was secretary of SCAPA, and eventually its historian: *An Account of the SCAPA Society* (London, 1926).

10. *A Beautiful World*, no. 5, December 1895: letter from Kipling accepting an invitation to join the Council of the Society for Checking the Abuses of Public Advertising.

11. *Fors Clavigera*, Letter 21 (September 1872). Ruskin refused to advertise his series of 'Letters to Working Men' and for many years prevented his publishers from even announcing his books in newspapers.

12. Michael Hiley, *Frank Meadow Sutcliffe* (London, 1974), p. 138. No particularly remarkable examples have come to light in Sutcliffe's surviving work.

13. Morris seconded a SCAPA resolution at the Society of Arts in January 1896. As might be expected, Morris's Socialist convictions gave him a wider view of the problem of advertising beyond the issue of urban and rural disfigurement. In 1893 he wrote to a fellow-member of SCAPA: 'I fear that there would be no slightest chance of success in attempting to tax (and thereby regulate) advertisements, except *in the streets*, where they are much less offensive than along the railways. You must remember that the advertisements you are speaking of are always on *private property*, and that in consequence it would be a revolutionary act to meddle with them. To tell you the plain truth, much as they annoy me personally, I cannot help rejoicing at the spectacle of the middle classes so annoyed and so helpless before the results of the idiotic tyranny which they themselves have created …' (from a letter to Mrs E. J. Lowater, published in SCAPA's journal *A Beautiful World*, no. 10, September 1909, p. 94).

14. *A Beautiful World,* no. 10, September 1909, summarizing proposals made by Waterhouse much earlier in SCAPA's history and a consistent feature of SCAPA's programme from the beginning.

15. E. McKnight Kauffer, 'Notes on Advertising Designing as a Career' in *Art Education Today* (New York, 1948), pp. 53–7.

16. See two exhibition catalogues published by the Fine Art Society, London: *The Earthly Paradise, F. Cayley Robinson and the Painters of the Birmingham Group* (1969) and *Homage to Maxwell Armfield* (1970).

17. E. McKnight Kauffer, *The Art of the Poster*, p. x.

18. Ed R.W. Flint, *Marinetti: Selected Writings* (London, 1972), p. 67.

19. Guillaume Apollinaire, *Apollinaire on Art, Essays and Reviews 1902–1918* (London, 1972), p. 383.

20. Letter to the author, October 1970.

21. Kauffer's statement is from a pamphlet containing short personal texts by a number of designers, published under the title *The Art Preservative of All the Arts* by the Graphic Arts Production Yearbook, New York. A copy is in the Cooper-Hewitt National Design Museum, New York.

22. The woodcut is often found, like other Kauffer woodcuts, dated 1922. However, this was merely the date when he made a series of impressions. The British Museum dates its impression to 1917. The *Flight* woodcut was illustrated in *The Apple (of Beauty and Discord)*, vol. 1, no. 1, 1920, p. 38.

23. Bevis Hillier unearthed this fascinating source and published in his *Art Déco of the 20s and 30s* (London, 1968), pp. 32–3, Suiseki's woodcut beside Kauffer's woodcut (which he identified in error as 'McKnight Kauffer's *Daily Herald* poster design of 1920'). The colour of the final poster reinforces the validity of Hillier's comparison. Kauffer may also have known Nikkwa's design of sparrows in flight from the *Khuhodo Gwalu* (1856), which is printed predominantly in black and beige. See L. G. Dawes, *Japanese Illustrated Books* (London, 1947), plate 47.

24. 'Brief Biography' – see n. 3. A fourth version (with seven birds) was published in Kauffer, *The Art of the Poster* (1924), and a fifth in *Portfolio*, no. 1 (1950).

25. The entire poster campaign, the posting of which was handled by S. H. Benson Ltd, was presented to the Victoria and Albert Museum by Ogilvy Benson and Mather Ltd in 1973. See V&A exhibition catalogue *Posters of a Lifetime* introduced by M. Haworth-Booth, London, 1973.

26. 'An Appreciation' – see n. 1.

27. Bevis Hillier was the first to notice the connection with Kauffer's *Flight* design, *Art Déco of the 20s and 30s*, p. 32.

28. Colin Hurry, 'An American Painter: E. McKnight Kauffer', *Pearson's Magazine*, June 1920.

29. Information from the late Mrs Peter Rendall.

30. Penguin Books edition (Harmondsworth, 1969), p. 641.

31. 'Brief Biography' – see n. 3.

32. Some designs were based on photographs taken in South America by William Zimmern (eg *Pompe Espina*). The original gouache designs were presented by him to the City of Manchester Art Gallery.

33. Coburn's photograph is in the International Museum of Photography at George Eastman House, Rochester, New York; Kauffer's oil painting is in the collection of Mrs Grevis Duce, Crediton.

34. A copy of the exhibition catalogue is in the Cooper-Hewitt National Design Museum, New York.

35. The Birmingham catalogue is also at the Cooper-Hewitt National Design Museum, New York.

36. Fry's letter, dated 5 April 1918, is in the Pierpont Morgan Library, New York (part of a group of letters, MA 1681). The letter is published in Denys Sutton, *Letters of Roger Fry*, vol. 2, pp. 426–7. The two volumes of letters contain other interesting details of the Fry-McKnight Kauffer friendship.

37. Letter to the author, 19 March 1974.

38. Kauffer had attempted to enlist in the British Army at the outbreak of war but had been rejected on grounds of citizenship: he was on his way to join the American Army when the war ended. Information from the late Mrs Peter Rendall.

39. Ana M. Berry, 'A Survey: Some Younger Artists and the ALS', in *Design and Art* published by the ALS (London, 1928). p. 47. The article is a brief history of the ALS up to 1928 and it includes the puzzling remark (p. 53) that 'the first ALS dramatic tour in May, 1919, had been heralded (as have all subsequent tours) by a Kauffer poster'. At present only two are known – see checklist.

40. Catalogue of the exhibition held at the Mansard Gallery, 2–30 April 1921.

41. This and the following quotation are published in *Wyndham Lewis's Letters*, ed. W.K. Rose (London, 1963), pp. 112–15.

42. E. McKnight Kauffer. *The Art of the Poster*, p. x.

43. 'Brief Biography'– see n. 3.

44. Wyndham Lewis, *Blasting and Bombardiering* (London, 1937), p. 211.

Chapter 3: The Early Twenties

1. A.M. Cassandre, introduction to *Art International d'aujourd'hui no. 12: Publicité* (Paris, 1929): 'L'affiche n'est plus un tableau mais devient une "machine a annoncer". Le catalogue, l'annonce, l'enseigne lumineuse, autant d'objets vivants qui sont aujourd'hui partie de notre vie quotidienne comme le téléphone et la machine à écrire'. The statement is not quoted in full here but shows how close Kauffer was to Parisian artists working in publicity. For Cassandre, 'Toute une génération d'artistes trouve en lui [publicité] son mode d'expression le plus vivant.'

2. The Evansville Museum of Arts and Sciences holds an extensive collection of these.

3. 'E. McKnight Kauffer, Poster Designer', *Portfolio*, vol. 1, 1950, pp. 30–35.

4. Penguin Books edition (Harmondsworth, 1951), p. 27.

5. Reproduced in *Evelyn Waugh and His World*, ed. David Pryce-Jones (London, 1973).

6. A useful contemporary account is Frank Sidgwick, 'The Westminster Press – its History and its Activities', *The Studio*, vol. 99, 1930, p. 438. Priscilla Johnston characterized Gerard Meynell as 'small and dark with a hooked nose, a blue chin and flashing spectacles. He resembled the popular idea of a newspaper man, cocking his head like a sparrow, his hat pushed back and – almost – his thumbs hooked into his waistcoat': *Edward Johnston* (London, 1959), p. 191. For Meynell's taste as a typographer see his *Pages From Books* (Lanston Monotype Corporation, 1927).

7. Kauffer kept a copy of this all his life and it is now in the Cooper-Hewitt National Design Museum, New York.

8. *Commercial Art*, November 1923, p. 320.

9. *London Mercury*, October 1921, p. 16.

10. *Commercial Art*, December 1923, pp. 322–3, 327–8 record the debate.

11. *Penrose Annual*, 1924.

12. The company's appreciative letter is in the Cooper-Hewitt National Design Museum, New York.

13. *The Times*, 18 May 1927.

14. Tributes to Grace McKnight Kauffer have been preserved in a *Memorial of Grace McKnight*, privately printed by Peter and Ann Rendall, Bembridge, Isle of Wight, 1966.

15. Wyndham Lewis, *Blasting and Bombardiering* (London, 1937), p. 211.

16. *Commercial Art*, October 1923, pp. 274–5.

17. Ibid.

18. See *The Chap-Book: A Miscellany* (London, 1924) for the illustration to Eliot and the portrait of Monro. The original drawing for the latter is now in the Poetry Collection of the Lockwood Memorial Library State University of New York, Buffalo.

19. On an objection from the landlord the sign was placed flat against the front wall of the shop (rather than at right-angles); this explains the excellent state of preservation of one side of the board and the severe blistering to the other. A photograph of Monro with the board is reproduced in Robert H. Ross, *The Georgian Revolt: Rise and Fall of a Poetic Ideal 1910–22* (London. 1967), opposite p. 96.

20. See Eleanor Elder, *Travelling Players: The Story of the ALS* (London, 1939), in which a plate reproduces Kauffer's costumes for Anatole France's *The Man Who Married a Dumb Wife* (1923–4). Kauffer also designed a screen for Chekhov's *The Proposal* (1925–6), costumes for *Henry VIII* (1935–6) and symbols for *Lazarus*, presumably about the same date.

21. Sets of the printed posters are lettered for both Whitsuntide and Summer – presumably they were issued twice. The reasons for this are not known.

22. Catalogue of Kauffer's retrospective exhibition, Arts League of Service, London, 1925.

23. See n. 20.

24. *Vogue*, early August 1925, p. 54.

25. Sir Francis Meynell, 'An Appreciation', E. McKnight Kauffer Memorial exhibition, Victoria and Albert Museum, 1955.

26. As above.

27. Colour plate from an unidentified magazine, dated June 1926, in Kauffer's guardbooks, Victoria and Albert Museum.

28. The dress has a zig-zag pattern at the sleeves and a hem decorated with stylized roses and thistles. It is in the collection of Mrs Rosemary Pepler, Ditchling.

29. See n. 25. Meynell's side of the correspondence has now come to light in the Pierpont Morgan Library, New York. See John Dreyfus et al., *A History of the Nonesuch Press* (1981).

30. This and the following remarks are from Fry's essay 'The Author and the Artist', first published in the *Burlington Magazine*, July 1926, pp. 9–12, and collected by Fry in his *Transformations: Critical and Speculative Essays on Art* (London, 1926).

31. A typescript of notes taken at the lecture, perhaps by Kauffer himself, differs significantly from the pamphlet. It is preserved in the Pierpont Morgan Library, New York.

32. *Spectator*, 17 March 1923.

Chapter 4: The Late Twenties

1. Letter to the author, 17 January 1972.

2. Harold Acton, *Memoirs of an Aesthete* (London, 1948), p. 198.

3. *The Times*, 13 September 1958. A.L.F. Smith paid a splendid personal tribute to Tallents in the issue of 17 September. including praise for Tallents's 'brilliant nervous prose which he wrote down with a sliver of a pen which he must have used for 50 years'.

4. Gervas Huxley, *Both Hands* (London, 1970). Chapter 6 is the best inside account of the EMB yet in print. The quotation is from p. 126.

5. From Tallents's unpublished book on the EMB, *Empire Experiment*, which his son Mr T.W. Tallents kindly allowed me to see.

6. Quoted by Tallents in his article 'The Birth of British Documentary', *Journal of the University Film Association*, vol. 20, nos 1–3.

7. Ibid., 1.

8. Tallents, *The Projection of England*, 2nd edition (London, 1955), p. 34. His official report on the Barcelona exhibition is in the Public Record Office EMB/PC/135.

9. Letter to the author, 7 July 1972.

10. Mildred Constantine and Alan M. Fern, *Word and Image, Posters from the collection of the Museum of Modern Art* (New York, 1968), repr. p. 77 (original design in tempera).

11. Cooper-Hewitt National Design Museum records.

12. Letter to the author, 1 August 1973. For Ivor Montagu Kauffer also designed an international badge for the English Table Tennis Association – 'a Kauffer version of the English rose – very good indeed – which so surprised and bewildered the players – it was ahead of the taste of the time – that two at least sewed it on their blazers upside down'. Montagu presented an example to the Textiles Department of the V&A.

13. A preliminary sketch is in the Museum of Modern Art, New York.

14. See n. 5.

15. *Advertiser's Weekly*, 10 December 1926.

16. Public Record Office, EMB papers: CO.760.3. EMB/PC/93 (10.12.28) – Report on the efficacy of the Board's Poster Publicity.

17. Public Record Office, EMB papers: CO.760.22, Publicity Committee Papers 2, paragraph 5.

18. See Tallents, *Empire Experiment*, op. cit., for details of the poster campaign.

19. The original design is in the Victoria and Albert Museum: as it was used at bulletin-board, or 16 sheet, size Kauffer was paid 100 guineas for it. For his 'National Mark' design he received 35 guineas. Public Record Office. EMB/PC/Poster subcommittee papers 21.7.27 and 19.4.28. In general fees were £75 for a poster, £15 for a showcard – 29 September 1927.

20. Conversation, 12 January 1971.

21. *Empire Experiment*, op. cit., p. 43.

22. Ashley recorded how Stanley Morison introduced him to Kauffer's work in his Prologue to Michael Frostick, *Advertising and the Motor Car* (London, 1970), p. 12: 'Morison's advice to me on this occasion was: get out of advertising and find something worth while to do – or, alternatively, *do* something constructive to improve the dreadful appearance of advertising (this is 1923) which was still reflecting the visual vulgarity of the late nineteenth-century printing and advertising with its crude illustrations, ugly display typefaces and even worse body types for the setting of text matter. Morison continued by observing that if I must work in advertising, I should try to do something like this – and at that point he handed me a small printed showcard he had on his desk for "Eastmans" (the dry cleaners). This depicted a very "cubist" sort of design in bright colours signed by an artist entirely strange to me: "E Mc K K". Morison went on to say that if I didn't like this, then I ought to get to like it, because it was an example of what the modern poster was going to be.'

23. Conversations with Ashley and Mr Hellicar, 1972.

24. Stenberg's poster is reproduced in the University of Texas Art Museum exhibition catalogue *Russian Painters and the Stage 1884–1965* (1978), plate 99.

25. *Gebrauchsgraphik*, May 1929, p. 45.

26. Dr Desmond Flower, 'The Book Illustrations of E. McKnight Kauffer', *Penrose Annual*, London, 1956, pp. 35–40.

27. Ibid.

28. Letter from Eliot to Kauffer, 24 July 1930, carbon copy in collection of Mrs Valerie Eliot.

29. Roger Fry congratulated Kauffer on precisely this quality in a letter on the Robinson Crusoe illustrations: 'I trembled for you when I saw the title but once more you've found the way by a miracle of tact and sensibility. Its amazing to me how you manage never to block any of the avenues of the reader's imagination by any too precise image: how you manage by the subtlest allusions to show how much you have understood and how carefully you have refrained from imposing that on us. The images are all like Japanese stop-shorts, where the words stop but the sense goes on.' Unpublished letter dated 27 November 1929, Pierpont Morgan Library, New York (MA 1681).

30. Letter from Kauffer to Eliot, 15 September 1927, in the collection of Mrs Valerie Eliot.

31. Letter from Eliot to Kauffer, Pierpont Morgan Library, New York (MA 1667).

32. Letter from Kauffer to Eliot dated 10 October 1929, in the collection of Mrs Valerie Eliot.

33. Letter from Kauffer to Eliot dated 29 July 1930, in the collection of Mrs Valerie Eliot.

34. Letter from Eliot to Kauffer dated 8 August 1930, Pierpont Morgan Library, New York (MA 1667). This version of the design is in the Cooper-Hewitt Museum: an earlier version is in the collection of Lord Hutchinson QC, London.

35. Leonard Woolf, *Downhill All the Way* (London, 1967).

36. Collection of Mrs Valerie Eliot.

37. Letter from Eliot to Kauffer dated 15 December 1929, Pierpont Morgan Library (MA 1667).

38. Undated letter, source as above.

39. Letter from Eliot to Kauffer, 30 May 1949, including a 'profile' of Kauffer written at the artist's request: carbon copy in the collection of Mrs Valerie Eliot.

40. Notes by T. S. Eliot for the Memorial Exhibition of Kauffer's work at the V&A, opened on 6 October 1955. Eliot's address was given by tape-recording as he himself was indisposed, due to a foot infection. The notes are in the collection of Mrs Valerie Eliot.

41. See *The Studio*, January 1929, pp. 35–9. See also Valerie Mendes, 'Marion Dorn, Textile Designer', *Bulletin of the Decorative Arts Society 1890–1940*, no. 2, 1978, pp. 24–35. Also the exhibition catalogue introduced by Jacqueline Pruskin, *British Carpets and Designs: the Modernist Rug 1928–1938*, Royal Pavilion, Art Gallery and Museums, Brighton 1975.

42. The rug was item H12 in the exhibition catalogue *Victorian and Edwardian Decorative Art: The Handley-Read Collection*, Royal Academy of Arts, 1972 (pp. 130–31), and was later generously presented to the V&A by Lady Ashton.

43. Letter from Bennett to Kauffer, Pierpont Morgan Library, New York (MA 1664).

44. See *Architectural Review*, July 1931, for the only surviving photographic record.

45. Letter from Bennett to Kauffer dated 18.9.1930, Pierpont Morgan Library, New York (MA 1664).

46. 'E. McKnight Kauffer, Poster Designer', *Portfolio*, vol. 1, 1950, pp. 20–35.

Chapter 5: The Thirties (1)

1. Osbert Sitwell, *Noble Essences* (London, 1950), p. 304.

2. 'The Book Illustrations of E. McKnight Kauffer', *Penrose Annual*, London, 1956, pp. 35–40. Dr Flower himself owned two of the abandoned designs.

3. Recollections of Jeanette Rutherston Powell in conversation with the author, 1971. The Nicholson relief, of 1938, is reproduced in *Ben Nicholson: Paintings, Reliefs, Drawings* (London, 1948), plate 71.

4. Recollections of the late Freddie Mayor in conversation with the author, 1971. The Baumeister, whereabouts now unknown, was acquired in 1931–2.

5. The late Lord Clark in conversation with the author, 1971.

6. *Advertising Review*, vol. 1, no. 3, Winter 1954–5, p. 36.

7. See n. 5.

8. Letters to the author, July–August 1970.

9. Examples are in the Word and Image Department at the V&A.

10. Recollections of Mrs Peter Rendall in conversation with the author, 1970.

11. Illustrated in the *Architectural Review*, June 1933, p. 261.

12. *Architectural Review*, August 1937, p. 51.

13. The building and the photo-mural were featured in *Architectural Review*, vol. XXXIII, 1935, pp. 167–73. Details of the process were provided by Mr Eugene Mollo in conversation in 1979. The photo-mural at Embassy Court no longer exists.

14. Kauffer's statement was published in an *Architectural Review* 'Decoration' supplement on the photo-mural technique in February 1937, together with 14 illustrations: two of these show the photo-mural on Earl's Court referred to below.

15. The space-frame may derive from Herbert Bayer, whose poster for the German section at the *Exposition de la société des artistes décorateurs*, Grand Palais, Paris, 1934, certainly contains ideas which Kauffer used in 1937 (*Lubrication by Shell, Miles-Whitney Straight Aeroplane*) – see *Herbert Bayer: Painter, Designer, Architect* (London and New York, 1967), p. 31. The painted clouds often used by Kauffer in the later 1930s probably come from Bayer also – see the Cinzano poster (1934) in the Bayer monograph, p. 47. On the other hand Kauffer's Embassy Court photo-mural may well have

influenced Moholy-Nagy's brilliant layout, 'Leisure at the Seaside', for the *Architectural Review* in July 1936.

16. *The Times*, 12 February 1959. The obituary was published on the previous day: further tributes included contributions from Jane B. Drew (14 February) and Henry Moore (19 February).

17. Sir Herbert E. Read and Sir Charles Morris, *Eric Craven Gregory* (the addresses in tribute at the Cathedral, Bradford, on Monday 2 March 1959 by Sir Charles Morris and at St Luke's Church, Chelsea, on Thursday 5 March 1959 by Sir Herbert Read), London, 1959. See also the catalogue of the Gregory Memorial Exhibition, Leeds City Art Gallery, 1960, introduced by Herbert Read: 'his long and intimate association with E. McKnight Kauffer should not be forgotten. Kauffer is chiefly remembered as a poster artist, but he was a sensitive and extremely intelligent man whose talent was applied in many directions' (p. 5). For further information on Gregory's collection, see Sotheby's sale catalogues for 4 November 1959 (paintings and sculpture), 26 October 1959 (books), 11 February 1960 (lithographs and other prints). The first sale included a Kauffer oil, *Easel and Chair*, 1939, present whereabouts unknown.

18. The gallery is described and illustrated in Dorothy Todd, 'Marion Dorn, Architect of Floors', *Architectural Review*, October 1933.

19. See James L. Enyeart. *Bruguière: His Photographs and his Life* (New York, 1977), pp. 93–4, and plate 67.

20. Conversation with Man Ray, Paris, March 1970.

21. Reproduced in a cutting from an unknown publication, Cooper-Hewitt National Design Museum, New York.

22. *Guardian*, 15 March 1935.

23. *Spectator*, 5 April 1935.

24. Notes for BBC talk on Kauffer, The Library, King's College, Cambridge, 1955.

25. Conversation with Lord Clark, 1970.

26. *Advertising Review*, vol. 1, no. 3, Winter 1954–5, p. 35

27. See Christine Boydell's monograph, cited in the Bibliography (p. 117). This deals with Marion Dorn's work in England.

28. Conversation with Lady Robinson, January 1973.

29 Sir Colin Anderson, 'Ship Interiors – When the Breakthrough Came', *Architectural Review*, June 1967, pp. 449–52.

30. Reproduced in *Architectural Review*, October 1935, p. 157.

31. *Trend*, Spring 1936.

32. Ibid.

33. Tallents, *Empire Experiment*, op. cit.

34. Herbert Read, 'Novelism at the RA', *Architectural Review*, February 1935.

Chapter 6: The Thirties (2)

1. Conversation with Lord Clark, 1971. Beddington's career is described in an obituary in *The Times* for 15 April 1959; tributes were subsequently published on 16 April (Nicholas Bentley), 17 April (C.M. Vignoles and Bryan Robertson), 22 April (Paul Rotha), 27 April (John Betjeman). I am grateful to Colonel Freddie Beddington for supplying other details.

2. In *Fifty Years of Shell Advertising*, brochure of an exhibition held at 195 Piccadilly in 1969.

3. *The Times*, 17 April 1959.

4. The Kauffer paintings owned by Beddington were: *View at Cassis* (1935) and *Cornfield with Stooks and Distant Cottage*, lots 64 and 141 respectively in the sale of most of Beddington's collection, Christie's, 25 March 1960.

5. Collection of Mrs Christopher Lobb, Penzance, Cornwall.

6. Letter dated 17 November 1929, collection of Mrs Lobb, as are the other letters from Kauffer to Beddington quoted by her kind permission in this chapter and the next.

7. 24 November 1935.

8. 12 May 1936.

9. 21 May 1936.

10. Formerly collection of the late Whitney Straight.

11. *Architectural Review*, December 1929, p. 276 shows a country garage before, during and after the removal of advertising signs.

12. E. McKnight Kauffer, 'The Designer and the Public', *Journal of the Royal Society of Arts*, vol. 85, 1938, pp. 51 ff.

13. Ibid.

14. Kenneth Clark, Preface to Roger Fry's *Last Lectures* (Cambridge 1939), p. vi: '… we have seen a series of events so tragic and horrible that our indignation can hardly fail to overflow and swamp out detached contemplation of shapes and colours. To be a pure painter seems almost immoral.'

15. See n. 12.

16. *Morning Post*, 5 April 1932.

17. *Observer*, 10 April 1932.

18. A number of set and costume designs are preserved in the Cooper-Hewitt National Design Museum, New York, and in the collection of Dr Richard Wunder, Orwell, Vermont.

19. *Morning Post*, 9 June 1934.

20. *Sunday Times*, 8 June 1934.

21. Clive Barnes, 'Checkmate', *Dance and Dancers*, February 1963, pp. 31–3.

22. P. W. Manchester, *Vic-Wells: A Ballet Progress* (London, 1942), p. 38.

23. Details of the ballet can be added from Ninette de Valois, *Come Dance With Me: A Memoir* (London, 1957), p. 119 and Mary Clarke, *The Sadler's Wells Ballet* (London, 1955), p. 133.

24. Conversation with Irene Wellington, 1972 (also the source of the following remarks about the White House).

25. Letters in the collection of Simon Rendall, quoted with his kind permission.

26. Pierpont Morgan Library, New York (MA 1667).

27. Collection of Mrs Valerie Eliot.

28. See n. 27.

29. See n. 27.

30. Peter Gregory's diary (1940–41), entry for 15 July. Collection of Jane B. Drew, London, and quoted with her kind permission.

31. Ministry of Information records: INFI/33 Staff organization General Production *Division* – 13/5/40 OEPEC.

32. *Advertising Review*, vol. 1, no. 3, Winter 1954–5, p. 33.

Chapter 7: New York, 1940–54

1. By kind permission of Mrs Christopher Lobb.

2. By kind permission of Sir Colin Anderson.

3. Pierpont Morgan Library, New York (MA 1667).

4. Collection of Mrs Valerie Eliot.

5. Lady Ashton – conversation, 1970.

6. *Advertising Art Now* by E. McKnight Kauffer, from an address given before the Art Directors Club, New York, 1941 (16 pp. with illustration of *Flight* on cover), Cooper-Hewitt Museum, New York.

7. Introduction to Paul Rand, *Thoughts on Design* (New York, 1947).

8. J. I. Biegeleisen, *Poster Design* (New York, 1945), p. 1.

9. T. S. Eliot, notes for the opening of Kauffer's memorial exhibition at the V&A, October 1955 (Mrs Valerie Eliot).

10. He liked to visit Harlem's night-spots with young English friends like Jeremy Hutchinson (now Lord Hutchinson). He also carried out a set of illustrations for Carl Van Vechten's *Nigger Heaven* but an illustrated version of the book was never published. His original watercolours for this are preserved in the Museum of Modern Art, New York.

11. Speech printed on single sheet, author's collection.

12. D. Flower, 'The Book Illustrations of E. McKnight Kauffer', *Penrose Annual*, London, 1956, pp. 35–40

13. See Beeleigh Abbey Books, catalogue 12, pt. 1, 663: includes Kauffer letter to Eliot of November 1929 on this subject.

14. Letter to the author, 21 November 1973.

15. *Dance and Dancers* for December 1954 (p. 23) states that Kauffer revised his designs 'to fit in with de Valois' insistence on a more stylised less human interpretation of the leading roles', but Dame Ninette (letter to the author, March 1979) confirmed that the slight changes made were all of Kauffer's choosing, and she regretted most the simplification of 'the double-bass-shaped Red Bishops' costumes: 'the originals were wonderful – but cumbersome and difficult to travel, hence, no doubt, the change'.

16. Preserved by Grace Schulman, who very generously allowed me to quote the Marianne Moore texts in her possession. See chapter 1, n. 1.

17. Letter from Grace Schulman to Mrs Peter Rendall, 1974.
18. E. McKnight Kauffer, 'The Poster – What It Is and Why', *Travel USA*, April 1949.
19. *Portfolio*, vol. 1, 1950, pp. 20–35.
20. Letter from Eliot to Kauffer, 30 May 1949 – carbon copy in collection of Mrs Valerie Eliot.
21. Man Ray, *Self Portrait* (London, 1963), p. 323.
22. Sir Francis Meynell, 'An Appreciation', McKnight Kauffer memorial exhibition catalogue, Victoria and Albert Museum, 1955: 'Kauffer was a warm and generous man, but came to suffer from the delusion that his friends despised him for having returned to the USA early in the war. What nonsense! It was the only sensible thing for him to do. But no reassurance could prevail, and he insisted on his own sense of guilt which nobody shared; and this made him aloof from many who loved him, and wished him close and well.'
23. See n. 19.
24. Kauffer to Beddington, 31 October 1950 (Mrs Christopher Lobb).
25. Kauffer to Barman, 26 July 1950 (Christian Barman).
26. See n. 6.
27. Cooper-Hewitt National Design Museum, New York.
28. Marion Dorn bequeathed a collection of some 1,100 items of work and memorabilia of Kauffer's to the Cooper-Hewitt Museum, and collections of his posters were given to the Rochester Institute of Technology, New York, and to the American Museum at Bath in England. She died in Tangiers in 1964.
29. Eliot to Marion Dorn, 7 November 1954 (carbon copy with Mrs Valerie Eliot).
30. Eliot's notes for opening address, Kauffer memorial exhibition at the V&A, October 1955 (Mrs Valerie Eliot).
31. Marianne Moore to Eliot, 27 October 1954 (Mrs Valerie Eliot).

Appendix

1. The two lithographs were listed in the catalogue for Kauffer's one-man exhibition supporting *The New Movement in Art* exhibition: No. 1 'The Bridge', and No. 29 'Still life'. In *Artists at Curwen* the author Pat Gilmour noted that Harold Curwen had pasted a litho drawing of Don Quixote by Kauffer into a scrapbook and annotated it 'drawn by Kauffer on stone' (London, 1977, p.78). There is also a reference in a letter from Kauffer to the publishers Chatto & Windus to a book cover design drawn directly on to litho transfer paper: 12 July 1921, Chatto & Windus archives, University of Reading Library.

2. *The Technique of Colour Printing by Lithography*, by Griffits was first 'published' in 1940 by Faber & Faber but the warehouse was bombed before the book was distributed. It was re-issued in 1944. Griffits published two further books on the subject of lithography and wrote numerous articles, mainly for the *Penrose Annual*.

3. Griffits joined The Baynard Press (the imprint for the large and successful printing company, Sanders Phillips and Co Ltd) in 1935 to take charge of the litho works. The Baynard Press eventually absorbed Vincent Brooks, Day and Son (*c*.1950).

SELECT BIBLIOGRAPHY

Note: Kauffer's own press-cuttings books are preserved at the Cooper-Hewitt National Design Museum, New York City, and a file of cuttings is also held by the Evansville-Vanderburgh County Public Library, Indiana.

Further references are given in the Notes and checklist.

Exhibition Catalogues (one-man)

Paintings by E. McKnight Kauffer, Hampshire House, Hammersmith, London, 1916. Foreword by Alvin Langdon Coburn

Posters by E. McKnight Kauffer, Arts League of Service Galleries, London, 1925, and the Ashmolean Museum, Oxford, 1926. Foreword and notes by Roger Fry

Watercolour Drawings by E. McKnight Kauffer, Arthur Tooth and Sons Gallery, London, 1933

The Work of E. McKnight Kauffer, Lund Humphries & Co Gallery, London, 1935

Posters by E. McKnight Kauffer, Museum of Modern Art, New York, 1937. Foreword by Aldous Huxley. Note on Technique by McKnight Kauffer

Drawings for the Ballet and Original Illustrations for Edgar Allan Poe, American – British Art Gallery, Batsford House, New York, 1949. Foreword by Marianne Moore

Memorial Exhibition of the Work of E. McKnight Kauffer, Victoria and Albert Museum, London, 1955. Opened by T. S. Eliot, OM. Introduction by Ashley Havinden. Appreciation by Sir Francis Meynell. Note by Thomas Eckersley

Posters by E. McKnight Kauffer, IBM gallery, New York, 1969. Introduction by Paul Rand

E. McKnight Kauffer. Poster Art 1915–1940, Travelling exhibition arranged by the Circulation Department of the Victoria and Albert Museum, London, 1973. Text by Mark Haworth-Booth

Exhibition catalogues (group)

The London Group, London, 1916–19

Paintings and Drawings by E. McKnight Kauffer and Barry V. Jackson, Birmingham Repertory Theatre, 1917. Introduction by Roger Fry. Also shown as part of *The New Movement in Art*, selected by Fry, at the Mansard Gallery, London, later in the same year

Group X, Mansard Gallery, 1920. Foreword by Wyndham Lewis

Groupe de Peintres Modernes, Galerie Druet, Paris, 1921

The Friday Club, Mansard Gallery, London, 1921

Present Day Industrial Art, Victoria and Albert Museum, 1922

Mostra Internzionale delle Arti Decorativi, Milan, 1923

British Industrial Art for the Slender Purse, Victoria and Albert Museum, 1929

Modern Pictorial Advertising by Shell, New Burlington Galleries, London, 1931. Foreword by Robert Byron: 'Responsible Publicity'

British Industrial Art in Relation to the Home, Dorland Hall, London, 1933

Pictures in advertising 1935–38, Royal Watercolour Society Galleries, London, 1938

The Advance Guard of Advertising Artists, Katharine Kuh Gallery, Chicago, 1941 and then A-D Gallery, New York, 1942

Posters of a Lifetime, Bethnal Green Museum, 1973. Introduction by Mark Haworth-Booth

Artists at Curwen, Tate Gallery, London, 1977. Catalogue by Pat Gilmour

Teaspoons to Trains: The Work of Frank Pick, 1878–1941, Victoria and Albert Museum, 1978 (arranged by Barbara Morris, Jennifer Hawkins and Geoffrey Opie)

Thirties: British Art and Design Before the War, Arts Council of Great Britain and Victoria and Albert Museum, 1979

Statements by Kauffer

'The Poster', *Arts and Decoration*, New York, November 1921

'The essentials of poster design', *Arts League of Service Bulletin 1923–24*, London, 1924

'The Poster and symbolism', *Penrose Annual*, London, 1924

The Art of the Poster, London, 1924. Note: 100 copies of the book containing a poster by Kauffer were issued in addition to the ordinary edition

'When I design a poster …', *Daily Review*, London, 19 July 1933

'The Photomural', *Architectural Review*, London, February 1937

'Art and advertising, the designer and the public', *Journal of the Royal Society of Arts*, vol. 87, London, 1938, pp. 51–70

Advertising Art Now. An address to the Art Directors' Club of New York, New York, 1941

Foreword to *Thoughts on Design* by Paul Rand, New York, 1947

Statements about Kauffer

C. Hurry, 'An American painter E. McKnight Kauffer', *Pearson's Magazine*, June 1920

H. Taylor, 'The poster revival no. 1 – E. McKnight Kauffer', *The Studio* vol. 79, 1920, pp. 140–47

R. A. Parker, 'A commercial artist with ideals', *Arts and Decoration*, New York, November 1920

H. K. Willoughby, 'Modernism in poster art', *The Poster*, May 1923

A. A. Braun, 'Artists who help the advertiser – E. McKnight Kauffer', *Commercial Art*, December 1923, pp. 324–6

Raymond Mortimer (article unsigned), 'The Posters of E. McKnight Kauffer', *Vogue*, late May 1925

R. Gram Swing, 'Montana artist upsets another British tradition', *Evening Post*, New York, 12 June 1926

R. Fry, 'The author and the artist', *Transformations*, London, 1926

G. S. Sandilands, 'E. McKnight Kauffer', *Commercial Art*, July 1927

W. G. Archer, 'E. McKnight Kauffer and T. S. Eliot', *Cambridge Review*, 1 May 1931

G. Grigson, 'The Evolution of E. McKnight Kauffer, a Master Designer', *Commercial Art*, vol. XVIII, 1935, pp. 202–6

A. Blunt, *Spectator*, 5 April 1935, p. 567

Anonymous, 'E. McKnight Kauffer: poster designer', *Portfolio*, vol. 1, Cincinnati, 1950, pp. 20–35

H. Schleger, Sir F. Meynell, J. Beddington, C. Barman, E.C. Gregory, A. Havinden and Sir C. Anderson, 'E. McKnight Kauffer, a memorial symposium', *Advertising Review*, vol. 1, no. 3, Winter 1954–5

C. Rosner, 'In Memoriam: E. McKnight Kauffer', *Graphis*, vol. 11, 1955, p. 10

D. Flower, 'Book illustrations by E. McKnight Kauffer', *Penrose Annual*, 1956

K. Murgatroyd, 'E. McKnight Kauffer: the artist in commerce', *Print*, New York, January 1969

M. Haworth-Booth, 'E. McKnight Kauffer', *Penrose Annual*, 1971

P. Gilmour, *Artists at Curwen*, Tate Gallery, London, 1977

C. Barman, *The Man Who Built London Transport: A Biography of Frank Pick*, David & Charles, Newton Abbot, 1979

J. Dreyfus et al., *A History of the Nonesuch Press*, The Nonesuch Press, London, 1981

D. Ades, *The 20th-Century Poster Design of the Avant-Garde*, Abbeville Press, New York, 1984

S. Constantine, *Buy & Build: The Advertising Posters of the Empire Marketing Board*, HMSO, London, 1986

O. Green, *Underground Art: London Transport Posters 1908 to the Present*, Studio Vista, London, 1990

B. Cole, and R. Durack, *Railway Posters 1923–1947*, Laurence King, London, 1992

C. Boydell, *The Architect of Floors: Modernism, Art and Marion Dorn Designs*, Schoeser, London, 1996

G. Schulman, 'Gift from a Lost World', *The Yale Review*, October 1997

B. Costello, ed., *The Selected Letters of Marianne Moore*, Alfred A. Knopf, New York, 1997

D. Rothschild et al., *Graphic Design in the Mechanical Age: Selections from the Merrill C. Berman Collection*, Yale University Press in conjunction with Williams College Museum of Art, Williamstown, Massachusetts and Cooper-Hewitt National Design Museum, New York, 1998

M. Timmers, ed., *The Power of the Poster*, V&A Publications, London, 1998

M. Saler, *The Avant-Garde in Interwar England: Medieval Modernism and the London Underground*, OUP, New York, 1999

A. Powers, *Front Cover: Great Book Jacket and Cover Design*, Mitchell Beazley, London, 2001

G. Schulman, 'The Designer's Notebook: E. McKnight Kauffer, 1890-1954', *The Paintings of our Lives*, Houghton Mifflin, New York: 2001

CHECKLIST OF POSTERS BY E. McKNIGHT KAUFFER

Compiled by Graham Twemlow based on the1979 checklist by Alan Howell and Mark Haworth-Booth

Note: the dates given are those of publication, where known, rather than the date on the artwork. 'od' indicates original design

Clients

Where known, they are represented by a set of initials as presented in the key below:

AA	American Airways	GO	Greek Office of Information	Po	Pomeroy
AFN	American Friends of Norway	GPO	General Post Office	PWA	Prisoners' War Aid
AH	Aeolian Hall	GWR	Great Western Railways	Ri	Ringling Brothers and Barnum & Bailey
ALS	Arts League of Service	GWRA	Greek War Relief Association		
ARC	American Red Cross	HO	Home Office	SA	Subway Advertising Co
ARP	Air Raid Precautions	IA	Imperial Airways	SM	Shell-Mex Ltd
BEE	British Empire Exhibition, Wembley	IAA	Co-ordination of Inter-American Affairs, Washington DC	SMAC	Spanish Medical Aid Committee
CAA	Civil Aeronautics Administration			ST	Schubert Theater
CD	Office of Civilian Defence	IT	India Tyre Co	St	Stetson Hat Co
CM	Chrysler Motors	JD	Sir Joseph Duveen	TG	Theatre Guild, NYC
CMA	Chinese Medical Aid	LB	Lever Brothers	TMB	Tea Marketing Board
CO	Chesapeake & Ohio Railroad	LG	London Group	UCSSA	United Committee of South-Slavic Americans
CWM	Canadian War Memorials	LMF	London Music Festival		
D&T	Derry & Toms	LT	London Transport = London Passenger Transport Board (1933–)	UD	London Underground = Underground Electric Railways of London (1902–33)
DB	Defense Bonds				
DH	Daily Herald	LW	Labour Woman		
DSS	Disabled Sailors & Soldiers	MARS	Modern Architectural Research Group	UN	United Nations
DWC	Dependant & Wounded Aid Committee	MG	Manchester Guardian	US	US War Bonds
		MM	Metropolitan Museum of Art, NY	Vi	Villiers Motor Cycle Co Ltd
Ea	Eastman and Son, Acton, London	MoH	Ministry of Health	WB	Walker Brothers (Vigil Silk)
EMB	Empire Marketing Board	NC	News Chronicle	We	Welwyn Garden City Estates Office
En	J.C. Eno Ltd	OL	Orient Line, Anderson Green & Co Ltd	Wo	Wolseley Cars
FoG	Friends of Greece			WP	Westminster Press
Gi	W.A. Gilbey	P	Pratt's Oil		
GLCC	Gas, Light & Coke Co	PA	Pan American Airways		

Sources of information

A guide to where printed examples or references can be found. Public collection sources are abbreviated as follows:

AMB	The American Museum in Britain, Bath (donated by Marion V. Dorn)
CHNDM	Cooper-Hewitt National Design Museum, NYC
IWM	Imperial War Museum, London
JJC	John Johnson Collection, Bodleian Library, Oxford
LoC	Library of Congress, Washington DC
LTM	London's Transport Museum
MMA	Museum of Modern Art, NYC
NRM	National Railways Museum, York
PRO	Public Record Office, Kew
Shell	Shell Art Collection, Beaulieu
	Shell-Mex & BP Archive, University of Warwick
V&A	Victoria and Albert Museum, London
V&A (S)	Schreyer Collection at V&A
V&A (SG)	Sidney Garrad Collection in the V&A Art and Design Archive, Blythe Road, London

Sizes

HC	Half Crown	15″ x 10″	38.1 x 25.4 cm
C	Crown	20″ x 15″	50.8 x 38.1 cm
R	Royal	20″ x 25″	50.8 x 63.5 cm
DC	Double Crown	30″ x 20″	76.2 x 50.8 cm
DR	Double Royal	40″ x 25″	101.6 x 63.5 cm
QC	Quad Crown	30″ x 40″	76.2 x 101.6 cm
QR	Quad Royal	40″ x 50″	101.6 x 127 cm
DQC	Double Quad Crown	60″ x 40″	152.4 x 101.6 cm
LB	Lorry Bill	30″ x 45″	76.2 x 114.3 cm
	16-sheet	120″ x 80″	304.8 x 203.2 cm
	48-sheet	120″ x 240″	304.8 x 609.6 cm

Irregular sizes

ISa		22½″ x 16½″	57 x 42 cm
ISb		11½″ x 18¼″	29.5 x 46.5 cm
ISc		10″ x 20″	25.4 x 50.8 cm

Title	Client	Size	Collections
1915			
1. *In Watford*	UD	DC	V&A (+od), LTM, MMA, LoC
2. *Oxhey Woods*	UD	DC	V&A, LTM, MMA, LoC
1916			
3. *Godstone*	UD	DC	V&A, LTM (+od), LoC
4. *Route 160: Reigate* Version in MMA has 59b pasted over '160'	UD	DC	V&A (+od 'Above Reigate'), LTM, MMA, LoC
5. *The Heaths, No 178: Surrey*	UD	DC	V&A (+od 'Beyond Esher'), LTM, LoC
6. *The North Downs*	UD	DC	V&A (+od), LTM, LoC
1917			
7. *Derry & Toms: Economy and Smartness in Men's Wear*	D&T	DQC	V&A, MMA, LoC
8. *Derry & Toms: Autumn Offerings*	D&T		see *The Studio*, 15 June 1920, p.143
1918			
9. *Canadian War Memorials Exhibition*	CWM	DC	IWM
10. *The London Group Exhibition: 2 May–2 June*	LG	DC	V&A, MMA
11. *Exhibition of Modern Painting and Sculpture by the London Group: 1–29 Nov*	LG	DC	V&A (SG)
1919			
12. *Soaring to Success! Daily Herald – The Early Bird*	DH	297.7 x 152.2 cm	V&A
13. *Soaring to Success! Daily Herald – The Early Bird* Large version (12) has 8 birds in flight, the smaller version (13) has 7 birds	DH		see E. McKnight Kauffer, *The Art of the Poster*, (London, 1924), p.165 and V&A (SG)
14. *Summer Sale at Derry & Toms*	D&T	DQC	V&A, MMA, LoC
15. *Objects from the East at Derry & Toms*	D&T	DQC	V&A, MMA, LoC
16. *Winter Sale at Derry & Toms*	D&T	DQC	V&A, MMA
17. *Vigil the Pure Silk*	WB	93.5 x 60.5 cm	MMA, V&A od
18. *The Golden Ballot – in Aid of Settlement for Disabled Sailors and Soldiers*	DSS	DC	MMA
19. *Exhibition of Modern Painting and Sculpture by the London Group: 12 April–17 May*	LG	DC	Private Collection
20. *Exhibition of Modern Art: The London Group: 1–29 Nov*	LG	DC	V&A (S)
21. *Arts League of Service*	ALS		Private Collection
1920			
22. *Blue Bells, Kew Gardens*	UD	DC	LTM
23. *Flowers of the Riverside*	UD	DC	V&A, LTM (+od), LoC
24. *The Forest Glades of Epping*	UD	DC	V&A, LTM
25. *Flowers o'the Corn*	UD	DC	LTM, LoC, V&A od
26. *Flowers of the Hills*	UD	DC	V&A, LTM, LoC
27. *Aster Time Kew Gardens*	UD	DC	V&A, LTM
28. *Uxbridge by Tram*	UD	DC	V&A (+od), LTM, LoC
29. *Hainault Forest by Motor Bus*	UD	DC	V&A, LTM
30. *Hatfield by Motor Bus*	UD	DC	V&A, LTM, JJM
31. *Windsor by Motor Bus*	UD	DC	V&A, LTM, LoC
32. *Chingford by Motor Bus*	UD	DC	V&A, LTM, LoC
33. *Epping Forest by Motor Bus*	UD	DC	V&A (+od), LTM, LoC
34. *St Albans by Motor Bus*	UD	DC	V&A (+od), LTM
The V&A holds a set of 10 proofs showing progressive stages of the printing process			
35. *Group X Exhibition*	Group X	DC	MMA
1921			
36. *Reigate – Priory Park by Motor Bus*	UD	DC	V&A, LTM
37. *Winter Sales Are Best Reached by Underground*	UD	DR	V&A (+od), LTM, MMA
38. *Shop Between 10 & 4 the Quiet Hours*	UD	DR	LTM (+od), MMA
39. *Eastman's Tailor Valet Service*	Ea		see *Commercial Art*, Dec 1923
40. *London Dyers and Cleaners For Over 100 Years: Eastman and Son (Magic Dyers)*	Ea	ISa	V&A
41. *Vigil the Pure Silk – for Lovely Frocks*	WB	DC	MMA
1922			
42. *London Museum of Practical Geology*	UD	DR	V&A, LTM, MMA
43. *The Royal United Service Museum*	UD	DR	V&A (+od), LTM
44. *Victoria & Albert Museum, South Kensington - Kuan-Yin*	UD	DR	V&A (S), LTM, MMA
45. *Winter Sales Are Best Reached by the Underground*	UD	DR	V&A, LTM
46. *Gloves Cleaned – Colour and Beauty Restored: Eastman and Son*	Ea	ISa	MMA
47. *London Dyers and Cleaners For Over 120 Years: Eastman and Son (storm and rainbow)*	Ea		V&A (SG)
48. *London Dyers & Cleaners For Over 120 Years: Eastman and Son – Magic Dyers (magician)*	Ea		see G. Warren and D. Klein, *Art Nouveau and Art Deco* (London: Galley Press, 1978), p.12
49. *The Westminster Press*	WP	DC	MMA
50. *Pomeroy Day Cream*	Po	DC	V&A (SG), see *The Year-Book of the Design & Industries Association*, 1923–4, pl.6
51. *He Who Gets Slapped*	TG	24S	V&A (SG)
52. *Back to Methuselah*	TG	24S	V&A (SG)
Four handbills publicising *Back to Methuselah* in Kauffer guard book (SG); also one example in Kauffer, *The Art of the Poster* (1924), p.183			
53. *The SS Tenacity*	ST		
54. *The Dover Road*	ST		
The posters for the Schubert Theater were reported in a newspaper cutting (8 June 1922) in Willard Library, Evansville, Ia, USA			

Title	Client	Size	Collections
1923			
55. *London History at the London Museum*	UD	DR	V&A (+od), LTM, MMA
56. *The Rocket of Mr Stephenson of Newcastle at the Museum of Science*	UD	DR	V&A (+od), LTM
57. *Museum of Natural History, South Kensington*	UD	DR	V&A, LTM (+od), LoC
58. *Regatta Time Hampton Court and Dittons by Tram*	UD	HC	LTM
Another version using same image: *Regatta Time Molesey by Tram*			
59. *London Dyers & Cleaners For Over 120 Years: Eastman and Son* (dove and rainbow)	Ea	ISa	V&A
60. *Since 1802 The London Dyers and Cleaners: Eastman and Son*	Ea	ISa	V&A
61. *Pomeroy Day Cream*	Po	DC	V&A
Also issued with alternative wording, 'Pomeroy Skin Food', in *Advertising World*, September 1926, p.ii and *Commercial Art*, vol.1, 1926, p.70			
62. *The Arts League Travelling Theatre at Royal Court Theatre*	ALS		Private Collection
63. *Vim Zum Putzen und Polieren*	LB		V&A (SG)
64. *Read 'Cricketer' in the Manchester Guardian*	MG	DC	V&A(S), MMA
65. 'Poster for a book' (listed in catalogue to ALS retrospective exhibition of posters, 1925, group H)			
1924			
66. *Bushey Park by Tram*	UD	DC	V&A, LTM (+od)
67. *Hadley Wood by Tram*	UD	DC	V&A (+od), LTM, MMA, LoC
68. *Combined Seasons*	UD	DR	LTM
69. *Twickenham by Tram*	UD	DC	V&A, LTM, LoC
70. *The Colne River at Uxbridge by Tram*	UD	DC	V&A (+od), LTM
71. *Near Waltham Cross by Tram*	UD	DC	V&A (+od), LTM
72. *Winter Sales Are Best Reached by Underground*	UD	DR	V&A, LTM (od), MMA
73. *Imperial War Museum: The Vindictive Howitzer*	UD	DR	V&A (+od), LTM, MMA
75. *Olympia Show, October 17–25*	UD	ISb	LTM
76. *Edgware & Hampstead Extension* (illustrative border by Kauffer)	UD	ISb	LTM
77. *Clapham Common – Morden* (illustrative border by Kauffer)	UD	ISb	LTM
The above three 'panel posters' were intended for display inside Underground carriages			
78. *Spring Cleaning: Eastman's The London Dyers & Cleaners*	Ea	ISa	V&A
79. *Eno's Fruit Salt – First Thing Every Morning* (cock crowing)	En	DC	V&A, MMA
This design was adapted for a number of different poster sizes including 16-sheet and another version has the cockerel facing to the left: in *Poster Points* (July 1927), the journal of the British Poster Advertising Association. The design was also adapted to be used for other promotional items including magazine advertisements and show cards.			
80. *Eno's Fruit Salt – First Thing Every Morning* (cock on weather vane)	En	DC	MMA
81. *The Arts League Travelling Theatre – The Travelling Players are Coming*	ALS		see Haworth-Booth (1979), pl. 21
82. *The Arts: British Empire Exhibition*	BEE		
83. *Chemistry: British Empire Exhibition*	BEE		
84. *Electricity: British Empire Exhibition*	BEE		
85. *Food: British Empire Exhibition*	BEE		
86. *Homemaking: British Empire Exhibition*	BEE		
87. *Pottery: British Empire Exhibition*	BEE		
88. *Sport: British Empire Exhibition*	BEE		
89. *Mining: British Empire Exhibition*	BEE		
90. *Theatres: British Empire Exhibition*	BEE		
Six of the posters are reproduced in *Commercial Art*, July 1924, p.64. They were displayed in the 'poster street' at the 1924 Empire Exhibition, Wembley – and were probably all 16-sheet in size			
1925			
91. *Whitsuntide Pleasures by Underground* (Jack i'the green)	UD	DR	LTM
92. *Whitsuntide Pleasures by Underground* (Pierrot)	UD	DR	LTM (+od)
93. *Summertime Pleasures by Underground* (Jack i'the green)	UD	DR	V&A, LTM
This is the same design as *Whitsuntide* (Jack i'the green) with alternative heading			
94. *Summertime Pleasures by Underground* (Pierrot)	UD	DR	V&A, LTM
This is the same design as *Whitsuntide* (Pierrot) with alternative heading			
95. *Whitsuntide in the Country*	UD	QR	LTM
96. *Summertime in the Country*	UD	QR	V&A
This is the same design as *Whitsuntide in the Country* with alternative 'Summertime' heading			
97. *The Wallace Collection – Book to Bond Street*	UD	DR	V&A (+od), LTM
98. *The Indian Museum – Book to South Kensington*	UD	DR	V&A (+od), LTM, MMA
99. *The New Trade Mark of Eastman and Son* (bell)	Ea	ISa	V&A
100. *Eastman and Son – Spring Cleaning and Dying* (swan)	Ea	ISa	V&A
101. *The London Group – RWS Galleries 6–26 June*	LG	DC	MMA
102. *The London Group – New Burlington Galleries 13–31 Oct*	LG	DC	V&A
The autumn London Group poster design is the same as the summer show poster but with alternative lettering and different second colour			
103. *England to India – a World Record in a Wolseley*	Wo	DR	MMA
104. *Welwyn Garden City*	We		see Haworth-Booth, (1979), pl.12
105. *The Labour Woman*	LW	DC	MMA
1926			
106. *Socrates at the British Museum*	UD	DR	V&A, LTM (+od), MMA, LoC
107. *The Flea at the Natural History Museum*	UD	DR	V&A (+od), LTM, MMA
108. *Eastman and Son – Since 1802*	Ea	ISa	MMA
109. *Gloves Gloves Cleaned: Eastman and Son*	Ea	ISa	V&A (S), MMA

Title	Client	Size	Collections
1927			
110. *Cheap Return Tickets –* *From this Underground station*	UD	DR	LTM, MMA
111. *Season Tickets Weekly –* *From this station*	UD	DR	LTM
Kauffer's designs for the above two posters formed decorative borders which left an area for overprinting (using Johnston Sans) the names of different Underground stations			
112. *From Winters Gloom to* *Summers Joy*	UD	DR	V&A, LTM (+od), MMA
Kauffer neglected to insert apostrophes in *Winter's* and *Summer's*			
113. *Publicity – For all Advertising* *Spaces on This Railway*	UD	DC	LTM
114. *Eastman and Son – The London* *Dyers and Cleaners (harlequin)*	Ea	ISa	MMA
115. *Cocoa Pods*	EMB	DQC	V&A od, PRO
116. *Banana Palms*	EMB	DQC	MMA, PRO
117. *Jungles Today Are Gold Mines* *Tomorrow – Growing Markets for* *Our Goods*	EMB	DQC	PRO
118. *Cocoa – Three-Fifths of the* *World's Supply from Empire Sources*	EMB	DR	PRO
119. *Bananas – The Empire Exports* *12,000,000 Bunches a Year*	EMB	DR	PRO
120. *EMB – Today's Pick of the* *Empire Basket*	EMB	16-sheet	V&A od
121. *Hearts and Diamonds – Strand Theatre* Possibly not used			see *Commercial Art,* July 1927, p.7
1928			
122. *British Industries Fair –* *White City*	UD	ISb	LTM
123. *Chrysler Prices are Down!*	CM	DC	MMA
124. *Artistas Britanicos – Buenos Aires* *Junio MCMXXVII*	JD		see *Advertising World,* August 1928, p.403 and *Commercial Art,* Sept 1928, p.106.
125. *Well Done! 11 World Records –* *Villiers*	Vi	DC	MMA
1929			
126. *Exhibition: Native Art from* *British Columbia*	UD	DR	V&A, LTM, MMA
127. *St Albans: Route 84 from* *Golders Green*	UD	DR	LTM
128. *TOT Seasons – Combined* *Season Tickets available by Train –* *Bus – Train via this Station*	UD	DR	LTM
129. *International Aero Exhibition* *1929 – Shell*	SM	LB	V&A, MMA, Shell
1930			
130. *National Safety Week –* *Be on Guard Against Accidents!*	UD	29.7 x 73.7 cm	LTM, MMA
131. *Green Line Motor Coaches –* *Welwyn Garden City from* *Charing Cross*	UD	DR	LTM
132. *For Pull Use Summer Shell*	SM	LB	V&A, MMA, Shell

Title	Client	Size	Collections
1931			
133. *For All Theatres Travel* *by Underground*	UD	DR	V&A, LTM, MMA
134. *Play Between 6 and 12 –* *the Bright Hours*	UD	DR	V&A, LTM (+od)
135. *Shop Between 10 and 4 –* *the Quiet Hours*	UD	DR	V&A, LTM (+od), MMA, LoC
An amended version was re-issued in 1947			
136. *Power – the Nerve Centre of* *London's Underground*	UD	DR	V&A, LTM (+od), MMA, LoC
137. *Underground Progress*	UD	DR	LTM
138. *Roman Britain St Albans –* *Excavations Now in Progress*	UD	49.7 x 32.9 cm	LTM
139. *Stonehenge –* *See Britain First on Shell*	SM	LB	V&A, MMA, Shell
140. *Summer Shell – I Certify that* *the Summer Blend of Shell…* *(imitation of signed certificate)*	SM	LB	Shell
141. *The Quick Starting Pair –* *Shell Oil & Petrol*	SM	LB	Shell
142. *You Can Be Sure of Shell (chain)* Also smaller version with variant design	SM	LB 27.3 x 61 cm	V&A (S), MMA, Shell MMA
143. *The New Forest – See Britain* *First on Winter Shell*	SM	LB	V&A, MMA, Shell
144. *Michael Faraday Centenary* *Exhibition – Royal Albert Hall*		DR	MMA
c. 1931			
145. *To Get a Move On –* *Move On Pratt's High Test*	P	16-sheet	V&A
1932			
146. *Publicity Pays on the Underground*	UD	DC	LTM, MMA
147. *A pillar'd shade… (Milton)*	UD	DR	V&A, LTM LoC
148. *Now the pine-tree's waving top…* *(Cunningham)*	UD	DR	V&A, LTM, LoC
149. *By the rushy-fringed bank…* *(Milton)*	UD	DR	V&A, LTM, MMA, LoC
150. *Look! Under that broad beech* *tree…(Walton)*	UD	DR	V&A, LTM, LoC
151. *Piccadilly Express Trains –* *from 4th July (red and black)*	UD	DR	LTM
152. *Piccadilly Express Trains –* *from 4th July (blue and black)*	UD	DR	LTM
153. *Piccadilly Extension –* *Finsbury Park to Arnos Grove*	UD	DR	LTM, MMA
154. *Everywhere You Go* *You Can Be Sure of Shell* *Bodiam Castle*	SM	LB	V&A (S), MMA, Shell
155. *Aeroshell Lubricating Oil –* *The Aristocrat of Lubricants*	SM	LB	V&A, MMA, Shell, LoC
156. *Wherever You Go –* *You Can Be Sure of Shell* *River Yeo near Barnstaple*	SM	LB	MMA, Shell
157. *Economise in Time, Temper,* *Petrol by Using Winter Shell*	SM	LB	MMA, Shell
158. *Lewis Carroll Centenary*	J&E Bumpus		see *Commercial Art,* vol. XII, no. 71, 1932, p.212

Title	Client	Size	Collections
1933			
159. *At London's Service*	UD	DR	V&A (S), LTM
160. *Whitsuntide Holiday*	UD	DR	V&A, LTM, MMA
161. *BP Ethyl Controls Horsepower*	SM	LB	V&A, MMA, Shell, LoC
Also issued as a 48-sheet poster			
162. *Ask for BP Not Just Ethyl*	SM	LB	V&A, MMA, Shell
163. *Aladdin the Best Paraffin*	SM	LB	Shell
164. *Recommended for Winter – Double Shell Lubricating Oil*	SM	LB	V&A (S), MMA, Shell
165. *Merchants Prefer Shell*	SM	LB	V&A, MMA, Shell
166. *Go Great Western to Devonshire (no.10)*	GWR	DR	V&A, NRM, MMA
167. *Go Great Western to Devon (no.11)*	GWR	DR	V&A, NRM
168. *Great Western to Devon's Moors (no.12)*	GWR	DR	V&A, NRM, MMA
169. *Great Western to Cornwall (no.13)*	GWR	DR	V&A, NRM, MMA
170. *Go Great Western to Cornwall (no.14)*	GWR	DR	V&A, NRM, MMA
171. *Go Great Western to Cornwall (no.15)*	GWR	DR	V&A, NRM, MMA
172. *Gilbey's Castle Port*	Gi	ISc	V&A, MMA
173. *W&A Gilbey Rubicon Australian Burgundy*	Gi	ISc	V&A, MMA, LoC
174. *Gilbey's Invalid Port*	Gi	ISc	V&A, MMA, LoC
175. *Gilbey's Bonita Sherry*	Gi	ISc	V&A
176. *Gilbey's Spey Royal Scotch Whisky*	Gi	ISc	V&A, MMA, LoC
177. *Gilbey's Wrangoo Austral Red Wine*	Gi	ISc	V&A, MMA
178. *Gilbey's Invalid Port*	Gi	ISc	V&A, MMA, LoC
179. *Quickest By Airmail*	GPO	DC	MMA
1934			
180. *Road Accidents – Mostly Through Somebody's Carelessness*	LT	29.8 x 73.6 cm	LTM
181. *National Road Safety Campaign*	LT	30.5 x 66.0 cm	LTM
182. *Publicity Pays – Tell the World*	LT	DC	V&A, LTM, MMA
183. *Westminster Abbey*	LT	DR	V&A, LTM, MMA
184. *The Tower of London*	LT	DR	V&A, LTM, MMA
185. *Buckingham Palace – from St James's Park*	LT	DR	V&A, LTM, MMA, LoC
186. *Westminster from the Thames*	LT	DR	V&A, LTM, MMA, LoC
The above four posters were re-issued at half-royal size in 1936			
187. *7-Day Season – holidays in the West Country*	GWR	DR	MMA
188. *Contact With the World – Use the Telephone*	GPO	DC	V&A, MMA
189. *Come On The Telephone*	GPO	53.3 x 61 cm	MMA
190. *Come On The Telephone*	GPO	38.1 x 142.2 cm	MMA
191. *Orient Line Cruises*	OL	DR	V&A, MMA, LoC
192. *Orient Line to Australia*	OL	DR	V&A (S), MMA, LoC
193. *Keep Well – Eno's Fruit Salt First Thing Every Morning*	En		See *Commercial Art*, vol. XVIII, p.206
194. *Regent Exhibition of 1934 – Dorland Hall*		DC	MMA
1935			
195. *Train Yourself to Better Work*	LT	DR	V&A (S) (+od), LTM, MMA
196. *Treat Yourself to Better Play*	LT	DR	V&A, LTM, MMA
197. *News of Evening Classes*	LT	DR	LTM, MMA
198. *Shell is Always First*	SM	LB	MMA, Shell
199. *Magicians Prefer Shell*	SM	LB	V&A, MMA, Shell
200. *Explorers Prefer Shell*	SM	LB	V&A, MMA, Shell
201. *Actors Prefer Shell*	SM	LB	V&A, MMA, Shell, LoC
202. *Winter Shell On Sale till Next May*	SM	LB	MMA, Shell
203. *Royal Windsor, GWR*	GWR	DR	V&A (S), NRW
204. *Orient Line to Australia and Back*	OL		LoC
205. *Quickest Way by Air Mail*	GPO	DC	V&A (S), MMA
206. *Air Mail Routes*	GPO	101.6 x 127 cm	V&A
207. *Travel in Comfort by Imperial Airways*	IA	DR	V&A, MMA
208. *The New Gas Fires Light Themselves Says Mr Therm*	GLCC	DC	V&A, MMA
209. *Stop on India Non-Skid Tyres and Feel the Difference*	IT	DC	V&A
1936			
210. *Toys of All Ages (1–6 in a series of images of toys)*	LT	DR	V&A, LTM
211. *Toys of All Ages (7–12 in a series of images of toys)*	LT	DR	V&A, LTM
212. *Toys of All Ages (13–18 in a series of images of toys)*	LT	DR	V&A, LTM
213. *Special Areas Exhibition – Ticket Hall at Charing Cross Station*	LT	DR	LTM, MMA
214. *Evening Tourist Tickets – 6d*	LT	DR	LTM, MMA
215. *Spring in the Village (photo by Kate Jacob)*	LT	DR	V&A, LTM
216. *Spring on the Hillside (photo by J. Dixon Scott)*	LT	DR	V&A, LTM
217. *Follow the Spring, Ripley (photo by Paul Shillabeer)*	LT	DR	
218. *Follow the Spring, Shardeloes Park (photo by Paul Shillabeer)*	LT	DR	See F.A. Mercer & W. Gaunt (eds), *Poster Progress*, (London 1939), p. 108
219. *An Evening in Town – Cheap Evening Return Tickets*	LT	DR	LTM
220. *Earls Court – See the Model of the New Building in the Ticket Hall at Charing Cross Station*	LT	DR	V&A, LTM, MMA, LoC
221. *Ford Approves Triple Shell Lubricating Oil*	SM	LB	Shell
222. *Austin Recommend Shell*	SM	LB	Shell
Three further variations of the above lorry bill state that 'Standard', 'Rolls Royce' and 'Morris' 'Recommend Shell'			
223. *To Visit Britain's Landmarks – Dinton Castle*	SM	LB	V&A, MMA, Shell
224. *Official for Winter – Single Shell Lubricating Oil*	SM	LB	Shell
225. *Official for Winter – Double Shell Lubricating Oil*	SM	LB	V&A, MMA, Shell
226. *Tea Drives Away the Droops Says Mr T. Pott*	TMB	DC	V&A

Title	Client	Size	Collections
1937			
227. *News Chronicle Schools Exhibition – Dorland Hall* (boy's head)	NC	DC	V&A, MMA
228. *News Chronicle Schools Exhibition – Dorland Hall*	NC	DC	V&A
229. *News Chronicle Schools Exhibition – Also in the Ticket Hall Charing Cross Station*	LT	DR	LTM
The London Transport version of the *News Chronicle* poster was adapted from the above design			
230. *Spring – Still the fresh Spring finds new plants to quicken, and new groves to green* (Thomson)	LT	DR	V&A, LTM, MMA
231. *Spring in the Country*	LT	DR	V&A, LTM, MMA
232. *August Bank Holiday – Out by London Transport*	LT	DR	LTM
233. *Motor Show Earls Court*	LT	DR	V&A, LTM
234. *It's Not Far to the New Earls Court*	LT	DR	V&A, LTM
235. *Lubrication by Shell – Miles-Whitney Straight*	SM	LB	V&A, MMA, Shell
236. *Lubrication by Shell – Imperial Airways Empire Flying Boat 'Canopus'*	SM	LB	V&A, Shell
237. *New Shell Lubricating Oils*	SM	LB	V&A, MMA, Shell
Above design also issued as 48-sheet poster			
238. *Outposts of Britain – The North of Scotland*	GPO	R	V&A
239. *Outposts of Britain – Land's End*	GPO	R	V&A
240. *Outposts of Britain – Northern Ireland*	GPO	R	V&A
241. *Outposts of Britain – The Pool of London*	GPO	R	V&A
242. *Post During the Lunch Hour*	GPO	DC	MMA
243. *Post Office Savings – Bank Your Money Here*	GPO	DC	MMA
244. *Letter Mails by Air to East & South Africa, Egypt, Palestine, India, Ceylon, Burma, Malaya*	GPO	DC	V&A, MMA, LoC
245. *South and East African Air Mail*	GPO		MMA
246. *Towards a Fitter Britain – Use Your Health Services*	MoH	88.8 x 63.2 cm	V&A
247. *Study Success at the Advertising Exhibition – Olympia*		DC	V&A, MMA
248. *Help Wounded Beings – Help to Send Medical Aid to Spain*	SMAC	DC	V&A (S), MMA
1938			
249. *Countryside in Autumn*	LT	DR	V&A, LTM
250. *Autumn Woods*	LT	DR	V&A, LTM
The above posters carried no text. Each one was displayed alongside a text poster with a decorative border designed by Kauffer. *Autumn Woods* was re-issued in 1955 and advertised the E. McKnight Kauffer memorial exhibition at the V&A. It additionally contained the lines from a Thomas Hood poem: 'How bravely Autumn paints upon the sky The gorgeous fame of Summer which is fled.'			
251. *Exhibition of Modern Silver Work – Goldsmiths Hall*	LT	DR	V&A, MMA
252. *Whitsuntide*	LT	24.8 x 75.2 cm	LTM
253. *TVO For Maximum Draw-bar Pull!*	SM	LB	V&A, MMA, Shell
254. *Shell For Go For Shell*	SM	LB	MMA, Shell
Above design also issued as 16-sheet poster no. 58 in V&A exhib cat 1955			
255. *You Can Be Sure of Shell – Turns the Wheels of the World*	SM	16-sheet	V&A
256. *Nuffield Trophy Won on Shell Oil Lubrication*	SM	LB	Shell
257. *Cheaper Empire Telegrams*	GPO	DC	V&A, MMA
258. *New Architecture Exhibition of the Elements of Modern Architecture organised by the MARS Group*	MARS	DC	V&A
259. *ARP: Air Raid Precautions – Calling You*	ARP	DC	V&A, MMA
Also issued at HC size by London Transport			
260. *National Volunteers Service – Wanted for Women's Ambulance Services*	ARP	26.5 x 107.5 cm	V&A (S)
261. *Exhibition of Chinese Art – Chinese Medical Aid*	CMA		V&A (SG)
262. *Support for the British Battalion International Brigade*	DWC	DC	V&A (S), MMA. LoC
263. *Webster Aitken Playing Schubert's Complete Pianoforte Sonatas, Aeolian Hall*	AH	DC	V&A (S), MMA
264. *Fame for Britain – Films/Art/ Music/Entertainment*		DR	V&A
265. *Festival of Music for the People*		DC	V&A (S)
1939			
266. *London Music Festival – London Transport Serves Them All*	LT	DR	LTM
267. *London Music Festival*	LMF	DR	V&A (S)
268. *May to October – Summer Shell*	SM	LB	V&A, MMA, Shell
269. *From October to May – Winter Shell*	SM	LB	V&A, Shell
270. *Shell Lubrication Oil – Stays on the Job*	SM	16-sheet	See V&A exhib cat no 142
1940			
271. *Lincoln Continental for 1941*			*20th Annual of Advertising Art*, Art Directors' Club of NY, 1941, p.200
1941			
272. *CIO Supports Red Cross*	ARC		CHNDM
1942			
273. *The Greatest Show on Earth – Ringling Bros and Barnum & Bailey*	Ri	QC	V&A (S), LoC
274. *Greece Fights On*	GO	QC	V&A, MMA, LoC
275. *El Nuevo Orden – Del Eje*	IAA		V&A (S), MMA
276. *Luchamos por la Libertad de Todos* also: *Lutamos pela Liberdade de Todos*	IAA		V&A, LoC
277. *Libertad de Cultos Liberdade Politica*	IAA IAA		V&A (S) V&A, LoC
278. *Keep It Under Your Stetson – Hitler Wants to Know What You Know*	St	QC	

Title	Client	Size	Collections
1943			
279. *Ringling Bros and Barnum & Bailey Present – Holidays*	Ri		V&A (S)
280. *Norway Fights On*	AFN		CHNDM
281. *Target No 1 – New York City – Protect it Enroll Now*	CD		V&A (S)
282. *Watch Out For Fires – CAA War Training Service*	CAA		V&A (S), LoC
283. *For the Conquered – Steel! Not Bread*	DB		V&A (S)
284. *Help a Greek Child to Survive*	FoG		V&A (S)
285. *Xairete Nikomen – Greek War Relief Association*	GWRA		LoC
286. *Civil Aeronautics Administration – Speeds the War*	CAA		V&A (S), MMA, LoC
287. *You Can Set Their Spirit Free – Prisoners' War Aid*	PWA		
1944			
288. *Yugoslav People Led by Tito, 1941–1944*	UCSSA		V&A (S), LoC
289. *Drainy Weather – Conoco the Motor Oil*	CO		*24th Art Directors' Annual of Advertising Art*, 1945, p.274
1945			
290. *Give*	ARC		
291. *Join the Diamond Jubilee*	MM		CHNDM
292. *The Rainbow to Europe – Pan American*	PA		CHNDM
c. 1946–1949			
293. *American Airlines – Boston*	AA	QC	AMB
294. *American Airlines to California*	AA	QC	LoC
295. *American Airlines – California, Switzerland, Canada, Scandinavia, New England*	AA	QC	
296. *American Airlines to England*	AA	QC	V&A
297. *American Airlines – all Europe*	AA	QC	LoC
298. *American Airlines to Europe*	AA	QC	MMA
299. *American Airlines – Holland*	AA	QC	V&A
300. *American Airlines to Ireland*	AA	QC	AMB
301. *American Airlines – Mexico*	AA	QC	AMB
302. *American Airlines to New England*	AA	QC	AMB
303. *American Airlines to New York*	AA	QC	
304. *American Overseas Airlines – to New York*	AA	QC	
305. *American Airlines to Niagara Falls & Canada*	AA	QC	LoC
306. *American Airlines – San Francisco*	AA	QC	LoC, AMB
307. *American Airlines – Scandinavia*	AA	QC	
308. *American Airlines – The Tourist*	AA	QC	V&A exhib cat 1955 no
309. *American Airlines to Washington – Night and Day*	AA	QC	AMB
310. *American Airlines – Washington*	AA	QC	MMA, LoC
311. *Fashions in Flight via American Airlines*	AA	QC	LoC
1947			
312. *American Airlines to Mexico*	AA	QC	LoC
313. *American Airlines – Winter Sports*	AA	QC	LoC

Title	Client	Size	Collections
314. *American Airlines Over the World*	AA		
315. *United Nations – Your Peace is Our Business*	UN		see *Art & Industry*, vol. 43, 1947, p.119
316. *The United Nations – Nations Unite*	UN		
317. *Subway Posters Perform Daily Before 5 Million Pairs of Eyes*	SA		AMB
318. *MedaglioD'Oro – America's Favorite Italian Roast Coffee*			see *Portfolio* (1950), p.28
1948			
319. *American Airlines – California Arizona Texas New Mexico*	AA	QC	AMB
320. *American Airlines to the Sun Country*	AA	QC	
321. *American Airlines – East Coast*	AA	QC	LoC
322. *Pan American – Holland*	PA		
323. *Fly Pan America – Germany*	PA		
1949			
324. *For Quick Results – Ship by Clipper Cargo Pan Am*	PA		
325. *Clipper Service Around the Clock Around the World – Pan American*	PA		
326. *Mexico Festivals Old & New – Pan American*	PA		V&A
327. *Pan American – There's No Business in Slow Business*	PA		
328. *Subway Poster Pulls*	SA		
329. *28th National Exhibition of Advertising & Editorial Art*			
330. *Kentucky Derby – Go via Chesapeake & Ohio*	CO		V&A
1950			
331. *American Airlines to Chicago*	AA	QC	V&A, LoC
332. *Holy Year – Rome 1950 American Airlines*	AA	QC	AMB
333. *American Airlines – Paris*	AA	QC	V&A
334. *American Airlines – Sweden*	AA	QC	V&A
1953			
335. *American Airlines to Boston*	AA	QC	
336. *Aloha Hawaii – Pan American*	AA	QC	V&A LoC
337. *Ireland – Fly Pan Am*	PA		V&A (S)
338. *Round the World – Fly with Pan American*	AA	QC	V&A
1954			
339. *Japan via Pan American*	PA		V&A
1966			
Commemorating the Great Fire of London	LT		LTM
Reprint of 1923 London Museum poster			
1974			
Visit Your Museums – National History Museum	LT		LTM
Printed from original design completed in 1939			

By the rushy-fringed bank ... (Milton), 1932
poster, London Underground
E.3340-1932

INDEX

Note: Illustration references are shown in *italic*

Acton, Harold 46-7
Agate, James 89
Allen Lane 68
American Airlines 104
American Container Corporation 96, 101
Anderson, Sir Colin 61, 68, 72-3, 98
Andreyev, Leonid, *He Who Gets Slapped* 31, 44
Apollinaire, Guillaume 16
Architectural Review 61, 62
Armfield, Maxwell 10, 16
Armory Show (1913) 11
Arp, Jean 60
Art Directors' Club of New York 101
Art et Décoration 12
Arts and Crafts movement 14
Arts and Decoration 30, 34
Arts and Decoration Gallery, New York 30
Arts League of Service 24, 38, 42, 44, 55
Ashbee, C.R. 14
Ashton, Frederick 90
Asquith, Anthony 47-8
Attwell, Mabel Lucie 16
Auden, W.H. 74
Ayer, N.W. 96

Bacon, Francis 72, 79
Bacon, Frank 10
Bakst, Leon 39
Balcon, Sir Michael 48-9
Balla, Giacomo 18
Ballets Russes 33, 38, 39, 90
Barman, Christian 95, 107
Barnes, Clive 90
Barnum and Bailey's Circus 101
Barr, Alfred H. 98
Barr, Frank 86
Baumeister, Willi 61
Baynard Press 110
Beach and Bowers Minstrels 9
Beall, Lester 86
Beardsley, Aubrey 38
Beck, Maurice 77
Beddington, Jack 67, 74, 76-85, *76*, 95, 96-8, 104, 107
Beddington, Olivia 78, 91
Beddington-Behrens, Sir Edward 77
Beggarstaff Brothers 50
Bell, Vanessa 24
Bell, Clive 78
Bellamy, Edward, *Looking Backward 103*
Benchley, Robert 74
Bennett, Arnold 51, 53, 58
    Elsie and the Child 53-4, *54*, 58, 86
    Venus Rising from the Sea 54
Bentley, Nicholas 77
Bernstein, Sidney 48, 53
Betjeman, Sir John 46, 77
    Continual Dew 46, *47*
Bevan, Robert (fils) 94
Bevan, Robert (père) 21
Birkenhead, Lord, *The World in 2030* 62
Birmingham Group 16
Birmingham Repertory Theatre (1917) 22
Blakeston, Oswell 61
Blast 16, 17, 26, 31, 38
Blewbury, Berkshire *17*
Bliss, Arthur 90

Blumenthal, Joe 97
Blunt, Professor Sir Anthony 68-70
Boccioni, *Pittura e Scultura Futurista* 18
Bodley, George 14
Bomberg, David 17, 77
Brae, June 90
Brancusi, Constantin 11, 98
Braque, Georges 11
British Council 90
British Empire Exhibition 36, *36*, 44
British Instructional Films 47
British Overseas Airways Corporation 20
British Poster Advertising Association, 50
Britten, Benjamin 74
Brown, E.A. 58
Brown, Ivor 89
Bruguière, Francis 60, 61, 66, 67, 68, *76*
Bulletin 11
Burchfield, Charles 31
Burlington Magazine 44, 67
Burra, Edward 68
Burton, Robert, *The Anatomy of Melancholy* 42-3, *43*

Cahiers d'Art 61
Camargo Society 90
Carter, Alan 90
Cassandre, A.M. 31, 71-2, 78, 99
Cassells 59
Cerf, Bennett 102
Cézanne, Paul 11, 22, 24, 68
Chagall, Marc 12
The Chap-Book 38
Chappell, William 90
Charnaux 67
Checkmate (1937) 62
Chéret, Jules 14, 38
Chermayeff, Serge 61, 62, 68
Chicago 11
    Art Institute 11
    Art Students' League 11
Churchill, Winston 20, 97
Clark, Lord (Kenneth) 24, 51, 56, 61, 70, 76, 85
Cleverdon, Douglas 47
Coates, Wells 61, 62-4
Coburn, Alvin Langdon 17, 21
    Grace Kauffer 21
Cohen, Dennis 68
Cohen, Bernard 77
Colour 17, 18
Contact 77
Coster, Howard 68
    E. McKnight Kauffer 46
Coward, Noel 39, 53, 68
Crane, Walter 14
Crawford, Sir William 49
Crawford's Advertising Agency 49, 51-2
Cresset Press 68
Cresta Silk 64
Crick, Jesse 106
Cubism 11, 22, 70
Cumberland Market Group 21
Curwen, Harold 53, 91
Curwen Press 53

Daily Herald 18
Dante Alighieri, *Inferno* 94

Daviot, Gordon, *Queen of Scots* 89
Davis, Maud B., *E. McKnight Kauffer 13*
Delacroix, Eugène 11
Dell, M.O. 21
Derain, André 12, 43
Derry and Toms 21
Design and Industries Association 21, 36, 74, 75
Diaghilev, Serge 90
Dobson, Frank and Mary 108
Doré Gallery, London 16
Dorn, Marion 37, 46, 56, 58, 59, 60, 61, 67, 72, 73, 78, 80, 84, *89*, 92, 95, 96-7, 108, 109
Downman, Edward 33
Dronsfield 67
Duchamp, Marcel, *Nude Descending a Staircase* 11
Duchamp-Villon, Raymond 11
Duncan, Ronald 58
Durham 13

Earl's Court 66, 80
Eastman, Cyril 36
Eastman & Sons 36
Edinburgh 24
Edwards, Elizabeth 72
Ehrlich, Grace *see* Kauffer, Grace
Eight Commercial Artists 68
Elder, Paul 10
Eliot, T.S. 24, 38, 55-6, 58, 66, 67, 70, 94-5, *96*, 99, 103, 107, 108
Ellis, Richard 90
Elton, Arthur 77
Embassy Court, Brighton 64
Emberton, Joseph 61, 62, 64
Emerson, Ralph Waldo 106
Empire Marketing Board 47-51, *50*, 74
Eno's Fruit Salt 36-7
Epstein, Jacob 21, 61, 62
Etchells, Frederick 53, 61, 62
Evans, Richardson 14
Evans, Merlyn 77
Evansville, Indiana 9-10, 31

Faber & Gwyer (later Faber & Faber) 55
Faulkner, William, *Intruder in the Dust 103*
Fauvism 11, 16
Festival of Britain 104
Ffrangcon-Davies, Gwen 89
Film Society, London 48, 67
Filmer, A.E. 42
Flower, Dr Desmond 53-4, 59, 103
Fonteyn, Margot 90
Fortune 96
France, Anatole, *The Man Who Married a Dumb Wife* 42
'Friday Club' 25
Fry, Roger 22, 24, 26, 28, 31, 32, 43, 44, 61, 68
Futurism 16, 18

Games, Abram 104
Gardiner, Clive 50
Garland, Madge 57-8, 68
Garnett, Porter 11
Garrad, Sidney 83, 84, 86
Gaudier-Brzeska, Henri 77
Gauguin, Paul 11
Gebrauchsgraphik 53

General Post Office 74
Gentleman, Tom 77
Geology Museum, London 34
Gertler, Mark 50
Gibb, Sir George 14
Gielgud, John 89
Gill, Eric 33, 47
Gill, MacDonald 25, 50
Gilman, Harold 21
Ginner, Charles 21
Goncharova, Natalia 39
Goossens, Eugene 24
Grahame, Kenneth 17
Grant, Duncan 24
Great Western Railway 70, 70, 71
Gregory, Eric Craven (Peter) 60, 69, 76, 78, 95, 96, 104
Grierson, John 75, 47, 48, 78
Griffits, Thomas Edgar 110
Gropius, Walter 68
Guardian 68
Guinness, Bryan 60, 61
Guyatt, Professor Richard 76

Hall, Easton and Robertson 67
Handy-Heck plane 80
Harcourt Brace 101
Harper's Bazaar 94
Harris, H.H. 33
Hasigawa, Sabro 109
Hassall, John 14
Havinden, Ashley 51, 74
Hayward, John 60
Hellicar, W. 51
Helpmann, Robert 90
Hendy, Sir Philip 67
Herkomer, Hubert 19
Heron, Patrick 64
Heron, T.M. 64
Herrick, F.C. 36-7
Hitchcock, Alfred 48
Hohlwein, Ludwig 11-12, 16, 20
Holden, Charles 57, 61
Housman, A.E 38
Hudson, W.H. 62, 102
Hughes, Langston, Shakespeare in Harlem 101-2
Humphries, Eric 67
Hunt, William Holman 14
Hurry, Colin 12, 26
Huxley, Aldous 48, 67, 99, 103, 108
Huxley, Gervas 47

The Imprint 33
Indian Museum 39
Institute of Contemporary Arts 67

James, Henry 61
Japanese art 16, 18, 26
John Lewis Partnership 68
Johnston, Edward 32, 91
Jones, George W. 68
Joyce, James, Ulysses 20

Kandinsky, Wassily 11
On the Spiritual in Art 31
Karlowska, Stanislawa de 21
Karsavina, Tamara 11
Kauffer, Ann 28, 37, 57-8, 62, 80-81, 92, 94, 108
Kauffer, Anna 9-10
Kauffer, Edward McKnight 9, 46, 59, 76, 96

air-brush, use of 53, 86
appointments 68, 87
art collection 55
book illustrations 43, 53-4, 55-6, 58, 62, 86, 88, 101, 107, 108
chromolithography 110
dress design 42
exhibitions
    Armory Show (1913) 11
    Birmingham Repertory Theatre (1917) 22
    Heal's Gallery (1917) 22
    Mansard Gallery (1917) 110
    Practical Arts (1919) 24
    Parker Gallery (1921) 30
    Retrospective (1925) 44
    Neal Walden's studio (1921) 31
    Arthur Tooth and Sons Gallery (1929) 56-57
    Arthur Tooth and Sons Gallery (1931, 1933) 78
    Retrospective (1937) 110
    Katherine Kuh Gallery (1941) 86
    'Britain at War'(1940) 95, 97, 98
    New York World Fair (1940) 98
    A-D Gallery (1942) 99, 101
    American British Art Galleries (1949) 89
lorry bills 80-3, 86
Munich 11-12, 14-15
photo-montage, use of 52
photo-murals 64-6, 80
return to America 82
reverse lettering, use of 52
rugs 42, 56-8, 57, 62, 71
stencil or 'pochoir' process 54
studio 51-2
technique, note on 76
Kauffer, Grace (née Ehrlich) 12, 21, 21, 33, 37, 108
Kauffer, John (Johnny Kifer) 9
Keane, Thos, Caricature of Kauffer 9
Kepes, Gyorgy 86
Kipling, Rudyard 14
Klee, Paul 11, 61
Knopf, Alfred 101
Kokoschka, Oskar 77
Korda, Alexander 68

Laboureur, Georges 43
Lang, Fritz 48
Lansbury, George 18
Lawrence, T.B. 18, 42
Lawrence, D.H., Birds, Beasts and Flowers 68
Lawrence, Gertrude 53
Le Blon, Christof 43
Leach, Bernard 25, 37
Lee-Elliott, Theyre 20, 68
Léger, Fernand 16
Legg, Stuart 77
Leighton, Frederic, Lord 14
Lewis, Wyndham 16, 24, 26, 26-8, 38, 61, 77
Lewitt-Him 64, 68
Life 96
London Group 20, 21, 26, 28, 29
    Exhibition of Modern Art 22
London Mercury 36, 68
Lowry, L.S. 77
Lund Humphries 67, 67, 70

MacColl, D.S. 68
MacDowell, Edward 12
MacFisheries 64, 68
McGrath, Raymond 61, 62
Mackintosh, C.R. 29

McKnight, Joseph E. 10-11
Mairet, Mrs 37
Man Ray 60, 67-8, 78, 106
Manhattan Electrical Supply Co 31
Mansard Gallery 26
Marey, E.J. 18
Marinetti, Filippo, War, the World's Only Hygiene 16
Marion Dorn Ltd 72
Mason, James 89
Matisse, Henri 11, 12
Matter, Herbert 86
May, Pamela 90
Mayor, Freddie 61
Melville, Herman, Benito Cereno 53
Mendelsohn, Erich 68
Metropolis 48
Meynell, Esther 42
Meynell, Sir Francis 13, 18, 32, 35, 36, 42, 54
Meynell, Gerard Tuke 32-3, 36, 38
Mies van der Rohe, Ludwig 48, 64
Millais, Sir John 14
Miller, John Duncan 58
Milton, Ernest 42, 89
Ministry of Information 94, 95, 97
Modern Library 101
'Modern Tendencies in Art' (lecture series) 24
Moffat, Curtis 56, 56
Moholy-Nagy, László 86
    Malerei, Fotografie, Film 18
Mollo, Eugene 64
Monotype Corporation 37, 51
Monro, Harold 32, 38, 42
Montagu, Ivor 48
Moore, Henry 60, 61
Moore, Marianne 89-91, 94, 104-6, 109
Morgan, Peter 68
Morris, Cedric 64
Morris, Margaret 24
Morris, William 14
Mortimer, Raymond 44
Moscow Chamber Theatre 52
Mosley, Lady 61
Motley 89
Mucha, Alphonse 14
Munich 11-12
Munich realistic school 20
Munro, C.K. 42
Murray, W. Staite 36
Museum of Modern Art, New York 86, 94, 98, 110
Myers, L.H. 60

Nash, John 50, 61
Nash, Paul 21, 25, 50, 61, 64, 77
The Nation 44
New York 30-31, 96-101
New York Subways Advertising Co. Inc. 101
New York Times 31
Nicholson, Ben 61, 79
Nicholson, William 50
Night Mail 74
Nijinsky, Vaclav 11
Nolde, Emil 11
Nonesuch Press 39, 42, 50
Normandy 12

Observer 89
Olivier, Laurence 89
Olympia building 62, 64
Omega Workshops 24, 32
Orcades 73

Organic Design 98
Orient Line 72-4, *72, 73*
Orion 73
O'Rorke, Brian 73
Oscar, Henry 89

Pantheon Books 101
Paris 10-11, 12, 68, 78
Paris Exhibition (1925, 'Art Deco') 37
Paris Exhibition (1937) 66, 90
Parker, Robert Allerton 30
Pear's Soap 36
Pearse, Susan Beatrice (née Webster) 17
Pelican Press 33
Penguin Educational Books 68
Percy, Lund, Humphries 67
Perelman, S.J. 104
Petrie, Eric 13
Petrie, Maria Zimmern 12, 13, 21, 24
Pevsner, Nikolaus, *An Inquiry into Industrial Art in England* 74
Philippe, Isidore 12
Phoenix Theatre 53
Picasso, Pablo 11, 38–9, 43, 98
Pick, Frank 38, 44, 74, 75, 78, 95
   commissions 21, 28, 32-4, 35, 51, 61, 66
   early career 14-15
   early poster campaigns 21
   and Charles Holden 57
   and Alfred Waterhouse 14-15
Pirandello, Luigi, *Henry IV* 42
Poe, Edgar Allan 102-3, 104
Poetry Bookshop 38
Pomeroy Skin Food *33*
Pound, Ezra 16
Poynter, Sir Edward 14

Quennell, Peter 77
Quinn, John 26

Rand, Paul 86
Random House 68, 101
Read, Sir Herbert 67, 74
   Art Now 69
Red Cross 101
Rees, John M. 10
Reid, Nancy 109
Remington, Frederic 9
Rendall, Peter 108
Ricardo, Halsey 14
Rimbaud, Arthur, *Poésies* 92
Robertson, Bryan 77
Robson, Flora 89
Rotha, Paul 77
Royal Ballet Company, Covent Garden 104
Royal Flying Corps 20
Royal Pavilion, Brighton 64
Royal Society of Arts 84
   exhibition (1935) 74
Royal Wilton Carpet Company 56
Ruskin, John 14
Russell, Gordon 37
Russell, Phillips 38
Rutherston, Albert 25

Saint-John Perse 104, *107*
San Francisco, Elder Bookshop and Art Rooms 10, 11
Sassoon, Siegfried 18, 20
Scherrer, Hermann 12

Schiff, Sidney and Violet 77
Schleger, Hans (Zero) 68, 95
Schoenberg, Arnold, *Pierrot Lunaire* 11
Science Museum, London 34
Scotsman 68
Scott, Septimus 33
Senefelder Club 32, 110
Shaw, Bernard, *Back to Methuselah* 31
Shell company 28, 33, 67, 76, 95
Shell County Guides 77
Shell-Mex BP Ltd 74, 76
Sickert, Walter 77
Simon, A. P. 21
Simon, Oliver 50, 54
Simpson's 62
Sitwell, Osbert 54
Sitwell, Sacheverell, 'The Parrot' 32
Smith, Matthew 78-9, 84
Smith, S. Bernard 36
Soaring to Success! Daily Herald - the Early Bird 18
Society for Checking the Abuses of Public Advertising 14-15
Society of Industrial Artists 74
Somes, Michael 90
Soudeikine, Sergei 38
Spencer, Stanley 77
   Peace 50
Steinthal & Co. 21, 73
Stelletski, Dimitri 38
Stenberg, Vladimir A. 52
Stephens, R. A. 38
Stephenson, George 34
Stokes, Adrian 59
Storm over Asia 51
Strachey, Lytton, *Eminent Victorians* 32
Straight, Whitney 80
The Studio 12
Suiseki, Satô, *Flock of birds 18*
Sun Engraving 33
Sunday Times 89
Superrealism 70
Sutcliffe, Frank Meadow 14
Sutnar, Ladislav 86
Swan Court, Chelsea 60

Tallents, Stephen 64, 74
   documentary film 47-51
   early career 47
   Empire Experiment 49
   exhibition design 51
   at GPO 68
   poster advertising 49
   The Projection of England 51
Tallents, Tommy 73
Tatlock, R. R. 44
Taylor, Miss 11
Tchelitchew, Pavel 39
Tecton 61
Tester, Jefferson 101
Theatre Guild, New York 31, 44
The Times 37, 47, 51
Tooth, Arthur, & Sons Gallery 56-7, 78
Toscanini, Arturo 90
Toulouse-Lautrec, Henri de 12, 14, 28, 38, 84
Tschichold, Jan 68
Turner, Harold 90
typefaces
   Gill Sans 47, 51, 58, 64
   Johnston Sans 38
   Narcissus 68

Neuland 49, 68
Plantin 43
revival of old 38
Rockwell 73

Utamaro, *Yehon Shikino Hana* 28

Valéry, Paul 106
Valois, Ninette de 90
Van Gogh, Vincent 11, 12, 13, 15, 16, 22, 32
Vic-Wells Ballet 90
Victoria and Albert Museum, London 74
Vigil Silk 26, *26*
Vincent, Brooks, Day & Son 44, 110
Vlaminck, Maurice de 12
Vogue 44, 57
Vorticism 16, 17-18, *18*, 25-6, 28, 34, 37, 38
Voysey, C. F. A. 14

Waddington, C. H., *The Scientific Attitude* 101
Wadsworth, Edward 17, 30-1, 34, 64, 79
   Black Country, Blast Furnace 34
Walden, Neal 31
Waldman, Bernard 88, 93, 104, 106, 109
Waldman, Grace 106, 108
Walker, Alec 26, 64
Walton, William, *Portsmouth Point* 90
Washington, SS 95
Waterhouse, Alfred 14
Waugh, Evelyn 31–2, 61
Webster, S.B. 17
The Weekend Book 42
Wellington, Hubert and Irene 96
Wells, H. G., *Things to Come* 68
Westminster Press 32, 33
Wheeler, Monroe 98
Whistler, Rex, *A Plain Publicity Manager* 76
White House, North End 91-2, *91*, 96, 97, 108
Whitman, Walt, *Backward Glance O'er Travel'd Roads* 48
Wilde, Oscar 76
Williams-Ellis, Clough 44
Woolf, Leonard, *Quack, Quack! 69*
Woolf, Virginia 67

X Group 26-8, 48, 57

Young, Stark, *The Colonnade* 42

Zero *see* Schleger, Hans
Zimmern, William 21

AMAZING OCTOPUS

AMAZING OCTOPUS

Michael Stavarič ✦ Michèle Ganser

Translated from the German by Oliver Latsch

Pushkin Children's

✦

IN MEMORY OF MY DEAR FRIEND
MONIKA KÜLPER, THE BEST AND MOST
WELL-READ BOOKSELLER IN THE WORLD.

CHAPTER

01

OUR JOURNEY BEGINS

Infinite spaces. Infinite knowledge. Infinite ways to tell all about it.

Fortunately, I love to tell stories. Stories are among the best things in life because they can reveal everything about us humans (and our world). Stories don't have to be true, but this one is: everything in this book is the absolute truth. Maybe you're wondering how I came to know so much about octopuses. I'll tell you: from books, from magazines, from the internet, from television. Everything you really want to know in life is out there, waiting for you. You just have to start searching for it. Fortunately, you have already found this book (or did it find you?)—in any case, I think this is an excellent start.

The Far Stars

We look into the night sky and—with luck—see an infinite number of stars belonging to countless galaxies (I'll explain that word in a moment). Why only with luck? Well, you may have noticed this already: you can't see that many stars in the sky any more, not in cities anyway. Even in the countryside, they have become rarer because of so-called "light pollution". We humans produce too much artificial light on our planet, which is why we see fewer stars. It is only where you find natural darkness that you can marvel at what you should actually be able to see from anywhere: the vast, brilliant, majestic universe right above our heads.

As for this light pollution, fortunately it has been recognized as a significant problem. Various European agencies and authorities are now working to make the nights darker again. This will not only be good for nocturnal animals, but it will help us sleep much better too. It will also allow us to see the Milky Way in the sky—the beautiful galaxy to which Earth belongs (sixty per cent of Europeans can't even do that right now). Ah, yes, I did want to explain the word "galaxy". It is a collection of stars and planets that belong together in space. Our Milky Way is truly a beauty. You really must check it out for yourselves in the night sky. Oh, you want to know exactly where it is? It's actually always hovering above our heads, where you can see it on dark and cloudless nights. And if you want to make sure, just visit a planetarium.

Do you want to know something strange? I saw an interview with a marine biologist (Dr Edith Widder) who regularly dives into the deep sea in a small submarine (for research purposes, of course). She claimed that when you're in the deep sea, you feel like you're in outer space. Especially when you look out of the window and observe the countless luminous animals and tiny creatures, billions and billions of them—and every single little animal shines like a star in the sky. By the way, I'll tell you more about luminous animals in the ocean later—and what that's all about. But think about this fact for a moment: in the ocean's depths, you also feel like you're looking up at the stars. Isn't that great? As if our oceans were a whole universe. Personally, I like that thought…

When I look at the stars, I can't help but think about how the starlight travels for an eternity before I can even perceive it. Imagine light being something like a car. It moves from point A to point B. Point A is the star that emits it. Point B—that's us. So the light darts along, yet it takes countless years to reach us on Earth. It is even possible that the star from which the light emanated no longer exists. But its light is still travelling towards us through the vastness of the universe. Don't you find it exciting to think about such things? The universe really is unbelievably vast and full of riddles and mysteries—something that has fascinated me since I was a child.

Do you want to learn more about this? Well, I certainly do! The following is not uninteresting: if light is like a car, you can, of course, measure its speed. It travels at about 300,000 kilometres per second. (Since I'm sure some of you will want to be exact: 299,792,458 metres per second. Your physics teacher will write that on the blackboard one day.)

And just for comparison: your parents' car does maybe 150 kilometres per hour! So light really does travel at a massive speed, but in the infinite expanse of the universe, it's still a snail's pace.

Maybe some of you are thinking—all well and good, but I was expecting a book about octopuses… so where are the octopuses? Please bear with me a little longer. In fact, we are already in the middle of the story of the octopus, even if it doesn't look like it.

And the history of the universe is not only the history of the octopus. It is also our own history.

Where were we? Oh yes, light! Without light, of course, nothing on our planet would work. I'm talking about starlight, not some light bulb in your house. After all, our sun is nothing other than a star. And without the Sun, as you probably already know, life on Earth would be impossible. Without the Sun, there would be no plants. And without plants, there would be no oxygen (and for those who really need to know precisely: all of that is called photosynthesis). Without oxygen, there could be no humans or animals. And, of course, that includes animals that live in the ocean.

I can already hear the question—is sunlight also a bit like a car? Absolutely. Light always travels through space at the same speed (see above). With a distance between the Earth and the sun of around 150 million kilometres, it takes eight minutes and nineteen seconds for sunlight to reach us. So if the Sun were to suddenly disappear (maybe a wizard could conjure it away), we would still have a perfectly normal day ahead of us for more than eight minutes.

Oh, I could tell you all kinds of stories about the Sun, but the octopuses are growing impatient, so just one for now: one day, the Sun will be so big that we'll be able to touch it with our hands from the Earth; scientists call this stage of its existence a "red giant". And at some point, the Sun will suddenly shrink again, then it will only be as big as the Earth and it will be called a "white dwarf". As a child, such names inspired me to make up all kinds of stories about "red giants" and "white dwarfs". Do you like the sound of that too? In that case, you should get to it!

FOR BRIGHT MINDS
THE STRANGEST OBJECTS IN SPACE

1. CLOWN FACE

A nebula is a luminous cloud of dust and gas in space—and there is one that looks like a clown's face. It has the rather dull scientific name NGC 2392. Because there are so many objects in space, they simply number them sequentially (in order). It reminds me a bit of the National Insurance numbers they have in the UK or the Social Security Number in the US. Ask your parents for theirs. I wonder if they know it by heart.

2. RASPBERRY RUM

In the centre of our Milky Way, there is a massive cloud of alcohol. Its name sounds a bit more interesting: Sagittarius B2. It is 150 light-years wide and millions of times heavier than our sun. The really curious thing is that the whole cloud smells of raspberries and rum. Well, more like rum, say the scientists. And that's a good thing because a bit of rum is also needed for making an excellent marbled bundt cake—my favourite.

3. SAURON'S ALL-SEEING EYE

Maybe some of you have seen the famous *The Lord of the Rings* movies, although I preferred the books. The evil wizard, Sauron, is almost always invisible. All we can see of him is a big fiery eye in the sky. And that very thing actually exists in space. It's called the Helix Nebula. In the centre of this nebula is a dead star embedded in a dust cloud that looks like an eye. Some also call this phenomenon the "Eye of God", and at only 650 light-years away, it is pretty close to Earth.

4. DIAMOND LAKES OR JUST LAVA, AFTER ALL?

There is a mysterious planet called 55 Cancri e, which is about twice as big as Earth. It orbits a kind of sun (like Earth), although it is not known for sure whether this sun is like ours. If it is, 55 Cancri e's surface must be very hot—1,790 degrees Celsius. And some people think the whole surface might be made of diamonds or littered with huge lava lakes. We have no idea (yet) whether either of these things is true: imagine a planet with diamonds everywhere—like rocks here on Earth. That would be quite a sight, wouldn't it?

5. SOMBRERO GALAXY

This galaxy is shaped like a disc with a bulge in the middle and got its name because it reminded astronomers of the famous Mexican sombrero hat! It's one of the brightest galaxies in the sky at night, but you'll still need a good pair of binoculars or a telescope to see it. By the way, *sombra* means "shadow" in Spanish, which makes sense for a hat.

6. RED RECTANGLE NEBULA

Angular objects are really rare in space, but the Red Rectangle Nebula is an exception. When first seen from earth, it looked rectangular, but astronomers have since taken a closer look, using a telescope in space, and it's actually shaped like a big X. We're not sure why, but it must have something to do with the dying star at its centre.

7. DEATH STAR AND PAC-MAN

Well, I was never a big fan of *Star Wars*, but to each their own. OK, fine, I admit there are some cool scenes and objects in it, like the Death Star. There is actually a real-life equivalent of the Death Star in space, if you look at everything through *Star Wars* goggles: one of Saturn's moons, Mimas. But its outer appearance isn't the only interesting thing about it. A thermal image from the Cassini space probe makes the moon look like Pac-Man. Do you know Pac-Man? Your parents certainly do!

8. SKULL KINDERGARTEN

Have you ever wanted to be a pirate? I mean one of the friendly pirates who sail the seas, live in freedom and have all kinds of adventures. Well, then you will be interested in the so-called Skull and Crossbones Nebula, which actually looks like the skull and crossbones on a pirate flag. It is otherwise known as NGC 2467 and is a birthplace and nursery for numerous young stars.

Who is this Michael, anyway?

Of course, I'll also tell you something about myself. After all, you should know who is writing this book—and who you are actually talking to here. On a typical day as a child, I wanted to do the following jobs when I grew up:

1. To be an astronaut so I could flick the light switch, which I assumed was on the back of the Sun, on and off by myself—whenever I wanted to.

2. Also, to be an astronaut so I could build a fishpond on the Moon's surface; as a child, I never thought about the problem of the vacuum (= no oxygen).

3. More precisely: to be a cosmonaut (that's what Russian astronauts call themselves). Because I had heard the Russian (at that time, still Soviet) national anthem on the radio for the first time and thought that the Russians were better singers.

4. Suddenly: to be a pilot because the astronaut/cosmonaut thing seemed somehow unrealistic to me after all.

5. Next: to be a marine biologist because ocean animals fascinated me (especially octopuses!)—and as a diver, one could also experience the weightlessness of space.

6. To be a cryptozoologist (those are people who search for unknown animals that no one has ever seen) who journeys deep into the sea (preferably in a small submarine) to discover new animal species and be the first human to give them a name. For example, "vampire squid"—unfortunately, someone discovered and named that one before me. Darn it!

7. Very briefly, even: to be a dentist, so I could look after my own teeth and avoid any visits to the dentist in the future. Does that sound familiar to you? And, shhh, once even: to be the best tennis player in the world, because I suddenly spent all my free time on the tennis court and some people there thought that I might even end up achieving something.

8. To be a writer, when I was given my first typewriter and realized that everyone liked my stories. I even wrote something about the waterways of the local region of Weinviertel, all the ponds and rivers I knew. The ocean was too far away—and seemed unreachable, like outer space!

You know what? All of you, take a piece of paper and write down what you want to be when you grow up. Or you can write it down right here in this book—we'll leave a few lines free for that. I'll wait for you to do that—and in the meantime, I'll think about how to continue.

Are you ready? Please read it out loud to me. I want to hear it too!

1. *Astronaut*

2. *Astronaut*

3. *Cosmonaut*

4. *Pilot*

5. *Marine Biologist*

6. *Cryptozoologist*

7. *Dentist*

8. *Writer*

1. ∼∼∼∼∼∼∼∼∼∼∼∼∼∼∼∼∼∼∼∼∼∼∼∼∼∼∼∼∼∼∼∼∼∼∼∼∼

2. ∼∼∼∼∼∼∼∼∼∼∼∼∼∼∼∼∼∼∼∼∼∼∼∼∼∼∼∼∼∼∼∼∼∼∼∼∼

3. ∼∼∼∼∼∼∼∼∼∼∼∼∼∼∼∼∼∼∼∼∼∼∼∼∼∼∼∼∼∼∼∼∼∼∼∼∼

4. ∼∼∼∼∼∼∼∼∼∼∼∼∼∼∼∼∼∼∼∼∼∼∼∼∼∼∼∼∼∼∼∼∼∼∼∼∼

5. ∼∼∼∼∼∼∼∼∼∼∼∼∼∼∼∼∼∼∼∼∼∼∼∼∼∼∼∼∼∼∼∼∼∼∼∼∼

6. ∼∼∼∼∼∼∼∼∼∼∼∼∼∼∼∼∼∼∼∼∼∼∼∼∼∼∼∼∼∼∼∼∼∼∼∼∼

7. ∼∼∼∼∼∼∼∼∼∼∼∼∼∼∼∼∼∼∼∼∼∼∼∼∼∼∼∼∼∼∼∼∼∼∼∼∼

8. ∼∼∼∼∼∼∼∼∼∼∼∼∼∼∼∼∼∼∼∼∼∼∼∼∼∼∼∼∼∼∼∼∼∼∼∼∼

Exciting, absolutely thrilling—I'm really keeping my fingers crossed that one of these career dreams will come true. And always remember, no matter what you might be told later: you can be anything you want to be! But you have to really, really want it with all your heart!

Bring on the colouring pencils!
This picture needs a lot of colour.

CHAPTER

02

THE DEPTHS OF THE OCEANS

How Did Life on Earth Begin?

What is the most sensible way to continue before we finally start talking (almost) only about octopuses? I think we should briefly deal with the question of how life came to Earth. This is, of course, quite a difficult question to which there is (so far) no definitive answer. Many scientists claim that life began in the ocean about 3.5 billion years ago. According to them, life came from the sea. At first, it was in the water—and then at some point, on land.

We can picture it like this: back then, there were an incredible number of living creatures in the water, but one fine day it became too much for some of them. Maybe it was too noisy, too stressful, too crowded—what do I know? So these creatures evolved. The fins became feet, and the gills became lungs. That's how scientists explain it. And for those who want to know more: it's called "evolution" and "evolutionary biology" (you can read about that later in other books, which will tell you a lot about the development of species).

By the way, a good seventy per cent of the Earth consists of water and only thirty per cent is land. So if you ask me, it would be more logical to live in the water. After all, they don't call Earth the "Blue Planet" for nothing. I also find it interesting that the human body consists mainly of water: in babies, the water content is up to eighty-five per cent and in adults, it is around seventy per cent. In old people, it's about fifty per cent.

Isn't it strange that the Earth consists of seventy per cent water—and our bodies too? As a child, I also found it extremely exciting that our tears contain salt, just like the ocean. Of course, this is not entirely true because the ocean has about three times as much salt as our tears, but never mind!

FOR BRIGHT MINDS

At the beginning of the seventh week of gestation, the human embryo is four weeks old and has the curved shape of a "C". The head sits at one end of the arch, the tail at the other. Everyone agrees that it looks more like a shrimp than a human being. It is therefore not surprising that some scientists even think that we once had gills. And supposedly this can still be seen around the ears in some people.

How Did Life Get into the Water?

One thing is indisputable: without water, there's no life!

Which brings us back to the question posed earlier: how did life get into the water? Quite a few scientists think it came from the cosmos. You must know that our Earth did not always look like it does today. Before this "real" Earth, there was just a cloud of gas and dust in space, where a huge number of celestial bodies of various sizes were whirring around. All kinds of lumps of rock and ice collided there and gradually formed a "first" Earth. But more objects (comets—also made of ice!) kept hitting it. There were seas of glowing lava; steam and smoke everywhere. Our world was a red-hot, uninhabitable ball.

I'd rather cut to the chase. Anything more would only delay us further: at some point, the Earth cooled down, the steam became water and everything took its course!

Incidentally, some comets that have collided with the Earth are said to have contained life, which could have found its way into the water and continued to develop there. Recently I read something about living plankton (as found in the ocean) being discovered on the outer hull of the International Space Station. Curious, isn't it?

FOR BRIGHT MINDS

Oh yes, something else about the word "plankton" (Greek πλαγκτόν, meaning "the wandering, the drifting"): this is the term used to describe all the organisms that live in open water, (floating, with little or no movement of their own) drifting along, their movement dictated by the current. Without plankton, there would be no life in the sea, no whales, no octopuses, no sharks and so on; it ultimately forms the lowest tier of the food chain.

This means that these and other building blocks of life could—as many scientists believe—have originated in the infinite expanse of the universe and reached our oceans with the help of comets (or large shooting stars). All life may therefore be extra-terrestrial—including us!

I think a creature like the octopus makes this seem entirely plausible. And, believe me, there are many other animals living in the depths of the oceans that we might consider highly peculiar. Would you have guessed that only about five per cent of our oceans are known and have been explored? That's practically nothing! So it's not surprising that people say humanity knows more about the Moon or Mars than it does about its own oceans. It is also believed that at least one million undiscovered species are still waiting to be identified in the world's seas.

Of course, I will happily give you my personal list of the strangest animals in the ocean, which, at least in my opinion, could well be from another planet. But you must promise me that you will add to and extend the list… there are indeed many more exciting creatures in the water.

1. The octopuses, squids and common cuttlefish (we will really deal with these in detail now!).

2. The jellyfish, sometimes called "medusa". There is actually a type of jellyfish living in the ocean that never dies! It is called, somewhat unsurprisingly, the immortal jellyfish (its scientific name is *Turritopsis dohrnii*). But I'd need to write another book to tell you all about it.

3. The cigar shark, which does actually look a bit like a thick, brownish cigar. It is not very big and it causes circular wounds when it bites. That's why it's called a cookie-cutter shark. You could use this shark in the kitchen at Christmas!

4. The goblin shark looks like it has an oversized nose. I probably found it exciting as a child because my mum often insisted that I was a goblin. My nose is average-sized though, honest!

5. The skeleton shrimp has always struck me as an underwater praying mantis. Praying mantises are insects that live on land, by the way. And they look pretty exciting, too—be sure to check them out!

6. The oarfish, which supposedly grows up to seventeen metres long and, I swear, it's a real underwater dragon snake.

7. The leafy sea dragon, which also looks like a dragon, or should we say, like a cross between a dragon and a seahorse.

8. The deep-sea anglerfish, which is truly incredible; the female grows a wand out of her head with a glowing orb at the end of it. This attracts prey in the deep sea, which is devoid of light. In addition, the males, which are much smaller, grow attached to the females because this is advantageous for both. So they look like one fish, even though they are two! Isn't that incredible?

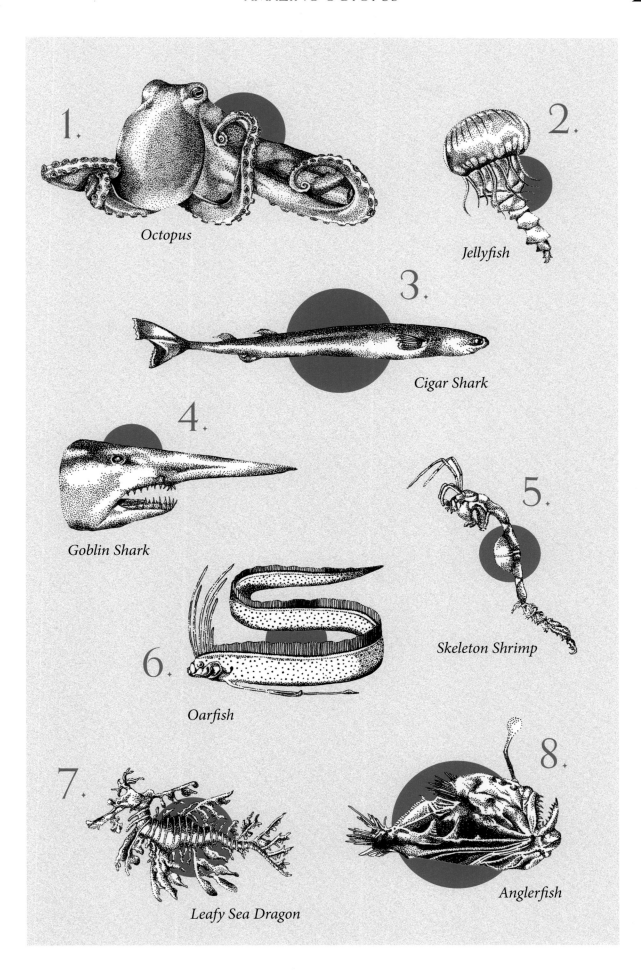

1. *Octopus*

2. *Jellyfish*

3. *Cigar Shark*

4. *Goblin Shark*

5. *Skeleton Shrimp*

6. *Oarfish*

7. *Leafy Sea Dragon*

8. *Anglerfish*

So let's summarize briefly: the depths of the oceans are just as unknown to us as the depths of the universe. And when I think about it, space is in some way just a vast ocean in which comets, planets, stars, galaxies and whatnot float in infinite space. And we're all floating too, rotating with our Earth around the Sun, which in turn dances around the centre of our galaxy, the Milky Way. So perhaps everything is just one huge cosmic merry-go-round!

We humans like to wonder whether there's life elsewhere in space, but we don't even know all the creatures on our own planet. So let's dive into the realm of the octopus together—incredible discoveries await us there.

EIGHT INK-REDIBLE JOKES
TO TELL YOUR FRIENDS

~~~~~~~~

1. Why did the octopus cross the ocean? To get to the other tide!

2. Where do octopuses prefer to work? At the inksurance company!

3. Why don't octopuses speak? Because they'd get a mouth full of water!

4. What do you get when you cross an octopus with a sheep? A blue jumper with eight sleeves!

5. How do little sea creatures travel to school? They take the octobus!

6. Why did the octopus blush? Because he saw the bottom of the ocean!

7. What sport do octopus wizards like to play? Squidditch!

8. How do you make an octopus laugh? Ten tickles!

CHAPTER
03

THE REALM OF THE OCTOPUS

The Eight-Footer

An octopus feels soft, moist, slippery and somehow stretchy if you touch it. In the mouth, octopus feels a bit like plasticine, a bit like a wet bathroom sponge, a bit like slimy fish, and smooth like chewing gum, but everyone has to try it out for themselves and find their own words.

It's an indisputable fact: these animals have long been eaten as seafood, especially in Asia and around the Mediterranean, and now people eat them in other places too. I can, for example, easily buy octopus to eat at Vienna's Naschmarkt. People eat animals, of course, but animals also eat animals. It is up to each person to make up their own mind. Octopuses are considered a delicacy, but they aren't impressed by this. In fact, I'd go as far as to say that they dislike it.

So let's look at it from a purely scientific point of view: octopuses are so-called "molluscs" and belong to the Cephalopoda genus. This difficult word, even for adults, comes from the ancient Greek *kephalē* (head) and *pod* (foot). Head-footer, then. That's kind of obvious because what do octopuses look like? A big head and a lot of feet! We humans tend to judge (and name) everything by its appearance. By the way, most scientific animal names come from ancient Greek and Latin. Do you want me to give you another example?

I'd love to! How about this one: "crocodile". The name "armoured lizard" is borrowed from the Latin *crocodilus*. Still, the word actually derives from the ancient Greek *krokódīlos* (κροκόδειλος), meaning "lizard". So the word lizard existed first and was then transferred to the crocodiles of the Nile, etc. The composition of the word in Greek is exciting: *krókē* (κρόκη) = "gravel" and *drīlos* (δρῖλος) = "worm". So the word crocodile means "gravel worm", which brings us back to human lack of imagination: people give simple names to animals and objects unknown to them. Head-footers, gravel worms—and let's not even get started on "balls for feet".

A long time ago people used to tell stories of a monstrous octopus that lived in the seas off the coast of Norway: the kraken. Its name comes from Danish-Norwegian and it means an "uprooted tree", again an allusion to the appearance of the animals. Lightning in the sky, which also branches out like tree roots, would certainly also have made a good symbolic image. A writer once wrote in a book that tree roots look like slowed-down lightning, but he didn't mention anything about octopuses.

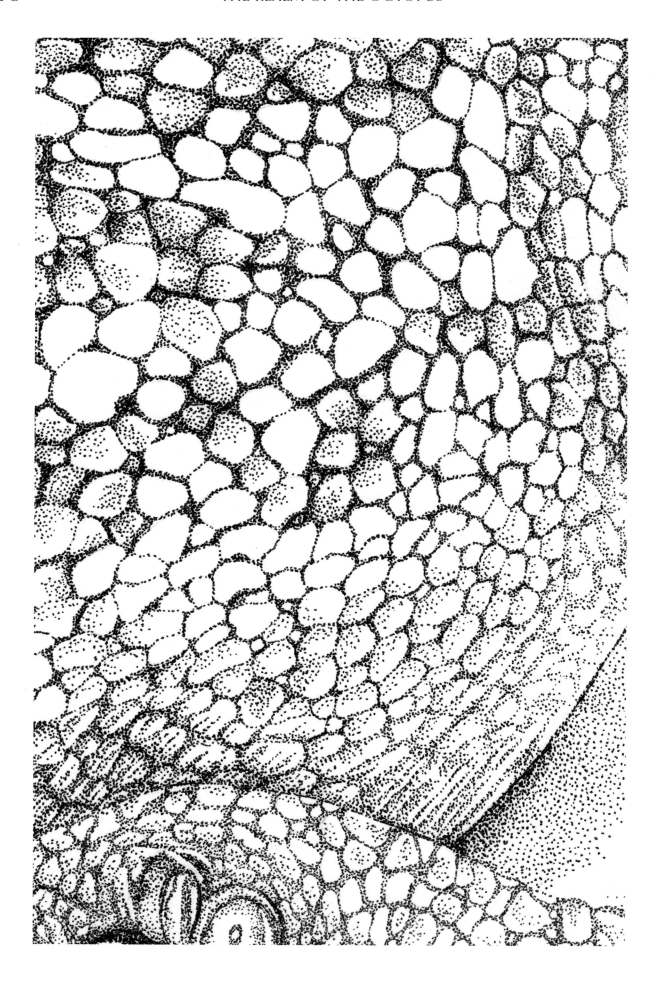

The name "octopus" translates (you guessed it, from the Greek!) as: "the eight-footed one". And that makes absolute sense because octopuses have eight "tentacles", but you could also think of them as limbs.

By the way, the number eight will constantly accompany us in this book. It is definitely the favourite number of all octopuses, which can easily count that far with their eight limbs. Did you notice, for example, that I gave you eight answers about what I wanted to be when I was a child? And that I chose eight of my favourite animals in the ocean? Well! Better concentr-*eight* harder in future! Oh, and just so you know, when the number eight topples over and lies horizontally, it becomes the mathematical symbol of infinity: ∞. This brings us back to the infinite cosmos!

FOR BRIGHT MINDS

And for the sake of completeness—again, only for those who are interested—the word "tentacle" comes from the Latin *tentare*, meaning "to feel" and "to touch". "Feeling and touching" arms are, after all, the main ingredients of an octopus. At this point, it should be revealed: octopuses do indeed have a favourite arm (or arms) that they particularly like to use. In addition, researcher Ruth Byrne at the University of Vienna has discovered that octopuses can theoretically use 448 possible combinations of their tentacles. But they only use forty-nine of these one-, two-, or three-arm combinations when touching objects. At least one thing seems certain: the animal's favourite arms are mostly found at the front, while the rear arms are used more for locomotion.

Are you left- or right-handed? That distinction also exists in the rest of the animal kingdom, among chimpanzees, for example. They are predominantly left-handed. On the other hand, walruses are usually right-handed and therefore like to use their right front flipper for everything. But that's just a quick aside.

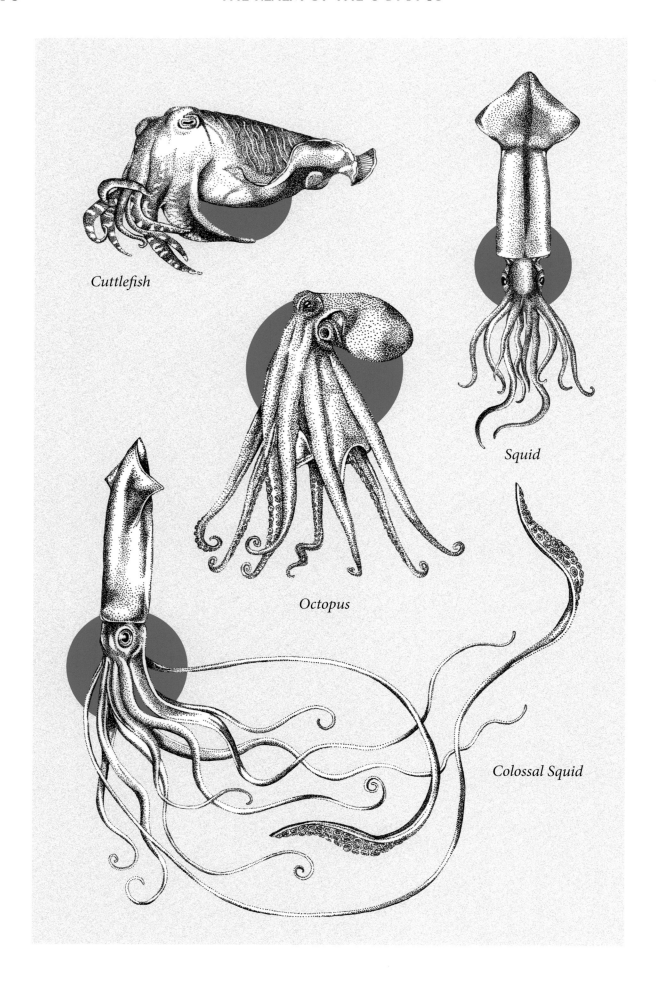

Cuttlefish

Squid

Octopus

Colossal Squid

Octopus, Squid or Cuttlefish?

Octopuses come in a wide variety of shapes and sizes. Some are a few centimetres long, others a good seven or more metres. The giant Pacific octopus is considered the most mighty octopus of them all. *The Guinness Book of World Records* in 2019 lists the largest specimen as weighing 136 kilograms and having an arm span of 9.8 metres.

Moreover, we should never confuse octopuses with (giant) squid, which are also cephalopods and usually have ten arms, two of them very long. They also have something like a spine—a stiff, backbone-like structure. They grow to more than ten metres long and are among the preferred prey of sperm whales. Have you ever heard of *Moby Dick*? Be sure to ask your parents about it!

If you see a picture of a whale fighting an "octopus", it is always a squid. The largest species have the scientific names "colossal squid" (*Mesonychoteuthis hamiltoni*) and "giant squid" (*Architeuthis dux*).

For the sake of completeness—and after this, I swear, we'll be through with the distinctions—we must also mention the cuttlefish, or the common squid (*Sepia officinalis*). They have a kind of "fin fringe" that runs all around their body and ten tentacles near their mouth. On page 40, if you look closely, you will see that our cuttlefish only has eight arms. This is because it usually hides two of its arms. These are only visible when it is hunting. So our cuttlefish is resting right now.

Spooky Tales About Octopuses

Many people only know cephalopods from scary stories that used to circulate all around the world, of tentacled beasts (like the kraken) clinging to ships and dragging them down into the depths of the ocean. These descriptions from Scandinavian, Greek and other sagas have often inspired books and films. For example, Homer's adventurous hero, Odysseus, has to watch six of his bravest friends being eaten by the twelve-footed and six-headed monster, Scylla (oh, always these literary exaggerations!). And the novel *Beast* by a certain Peter Benchley, a sequel to his horror classic, *Jaws*, stars a giant squid.

Jules Verne's *20,000 Leagues Under the Sea* is also recommended reading:

> "And wasn't its head crowned with eight tentacles that move on the water like a nest of snakes?" the servant Conseil asks Professor Aronnax on board the *Nautilus* in Verne's story.
> "Exactly."
> "And weren't its eyes rather large on top of its head?"

"Yes, Conseil."

"And did not its mouth resemble a parrot's beak, but a very large one?"

"Indeed, Conseil."

"*Eh bien!* If sir would care to look out of the window: if this is not Captain Bouguer's squid, it is at least one of its brothers."

Captain Nemo and his crew have the greatest difficulty saving themselves from this mollusc with a bird's beak. Hacking at the tentacles with axes seems to be their last resort…

In Victor Hugo's novel *The Toilers of the Sea*, a hero named Gilliat has to take on a terrible octopus. There it says: "Something flabby that has a will, what could be more horrible! Slime imbued with hatred." In the well-known pirate franchise *Pirates of the Caribbean*, a gigantic kraken appears, grabs an entire ship and one of the heroes falls into the water. At which point, another shouts, "Hey, comrade! Every man for himself!" And at that exact moment, one of the beast's extended arms shoots out of the water and kills him. In the Middle Ages, even bishops (Olaus Magnus from Uppsala in 1555 and Erik Pontoppidan at the beginning of the 18th century) reported swimming monsters, deceptive octopuses, as big "as an island lapped by floating seaweed, the back alone 1.5 English nautical miles long with many horns like the masts of medium-sized ships."

In some American lakes (Lake Thunderbird, Lake Tenkiller, and Lake Oologah in Oklahoma), there are rumours of a dangerous freshwater octopus, which is blamed for the drowning deaths of several people. Time and again, such news is reported in the American media, but no proof exists. It is probably a kind of Loch Ness Monster—you've heard of that one, right?

It's a simple fact: in movies, books and the like, octopuses and their cousins have acquired a nasty reputation. Irrational fears are fanned again and again. In reality, however, octopuses are among the most intelligent creatures on this planet—along with dolphins, monkeys, ravens, elephants and dogs. We should not fear them but show them respect and try to put ourselves in their place. We can try to understand how they perceive their environment and what they are capable of. In doing so, we would be expanding our horizons, which are often too narrow. We simply have to learn to look beyond our own noses.

I would like to recommend my eight personal favourite cephalopod species, two of which I have already mentioned:

1. The giant Pacific octopus (*Enteroctopus dofleini*) is considered to be particularly intelligent. As I said, it is also the largest of all known octopuses. In aquariums, it can quickly solve complex tasks, such as opening jars to get to the prey hidden inside. It can also recognize and distinguish between individual humans and is very sensitive to water pollution.

2. The vampire squid (*Vampyroteuthis infernalis*) owes its name to the fact that it can stretch out a webbing of skin between its arms (a bit like a bat). It grows to about thirty centimetres and can produce light with the help of luminescent organs (in science, this is called bioluminescence). It lives in the deep sea and has the largest eyes in the animal kingdom in proportion to its size.

3. The giant Antarctic octopus (*Megaleledone setebos*) grows to a solid ninety centimetres. The heaviest specimen to date weighed twenty-seven kilograms. It kills its prey with the help of a poison that is effective even at sub-zero temperatures. It is thought that many other octopus species have evolved from this animal (and are therefore also slightly poisonous). At least, this is what some research results suggest.

4. The mimic octopus (*Thaumoctopus mimicus*) is a true master of camouflage. It is the only living creature that can deceptively imitate up to fifteen other animal species, such as sea snakes, sea snails, mussels, rays, jellyfish, crabs, sea anemones, flounders and so on. The extraordinary thing about this animal is that it imitates not only the appearance but also the behaviour of those animals.

5. The wunderpus octopus (*Wunderpus photogenicus*) lives in the shallower seas off Indonesia and also likes to imitate other animals, preferably poisonous ones. Above all, it mimics the firefish almost perfectly.

6. The greater blue-ringed octopus (*Hapalochlaena lunulata*) grows to only fifty-five millimetres in diameter (without tentacles) and is one of the most poisonous animals in the world. With its bright blue rings, it is easy to recognize. It lives, among other places, off the coast of northern Australia. Its bite, which can be fatal for humans, releases the poison tetrodotoxin, which is also present in puffer fish.

7. The violet blanket octopus (*Tremoctopus violaceus*) is a relatively widespread octopus species with two unique features: the female is two metres long and weighs ten kilograms, while the male is just three centimetres long and weighs a quarter of a gram—making it barely the size of the female octopus's pupil. The males and young females like to

use torn-off, poisonous tentacles of the Portuguese man o' war (a kind of jellyfish to whose poison they are immune) for their defence.

8. The Casper octopus: this is probably the most recently discovered species of octopus and very little is known about it. It lives at depths of more than 4,000 metres off Hawaii. The animal lacks the skin texture responsible for the typical colour change of octopuses (we will discuss this in more detail later). Casper is only about ten centimetres long—and his appearance is indeed reminiscent of the well-known ghost from the animated film.

1. Giant Pacific Octopus

2. Vampire Squid

3. Giant Antarctic Octopus

4. Mimic Octopus

5. Wunderpus Octopus

6. Greater Blue-ringed Octopus

7. Violet Blanket Octopus

8. Casper Octopus

Well, those are "my" octopuses, but you will discover many more in the course of your life. After all, there are over 1,000 known species of cephalopods and who knows how many more are yet to be discovered! So let's follow these fascinating creatures on their journey through the seas. By the way, in ancient Greece the octopus was also a symbol for love! Oh, and not so long ago, in 2021, there was even an Oscar awarded to a film that documents the friendship between a diver and an octopus. It is called *My Octopus Teacher*. You absolutely have to see it!

EIGHT OTHER
Octythings

~~~~~~~~~~

1. Octagon—I like to go to the Oktogon in Vienna. But there's never an octopus waiting for me there, because the Oktogon is a restaurant where you can eat heavenly food—which is probably why it's on Himmelsstraße (Heaven Road). Oh, and an octagon is of course a shape with eight sides.

2. Octave—I have to confess: I can't play an instrument. And my singing is awful—I can't hit a single note! You can probably do much better. Octaves are mainly used by musicians and are a sequence of eight notes. Now hum eight notes in a row. *Voilà!*

3. Octogenarian—do you ever think about your age? As a child, I couldn't care less. It's different now. But I won't tell you my age—so there! I'm definitely not yet an octogenarian, which means someone between 80 and 89 years old. Do you know how old an octopus can get yet?

4. Octuplet—the German word for octuplet is funny: *achtling*. It's a diminutive form of the word *acht* which means "eight". Octuplets are kind of like twins, except there are eight of them!

5. *Octosyllabic*—in German, even children have no problem creating octosyllabic words. Want an example? How about: *kra-ken-fütt-er-ungs-ma-schi-ne* (octopus feeding machine). In other languages, like English, such long words are harder to make. My English publisher told me his favourite eight-syllable word: paleoarcheology. Even I know what that is. Do you?

6. *Octothorpe*—you've probably never heard the word, but you have definitely seen the symbol: #. It's on every computer and phone. Now search #octopus on Instagram, and you'll get a lot of information and pictures. We don't know for sure where the word comes from, but it's probably made up of "octo" (eight) and "thorpe" (field, or small village). Count all the ends of the symbol's lines. Yes, eight! And the centre could be a village or a field. So there. As good a theory as any!

7. *Octillion*—an octillion is definitely the octopus's favourite number. And it's huge: a 1 followed by 48 zeros! As for where the word comes from, well: we've all figured out that "octi" has something to do with eight. The "llion" comes from "million", as in six zeros. And $6 \times 8 = 48$, so forty-eight zeros. Which looks like this: 1,000,000,000,000,000,000,000,000,000,000,000,000,000,000,000,000.

8. *Octal*—I'm afraid it's time for another confession: I've always been bad at maths. And you can't get more maths than "octal" which refers to the mathematical octal system. It uses eight digits to represent any number: 0, 1, 2, 3, 4, 5, 6 and 7. The textbook says: "When counting in the octal system, note that 7 is not followed by 8, but must be increased one place to the left. In the octal system: $7 + 1 = 10$." Huh? I can't help you here. Ask your maths teacher. The internet tells me this system is used in air traffic control. 7+1=10? I'm never getting on a plane ever again.

CHAPTER

04

HUMANS AND OCTOPUSES

Would you have guessed that humans and octopuses have common ancestors? I'm not kidding! If we look way back down the timeline of the evolution of life on Earth, we can indeed find a common ancestor. Our planet is around 4.5 billion years old and the first life supposedly appeared about 3.8 billion years ago. Of course, we already talked about the fact that it probably happened in the ocean.

The Origin of Species

The common ancestor is thought to have been a worm-like creature (I also found it described as a "worm-like gloop") that lived in the ocean 600–700 million years ago. The history of biodiversity (it's easiest to think of it as a giant tree that keeps branching out) is linked to an era called the Cambrian, a time about 500 million years ago. After that, there were suddenly a lot of animals. Before that, there were actually very few.

Now we could debate what suddenly led to so many new species on Earth. Scientists still argue about this today. The so-called "Cambrian explosion" of life remains a mystery. Some say that it took until the Cambrian period for there to be enough oxygen in the sea for more complex forms of life to develop. Others think that a "biological arms race" took place. More complex animals with shells and skeletons would have been at a clear advantage from then on. Still others say that the Earth (including the oceans) was covered by a thick layer of ice at that time, so life evolved under the ice… never mind! We will never know exactly what happened for sure, but life on Earth flourished at that time.

One branch of this evolutionary development led to vertebrates (you know, spine and all), which includes us—another to invertebrates, such as oysters, snails, spiders, butterflies and so on. Almost all of these invertebrates are small and not exactly considered intelligent, cephalopods being the only exception. In his book *Other Minds*, philosopher and passionate diver Peter Godfrey-Smith concludes: "Cephalopods—octopods, squid and nautiluses—are an island of cognitive complexity amid an ocean of invertebrates." That's a nice but complicated way of putting it, so let's just remember: octopuses, squid and cuttlefish are by far the most intelligent invertebrate creatures on Earth. Unlike the octopus, however, the others do have something like a "back bone". Well, it's more like a "back reinforcement", the so-called "cuttlebone" (*Os sepium*). I must confess that I had almost forgotten the word. However, I remember that cuttlebones used to be (and probably still are) available in pet shops. My parakeets liked to chew on one. Supposedly it helped supply them with minerals. I think they were just sharpening their beaks and having fun.

In any case, the octopus does without this additional protection—and does quite well without it. Scientists agree that heavily armoured animals will never prevail against agile, fast creatures in the long run. So let's always stay fast and agile rather than squeeze ourselves into thick armour that makes us feel safe but also makes us incredibly slow. Remember the time of the knights? They also favoured heavy armour until they realized that they always got the short end of the stick against barely armoured, fast and agile opponents. By the way, you can build pretty amazing and light armour out of paper (Chinese soldiers have demonstrated this), which not even arrows can penetrate.

FOR BRIGHT MINDS

Chinese paper armour (*zhijah* or *zhikai*) is a traditional type of armour that was used in China until the 19th century. It consists of paper, made in this case from the fibres of the mulberry tree. First, the paper was folded several times, pressed and bonded together with the help of a glue. Then, the paper sheets were formed into individual scales and connected to each other with leather strips. These individual scales were used to make armour that protected the shoulders, chest, stomach, genitals, back and thighs.

When you think about it like this, the octopus is quite right to not carry the "back bone" that some other cephalopods have. And, intelligent as it is, it has developed many other protective and defensive mechanisms that make armour unnecessary.

The Body of the Octopus

So let's talk about the body of the octopus, which, after all, is responsible for it doing so well in the ocean.

Octopuses, as we know by now, are cephalopods—their legs, or rather their tentacles, are directly connected to their heads. This may give them a somewhat sack-like appearance to our eyes. Basically, they only consist of a huge head, two big eyes and eight arms, which are equipped with suckers on the underside. So it is not surprising that octopuses are also often called "aliens". Moreover, they have no skeleton or armour but only a soft mantle covering their internal organs. As an aside, nobody can really agree what the plural of "octopus" should be. Some say "octopi" (giving it a Latin plural ending) others prefer "octopodes" (Greek) but I'm going to stick with my good old English "octopuses" in this book.

Octopuses explore the world with their eight arms, and we do likewise, of course, with our two. We want and need to touch everything, especially new things we don't know and which fascinate us for that very reason. Evolutionary biology suggests that octopuses' tentacles evolved from a single muscular foot, which we can still find in other molluscs. Mussels, in particular, use this foot to move around. I recently read a purely fictional book set in night-time Prague (the capital of the Czech Republic), where a man feels he is being pursued by a colossal mussel. I don't want to deprive you of the part where this muscular foot takes centre stage. The author, Michal Ajvaz, writes:

> "On the pavement lay a mussel about two and a half metres long… it looked as if it were watching me hostilely through the narrow gap. Then it slowly threw its gelatinous foot over the edge of the lower shell, touched the pavement, shifted a little towards me, pulled the foot back in and waited."

Of course, we don't have to wait, we can turn our attention back to the octopus. It has over 250 suckers arranged in two rows on each of its eight arms. So it has a total of—hold on, I need to get the calculator—250×8. I'm sure some of you can work that out in your head, but I'd better play it safe: 2,000. So, an octopus has 2,000 suckers in total, which it can use independently of each other. Now imagine if we humans had 2,000 fingers, that's one thousand per hand. That would probably be pretty stressful for our brains.

Octopuses have found a fascinating solution to this, which shows how unlike us they are. Whereas in humans and other vertebrates, everything is controlled by the head, where the brain is located, octopuses have a different approach. Their whole body is somehow the brain, which branches out into the tentacles. You can never really tell where the brain stops. Certain sensory "information" (for example, if the octopus touches something, let's say our foot in the water) does not have to be passed on exclusively to the head, which then decides how to react. No, in the octopus, each sucker can handle this information—and communicate it to all the other suckers. This may sound a bit complicated, but imagine it like this: all arms of the octopus know at all times where the other tentacles and suckers are and what tasks they are currently performing, even without its "central brain" in the head.

This protects the octopus's central brain from an uncontrolled flood of information from each sucker. I imagine it as if every single one of my 2,000 fingers wants to talk to me personally. Maybe even via mobile phone. Imagine 2,000 phone calls all at once in your head, aargh! That would be a real pain in the neck!

What I find particularly remarkable about the octopus's body is its mobility. Vertebrates can only perform specific movements because they are limited by the shape of their joints. As a result, we humans simply cannot move our arms and legs in all directions at will, not even after doing a massive amount of yoga and Pilates.

Octopuses, however, can completely change their entire body shape. They are incredibly elastic and can stretch like rubber bands. And here's the thing: they can even deform their head and eyes. That's because they don't have a skeleton (you know, no spine and all). And now add their flexible muscles to that.

Speaking of muscles! By now, you may not even be surprised any more when I tell you that octopuses are pretty strong. Their suckers give them a good grip, much like we humans have with our thumb and forefinger.

Let's take a look at one particular octopus, and we may as well go straight to the largest of its kind, the giant Pacific octopus (yes, that's one of my eight favourite octopuses). The females of this species have a whopping 2,240 suckers, the largest of which are six centimetres in diameter. The octopus can pull or lift sixteen kilograms with a single sucker of this size—and can lift about twenty times its own weight in total. For an octopus with a body weight of fifty kilograms, that would be about one metric ton.

A metric ton is a lot—it's almost as if we could lift a hippo. Or two polar bears. Or ten large wild boars—at the same time, of course.

In reality, we humans can only lift twice our body weight at best. But you'd better not try that now. You'll quickly injure yourself. Anyway, we have all kinds of machines that lift really heavy things for us, such as construction cranes.

I read that researchers at Harvard University's John A. Paulson School of Engineering and Applied Sciences (SEAS for short) and the Beihang University of Aeronautics and Astronautics in Beijing have been able to create a robotic arm that looks and functions like the tentacle of an octopus. It can gently wrap around objects and hold them in place, and its suckers can grip and lift all kinds of things using a vacuum. Probably really heavy things, too—or at least they will be able to soon! If this robot with octopus arms were available in a smaller version, I might get one. I can picture how it would hand me eight books from the shelf simultaneously. Or cut eight onions at the same time with eight kitchen knives. Or carry eight shopping bags home from the supermarket. Oh, I'm sure you can think of many more examples.

FOR BRIGHT MINDS

Want to hear something even more amazing? Some scientists are working on a "self-healing material" which is able to repair itself when damaged, and guess where they got their inspiration from? That's right—cephalopods! Well, squid to be precise. They're hoping the material, which can repair itself in under a minute, can be used to make soft robots tougher. You see, sometimes it is useful for robots to be made of soft stuff. Then they can do all sorts of things better, including delicate tasks like performing surgery on people, or squeezing into tight spaces—just like a cephalopod—perhaps to rescue people trapped after an earthquake. Of course, the problem with soft material is that it gets damaged easily, but it seems our squid friends may have helped us to solve that problem!

This branch of science, which studies how natural phenomena and abilities can be transferred to technological devices, is called "bionics", by the way. We humans like to recreate (and use for ourselves) things that have existed in nature for ages. The robotic octopus arm is just one example. Others may be more familiar to you:

1. The Velcro fastener (burdock plants are the model for this).

2. Sonar (used in submarines to aid orientation underwater, copied from dolphins and bats).

3. Ventilation systems (copied from termites, who are so wonderfully capable of building ventilation into their structures).

4. Propellers (for aeroplanes; these were appropriated from the so-called wing fruit of the maple tree).

5. Flippers (these go back to frogs and water birds).

6. Swimsuits for top athletes (these are modelled on the skin of sharks who glide through the water effortlessly).

7. Adhesive foils (inspired by geckos, which can effortlessly walk up vertical walls).

8. Car chassis (we're trying to develop more crash-proof vehicles with the help of cockroaches, who have very resistant body armour). And so on and so forth.

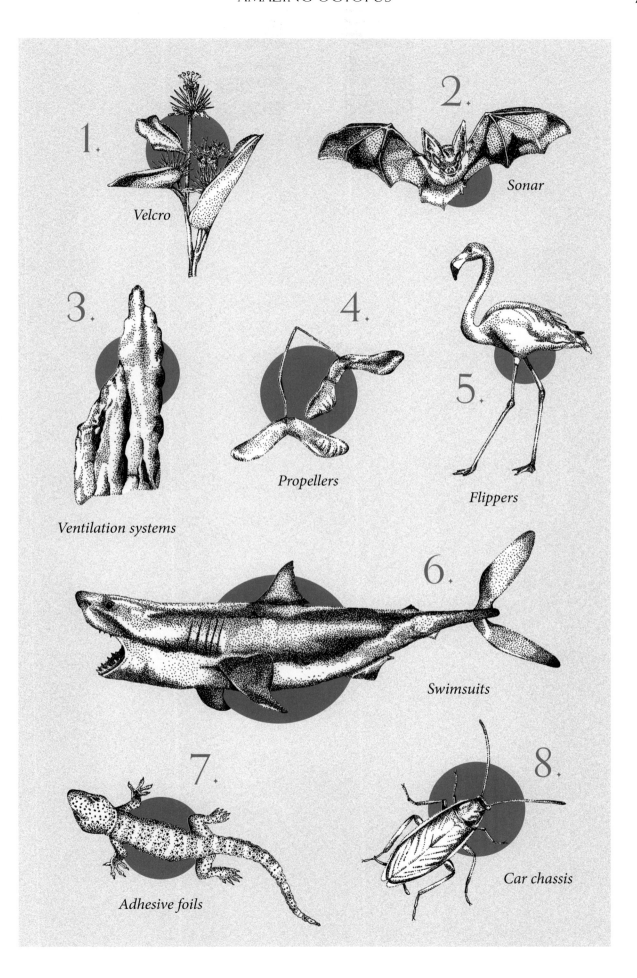

1. *Velcro*

2. *Sonar*

3. *Ventilation systems*

4. *Propellers*

5. *Flippers*

6. *Swimsuits*

7. *Adhesive foils*

8. *Car chassis*

CHAPTER

05

EVERYTHING IS IN MOTION

Have you heard one of the most famous quotes from ancient Greece? *Panta rhei!* Everything flows! A renowned philosopher named Heraclitus wrote it down. He wanted to express that everything in life is in motion, constantly changing and transforming. Or, if you will: nothing is ever still. I can appreciate this concept.

Of course, octopuses are also in motion. Like all other species, they've adapted to life on Earth over millions of years—and those creatures that don't manage to do this are in danger of going extinct. Think mammoths, woolly rhinoceroses and sabre-toothed tigers, for example, which were once unable to adapt to new climate conditions. Everything flows—and we flow with it.

Where Does the Octopus Actually Live?

In that spirit, let's keep moving and look at how octopuses move underwater—and how they live. First, it is essential to note that octopuses can move almost like humans if they want to. They can walk across the ground with two legs, erm, I mean arms. Some octopuses off the coast of Indonesia even collect coconut shells, clean them and use them as shelter. Then, if need be, they can take them with them when they hurry across the seabed (like we take tents for camping or, even better, a caravan).

Octopuses live in all the seas, no matter how cold or warm or deep. They are also found in brackish water areas, where freshwater mixes with salt water (pike, which are otherwise only found in freshwater, live here too). As you read earlier, there are even said to be freshwater octopuses, though their existence has not been proven. Plenty of other sea creatures can thrive in freshwater rivers and lakes. Bull sharks immediately come to mind. Salmon, of course, and saltwater crocodiles. So why not some octopods in the future? But that is, as I said, speculative.

By the way, octopuses certainly have a clear preference for ingenious shelters. They don't just collect coconut shells but also stones, shells, bottles, ropes, old sandals, rusty tins and whatnot. They transport these to a crevice in the reef, for example, where they stack all that stuff in front of the entrance (so they are better protected there). Sometimes octopuses even fight over particularly fine dwellings, like flower vases and clay pots that have somehow found their way into the sea.

Help the octopus find eight things
that allow it to hide from its enemies.

Solution: page 134

From Old Lady to Missile

The octopus offers another impressive spectacle when it walks across the seabed, slow and wobbly, like an old lady in a flowing dress. It tries to imitate the movement of the kelp in the current to avoid attracting attention. Recently, as I was writing another book, I came across a new way of describing a current: water that moves in the sea like a river. Nice, don't you think? In any case, octopuses love calm seas or a current that is not too strong.

Light currents, however, can be convenient for octopuses, as they can let themselves drift along with the flow. Still, they have, of course, developed their own means of propulsion. Every octopus has a "siphon", also known as a "funnel organ". This is basically a small tube through which the octopus can breathe but also expel water, ink and excrement. We'll talk about the ink part in more detail, but for now, it's interesting to note that an octopus can propel itself from A to B like an underwater rocket.

OK, maybe they don't move quite as fast as a rocket, but nevertheless rocket engineers have copied the "recoil principle" from the octopus (you guessed it, keyword: bionics). The one drawback is that the octopus can only move backwards, so it can't see where it's swimming. That's why it wraps its arms around its body to create a streamlined shape and prevent injuries when it crashes into underwater rocks, for example.

Like almost all sea creatures, octopuses have a slimy layer on their skin. Have you ever held a fish in your hand? That's what it feels like. The mucus protects the surface of their skin and helps them glide more quickly through the water or squeeze into very narrow crevices. If octopuses have to leave the water for a short time (which they can do) this layer protects them from drying out. The mucus has another unique feature too—it allows octopuses to taste with their whole body. Imagine if we could taste chocolate with our entire body—mmmm!

Researchers have also observed an octopus in an aquarium ejecting a jet of water through its siphon at a plastic container. It kept shooting the container against the aquarium wall as if it were passing the time—or just playing. Another octopus (at the Sea Star Aquarium in Coburg, Germany) was known to throw stones at the aquarium's windows. It could even aim its water jet at a lamp, causing regular electrical short circuits. Octopuses don't like bright light and can actually "spit" water at anything that bothers them.

Octopus Ink

Almost everyone knows octopuses can squirt ink—as can squid and cuttlefish. So naturally, you want to know right away whether this ink can also be used for writing. And yes, you can theoretically write with octopus ink, but it is too viscous to be used in a fountain pen or ink cartridge. The Romans (you know, Julius Caesar and his friends) had a recipe that involved drying the cephalopods' ink sacs and then grinding them. The resulting dye was called sepia. But I think the Romans used it more for cooking than for writing. Even today, sepia ink is used to dye black pasta, for example. The use of sepia ink for writing is documented from the year 1780.

More importantly, however, octopus ink is a highly effective defence strategy. When an octopus feels threatened (for example, by sperm whales, moray eels, conger eels, pyjama sharks, groupers, sharks in general, seals or dolphins), it sucks up water. Then, it shoots it out again as fast as an arrow, but this time the water is mixed with ink, allowing the octopus to hide its entire body within a thick cloud, which as you can imagine is really annoying for its predators. On top of that, the ink makes the hunter's eyes burn and can even clog the gills of some fish.

Ingeniously (octopuses really are ingenious), the ink secretion contains an active ingredient called "dopamine", also known as the happiness hormone, which tricks the octopus's enemies by giving them the feeling that they have already caught it and are gobbling it down. That's really clever, isn't it? If necessary, the octopus can do this up to six times in a row; it always carries enough concentrated ink in a small gland. In any case, this trick gives it plenty of time to get away.

Masters of Deception

Of course, the octopus would rather avoid predators in the first place. And it is ideally equipped for this too, because it is a master of deception. You will be amazed at what it can do with its skin.

Octopuses can change the colour of their skin to match that of their surroundings, even taking on patterns to camouflage them better—and all within the blink of an eye. They can even change the texture of their skin, from smooth to grainy like gravel, wavy like seaweed, or jagged like coral. If you ask me, chameleons look like amateurs in comparison. Octopuses are truly unsurpassed masters of transformation. They can produce stripes, dots and spots on almost any part of their body, forming many patterns— and all this despite the fact that octopuses are colourblind. If you want to visualize just how impressive these colour changes are, just imagine that the octopus's skin is something like a TV screen, and you're getting pretty close.

These colour changes aren't just for camouflage either—they express feelings too. So you can actually watch octopuses think! When angry they usually turn brick-red. If they are afraid, black circles can appear around their eyes. When they quickly change colour lots of times (and there are no enemies around), they are simply thinking about something. Octopuses often change colour when they are hunting. For example, they can send a pattern rippling across their skin that looks like dark clouds. To their prey, it looks as if the octopus is on the move while it is actually lurking motionless in one spot. I have been told that this is an excellent way to catch crabs.

When the octopus wants to escape from a hungry predator, it changes its colour, pattern and shape in rapid succession. The predator quickly gets confused and abandons the hunt. Sometimes it is enough for the octopus to turn dark red (we already know what that means: rage!), inflate and suddenly appear much larger than it really is.

Can you find all eight octopuses hiding here?

Solution: page 136

Superpowers

Octopuses often have to fight to survive in the ocean, regularly resulting in serious wounds. During such confrontations, they can quickly lose one of their tentacles. But then another of the octopus's superpowers comes into play: the severed arm grows back within a very short time! After just one week, it is already visible; in one hundred days at most, the arm will have completely grown back. Sometimes octopuses even shed their own arms if they are too severely injured. Just imagine if we could do the same; grow a new foot or hand whenever we wanted. But, of course, only superheroes in films can do that. I'm sure they copied octopuses (the bionics thing again).

Other animals on Earth can do this too, in their own way. I used to love catching lizards and would even take them to school. Once I accidentally let some loose in the cloakroom; they climbed into all the shoes and jackets. You wouldn't believe the fuss it caused! It just so happened that these lizards shed their tails (scientists call this "autotomy") when they were caught to confuse their hunters. And, of course, they also grew back completely. I saw it with my own eyes; that was something, I can tell you!

When I was writing this book about octopuses for you, I actually read about the following in the newspaper: the gullet snail (*Sacoglossa*) can regrow its entire body (with all its organs and stuff) from the head down. Just imagine it: this snail (which I had never heard of before) loses its entire body. It drops off below the head. And then everything grows back underneath, including a new heart. The researchers speculate that perhaps the snails do this to eliminate parasites or diseases in the body. Isn't it ingenious what animals can do?

But back to our octopus, which has a few more tricks up its sleeve. For example, it can squeeze into and slip through narrow gaps, which is also quite handy. You have to understand that its only hard body part is an immovable cartilage between its eyes—apart from its beak, of course. Yes, you heard me right. The octopus has a beak like a parrot, located between the eight arms on its underside, with teeth inside called "radula". Have you ever had your finger pinched by a parrot? You have to be really careful because they can bite quite hard. So you should never stick a finger in a big octopus's mouth either.

Once, researchers locked a giant Pacific octopus in a transparent container. Its only way to escape was through a hole just six centimetres wide. Six centimetres was also precisely the width of the inflexible cartilage between its eyes. The octopus felt the gap with its tentacles and, without hesitation, squeezed through. Then the octopus was returned to the container and the escape hole was reduced to four centimetres wide—the octopus again felt the opening with its tentacles, but this time did nothing. This experiment proves that the octopus has a clear sense of its body size and can accurately estimate how big a hole or crevice needs to be for it to venture in. What an escape artist!

FOR BRIGHT MINDS

FOR THE CEPHALOPOD GEEKS AMONG YOU, HERE ARE THREE EXCITING FACTS ABOUT SQUID:

1.

So-called "glass squid" live in the ocean and are barely visible, especially when the water is flooded with light. That's because their bodies are completely transparent, apart from their bulging eyes and an internal organ called a digestive gland. You can also see their tentacles, which they fold up on top of their heads into a crest, giving them their other name: "cockatoo squid"!

2.

The strawberry squid has a rather unusual appearance, with one small blue eye and one big yellow one. In fact, this species, and others like it, are sometimes known as "cock-eyed squids".

For a long time, nobody could work out the reason for these mismatched eyes, but now scientists think they have cracked the puzzle: as the strawberry squid drifts through the sea, its large yellow eye looks upward to spot prey, lit up by the dim sunlight filtering down from the surface; meanwhile, its small blue eye looks downward, watching for naturally glowing bio-luminescent creatures that live in the ocean depths. Each eye is perfectly suited to its job!

3.

The Humboldt squid has a fearsome reputation, with stories of divers and deep-sea cameras being attacked by swarms of these creatures. Fishermen off the coast of Mexico have even nicknamed them "red devils". Humboldt squid live in large shoals and hunt other sea creatures, including smaller cephalopods, making them true cannibal squid!

And since we mentioned octopus teeth, what do they like to eat? I wish I could write pizza, lasagne or French fries (my favourites), but octopods actually prefer to feed on crabs, shrimp and other crustaceans. Octopuses can even use one of their arms like a fishing rod, waving it around in front of a crab's home until the crab snatches it—and then the poor crustacean is done for. It takes the octopus half an hour to eat a medium-sized crab— about as long as it takes me to eat a pizza, but that is of no interest to anyone.

Can you find all eight animals that are a danger to the octopus?

Solution: page 138

CHAPTER
06

WITH THE EYES OF AN OCTOPUS

"One sees clearly only with the heart. Anything essential is invisible to the eyes," says the Little Prince in Antoine de Saint-Exupéry's world-famous book. "The eyes are a mirror of the soul" is another familiar saying. Which leads me to the question: what do we see when we look into the eyes of an octopus?

Panoramic View

The eyes of octopuses are, in fact, quite similar to ours—we both perceive the world through a lens. We both have a transparent cornea, an eyelid, an iris to regulate brightness and a retina that forms the background of the eye. Unlike us, the octopus can see in a "wide-angle format". You could almost say it has panoramic vision. To get a better idea of all this, borrow your parent's mobile phone and ask them to set the camera to a "wide angle" (most mobile phones can do this). Then take a few photos in your home and look at them closely. You will notice that with a wide angle, you can see much more of a room without having to rotate your head to the left and right. Our field of vision is much narrower—if we want to know what's going on behind our backs, we have to turn around or turn our heads. A cephalopod does not have to do that. Besides, the octopus can move its eyes individually and look in different directions, like a chameleon. Octopuses can't actually see very far—just 2.5 metres. But underwater visibility is usually limited anyway. You can't see as far as you can on land, so animals prefer to rely on other senses.

Do you want to know which animals can see the best? Well, as I said, those on land, probably birds—in particular, buzzards or eagles. They actually have binoculars built into their eyes, so they can see clearly at great distances (a tiny mouse at 500 metres). And all cats, of course, see pretty well at night. This is due to a reflective layer in their eyes, the *tapetum lucidum* (Latin for "glowing carpet"), with which they can "amplify" what little night light there is. That's why cats' eyes gleam when you shine a torch on them in the dark. Maybe you've seen some when you're driving on the motorway at night, because those reflectors on the road that shine so brightly in the dark are called cat's eyes. And I'd also like to mention dragonflies, which see movement particularly well (even when moving quickly themselves). That's because their compound eye consists of more than 30,000 individual eyes. This gives them 360 degrees of true panoramic vision, and they can also see ultraviolet light, which means that some things in their environment shine brightly for them—and are thus particularly easy to recognize. On top of that, they can actually see very deep into water. Isn't that cool? But enough now!

The pupil of the octopus looks quite strange to our eyes because it is a black rectangle. My old maths teacher would have liked that. He liked rectangles. But there is one vision-related thing that octopuses and humans have in common—both species have a dominant eye. It's funny, everyone knows whether they are right- or left-handed, but hardly anyone thinks about which of their eyes is dominant.

By the way, the dominant eye isn't always the one you use to look through the viewfinder of a camera or a telescope. Do you want to quickly find out which is your dominant eye? There is a fairly simple test: form a small circle with your thumb and index finger, stretch out your arm and aim it at any object around you. Now, if you alternate between closing one eye and then the other, you will notice that the object you are aiming at moves in and out of the circle formed by your fingers. When the object is inside the circle, you are looking through your dominant eye. I tried this, and now I know that my right eye is dominant. An octopus could theoretically do this test too, but I'm pretty sure it already knows the result.

FOR BRIGHT MINDS

Maybe you're wondering how octopuses perform in the famous "mirror test". In this test, researchers try to find out which animals recognize themselves in a mirror, i.e. know they are looking at themselves and not just another animal. All the great apes, but also dolphins, magpies and ravens, are on record as having passed this test. Octopuses do not belong to this select circle. Still, some of them have become famous even without passing this intelligence test—Paul the octopus immediately comes to mind.

Paul the octopus, who lives in the Sea Life Centre in Oberhausen, once surprised the public in Germany when, during the 2010 World Cup, he became an oracle and correctly "predicted" the outcome of all matches involving the German team. Since every football club that can afford it now keeps an Atlantic octopus in their aquarium, the price of these animals has increased more than tenfold. Whatever you think of the whole story, the reputation of molluscs has improved enormously as a result. But what does that actually say about us humans?

Octopuses Think Differently from Us

I've already told you about how octopuses think entirely differently from us because they have not only a "central brain" but effectively eight extra brains in their tentacles too, bringing the total to nine. The central brain is located just behind the mouth, where it is arranged around the oesophagus. This means that when they eat, octopuses' food travels right through their brains, so they have to be careful not to take too big a bite, in case they accidentally damage their brains.

Since octopuses don't live in social groups like us and are strict loners, they must learn everything for themselves. This makes it all the more surprising that they learn to solve many complex problems independently. Or, to put it another way: if octopuses lived together as families (and lived longer), they would undoubtedly be our absolute equals. And before you ask: octopuses only live for two or three years in the wild. Then they die, and everything they know is lost again. Their skin turns pale and white when they die as if they have suddenly decided to quietly disappear from the world…

But let's talk about something less sad, how octopuses sleep, for example. Animals sleep every day just like we do, and I'm sure some of them are even real sleepyheads, just like some of us humans. Scientists agree that some animals also dream like humans. This has been proven for dogs and cats, and researchers

also tend to agree about octopods. On the other hand, why we dream in the first place has not been conclusively clarified—not even for us humans. They say it has something to do with how our brain processes and stores memories. Do you want to know which animals have been proven to sleep the longest?

1. Bats *(up to 20 hours)*
2. Sloths *(15–20 hours)*
3. Hedgehogs *(18–20 hours)*
4. Lions *(18–20 hours)*
5. Koalas *(14 hours)*
6. Cheetahs *(12 hours)*
7. Chimpanzees *(10 hours)*
8. Gorillas *(10 hours)*

And which animals sleep the least? I'm sure you'll find out for yourselves—a little hint: take a look at giraffes, horses and wasps, for example. And then there's the okapi—wow!

Like us, octopuses have extremely well-functioning short- and long-term memory, which speaks for their remarkable thinking ability. You already know that they can open jars and unscrew caps. They can also learn from other octopuses by observing them, which is irrefutable proof of their intelligence.

Octopus Personality

I saw on TV only recently (in 2021) that some octopuses had passed the marshmallow test, which children can only manage from about the age of four. Do you want to know about the marshmallow test? It was invented by psychologists to test intelligence. It's all to do with "delayed gratification". That sounds complicated, but it's not. Imagine you're starving and you love chocolate. And then I come to you (I'm playing the role of the psychologist now) and give you a piece of chocolate. But I also tell you that you'll get a second piece of chocolate if you don't eat the first one. Then I leave the room again. Would you wait for me—or eat the first piece of chocolate? Anyway, the octopuses waited (by the way, apes, dogs and crows have also passed this test).

Like us, octopuses naturally develop personalities—some are curious, trusting and courageous, for example. In contrast, others are timid or reserved. This, of course, depends on their experiences or living conditions. An experiment by marine biologist Joshua Rosenthal showed that the behaviour of two sibling octopuses changed rapidly in response to different living conditions. One octopus usually sat hidden in a flowerpot in his aquarium, which made him very shy and untrusting after a while. The other octopus, who had no good hiding place in his aquarium, was open-minded and inquisitive. Sounds perfectly understandable, doesn't it? Imagine if we spent most of our lives

indoors, maybe even in our own room. If we suddenly had to go to the park or the supermarket, we would be scared to death.

Here's another unique feature of octopuses that I haven't mentioned at all yet: they have three hearts! One central heart—and two supporting gill hearts. Scientists agree on the reason for this—it is to compensate octopuses for what is their greatest disadvantage: their blood! Octopus blood is transparent to blue-green in colour and looks very different from ours. Our blood can transport oxygen quite well (among other things, because of the iron it contains). Octopuses also need a lot of oxygen, but their blood is not so good at transporting it (no iron). And that is why, scientists say, the octopus has developed three hearts. The two extra ones by the gills help to pump more blood, and therefore more oxygen, around their body.

FOR BRIGHT MINDS

I must confess, when I discovered this, I tried to find out whether octopuses can have heart attacks like humans. In the process, I learned that humans can die from "broken heart syndrome". This is diagnosed when the heart's left ventricle becomes strangely deformed (there are various triggers, such as grief and suffering). This single-ventricle deformation reminded Japanese doctors of something they had seen before: octopus traps. These are clay vessels with narrow necks that fishermen lay on the seabed. These traps are called *Tako-Tsubo* in Japanese, and cardiologists (heart specialists) all over the world now call this condition Tako-Tsubo Syndrome. So I'm beginning to get the impression that cephalopods really are everywhere.

Ocean Facts

~~~~~~~~~

1. It's not something you normally think about, but the Atlantic Ocean is getting bigger! And the Pacific is shrinking. Something to do with the North American continental plate moving away from the European plate. Strange to think that the land we're standing on is moving like an ice floe.

2. I once wrote a grown-up book in which the hero was Inuit. The Inuit people live in Greenland, northern Canada and other very cold places. The Inuit don't have a word for current. They say "sea water moving like a river". How beautiful is that? One of the most important ocean currents for the Earth's climate is called the Gulf Stream—it moves 150 million cubic metres of warm water towards Europe. Per second! That's one hundred times more than all the world's rivers combined.

3. There are huge underwater meadows in the oceans, and the most common sea grass is called neptune grass after the Roman god of the seas. It's one of the oldest known organisms in the world. For example, genetics show that a sea-grass meadow off Spain may be around 100,000 years old. That's definitely older than your grandpa!

4. Seawater contains 3.5% salt on average—so there are thirty-five grams of salt, or two level tablespoons, in one litre. The water is less salty where a lot of rivers flow into the ocean. The Baltic Sea contains very little salt, but the Mediterranean Sea is amongst the saltiest. The Dead Sea has up to thirty per cent! That much salt means your body actually floats on the water like a cork!

5. If you asked me to name the highest mountain, I wouldn't hesitate to answer: Mount Everest. But that's not really true, because Mauna Kea in Hawaii rises more than 10,000 metres from the bottom of the sea. Only 4,200 metres poke out of the Pacific Ocean. But it should still count, don't you think? And do you know the name of the highest mountain in our Solar System? It's called Olympus Mons and it's on Mars. It's 22,000 metres high—and it's almost as big as Germany!

6. As a child, I liked to imagine travelling across all the world's oceans from island to island, looking for pirate treasure. You would probably be better off looking under water—much more treasure has sunk with ships than would ever have been buried on land. Historians estimate three million ships have sunk in the past 4,000 years. The *Flor de la Mar*, to name just one, went down in 1512 between Indonesia and Malaysia. It is said to have been loaded with diamonds, rubies, gold and gem-encrusted statues worth up to seven billion Euro. Who wants to go treasure hunting?

7. The sea can create real monster waves! Even modern captains are afraid of them because you can't escape them or outrun them. Monster waves are actually several waves stacked together. The confirmed record (measured in 2018 near Campbell Island, 700 kilometres south of New Zealand) is 23.8 metres! That's about an eight-storey building!

8. Ever heard of apnea divers? They're also called freedivers. They dive without oxygen tanks. You can do that in lakes and ponds, but freedivers find it more exciting to do it in the sea. Croatian apnoea diver Budimir Sobat is the current record holder—he can hold his breath for twenty-four minutes and thirty-three seconds. It's in *The Guinness Book of Records*. I can't even hold mine for one minute!

CHAPTER
07

THE MOST ANCIENT INTELLIGENT CREATURE

Octopuses have lived on Earth for a long time. They have been roaming our oceans for 400 million years, making them the oldest intelligent creatures on the planet. In 2015, an international research team decoded the "genome" of the California two-spot octopus (*Octopus bimaculoides*). The genome, also known as "genetic material", contains all the information that makes up a living being. You have probably heard a lot about genes, which make things look the way they do. Specific genes (or gene sequences) decide, for example, what colour our eyes are. And our whole genome (genetic material) is a mixture of our father's and mother's genes. It all sounds quite complicated; genetics is, after all, a science in its own right. So perhaps you should just remember that genes are a blueprint for living things. And I'm sure all of you have seen the film *Jurassic Park*, where they try to bring dinosaurs back to life with the help of old genetic material. I mean, who knows, maybe one day that will actually be possible. In any case, I've read that researchers have been trying to reintroduce the extinct woolly mammoth using genetic engineering.

But I just wanted to point out that the human and octopus genomes are almost the same size. Humans have about 25,000 genes, whereas octopuses contain about 33,000 genes. It seems to me that octopuses are often ahead of humans. Do you notice that too?

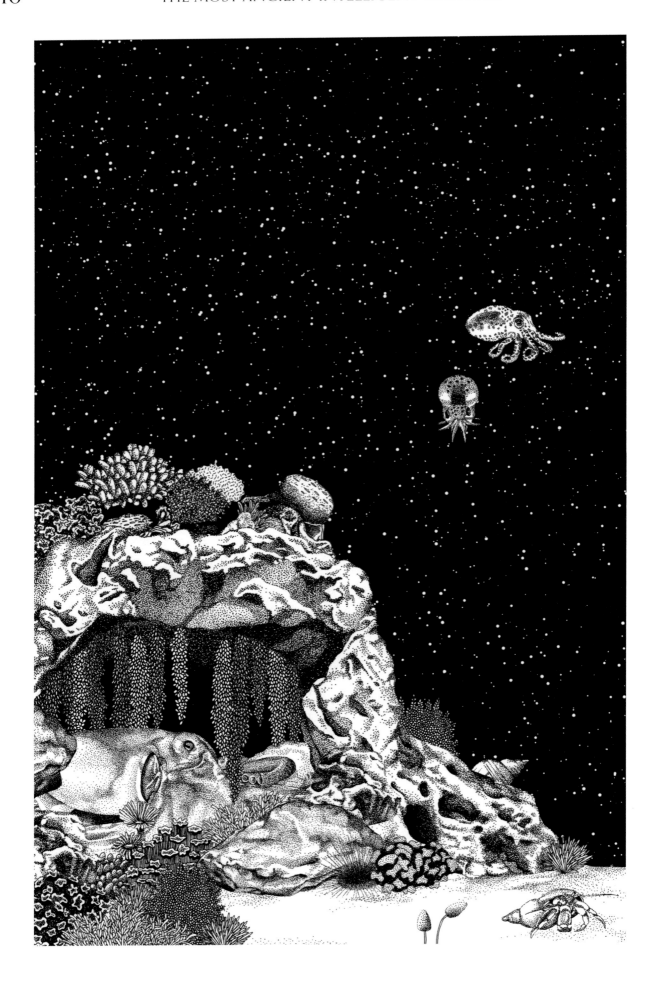

Reproduction

Octopus mating, by the way, is no big secret; it works more or less the same as in humans, although some female octopuses have developed a tendency to eat the males afterwards, so the males have to be pretty careful. After some time, depending on the water temperature and the time of year, the female octopus lays eggs. And not just a few like a hen. No! The giant Pacific octopus can lay between 67,000 and 100,000 eggs in three weeks! That sounds like a lot, but only two baby octopuses will emerge from a clutch of eggs like that!

The mother octopus watches over her eggs so attentively that she does not eat any food, so she can fully concentrate on her offspring (and their protection). When the little octopuses finally hatch, the mother octopus dies of hunger and exhaustion, having sacrificed herself. The young are left to fend for themselves.

I don't even want to imagine the dangers lurking in the ocean's depths for the mini octopuses, but we can rely on Mother Nature. There will always be enough octopuses to keep the species alive. Once again: octopuses have been living on Earth for 400 million years—and they've managed just fine up to now. On the other hand, humans as we know them have only lived on this planet for a paltry 40,000 years.

And we will see how the story continues for us bipeds.

Scientists (and futurologists) have long been thinking about which creatures will evolve on our planet in the future. There is an old, but excellent documentary about this called *The Future is Wild*. It speculates that octopuses and other cephalopods might one day leave the water to live on land! Then there might be elephant-sized land squids (called "megasquids" in the documentary) roaming the future forests. And, of course, there are bound to be smaller specimens that swing from tree to tree (the "squibbons") which might eventually become the next, even more intelligent inhabitants of the Earth.

Now that we are coming to the end of the book, how about a bedtime story? You've certainly earnt it after reading up to here. Besides, now you know as much as me about octopuses. And I'm sure it won't be too long before you know a lot more than me, because I have a hunch this won't be the only octopus book you read.

Perhaps you are wondering exactly what you should do with your new knowledge? Of course, you could share it with your parents, friends or classmates. Simply tell them everything you have learnt. Or you could do something that is (in my opinion) much better: write your own crazy story about octopuses. Let your imagination run wild and use all the knowledge you have acquired.

I know that's easier said than done, but how about I go first—and then it's your turn, OK?

Can you find eight differences between the two pictures?

Solution: page 140

You have to pay close attention
in the ocean!

CHAPTER
✦ 08

A STRANGE
METAMORPHOSIS

I woke up one morning in my crevice from a night of restless dreams, to find that I had been transformed into a human being. I know how that reads. *How weird!* you must be thinking. A human being! For us octopuses, this is unimaginable. We only occasionally encounter humans, after shipwrecks. Almost every one of our underwater playgrounds has a few of their skeletons scattered about, but we'll get to that later.

I wanted to stand up, but that was no easy matter with two arms and two legs. It's astonishing that humans manage to get by like that. Eight arms are clearly so much better. It took several minutes just to squeeze myself out of the crevice. When I had done so, I stood there for a bit, panting indignantly.

Of course, I was unsure how to deal with this new situation. Was I still dreaming, or had this nightmare actually become a reality? I stretched out both arms. Instead of my suckers, countless fine hairs were growing on them. I had a hard time suppressing a gag. This fuzzy feeling on my skin really rubbed me up the wrong way. A few sprats swam by unexpectedly. I gently moved my arms with their thousands of hairs through the current. The sprats seemed to enjoy the sight.

For a moment, I hoped that an octopus with two arms and two legs might not attract much attention in the ocean, but I quickly found out how wrong I was. As soon as one of my fellow octopuses caught sight of me, he disappeared into a nearby reef cave as if he had been bitten by a tarantula. I knew him quite well. We had never quarrelled before, so something really strange must have happened to me. "As if he had been bitten by a tarantula"—only now did I realize that such a phrase would never normally have occurred to me! I mean, I had no clue what tarantulas even were. They must be something truly terrible.

So not only did I look like a human, I was thinking like one too, and I even seemed to have acquired some of their strange land-animal vocabulary. I decided to put it to the test.

Usually, if a shark had swum up to me, I would have kept my cool and simply sprayed some ink at it—take that, gristle face! But now when I merely thought of a shark, I felt a cold shudder. I was paralysed by fear and found myself panicking, saying to myself, "A man-eater, a man-eater, run away!" Well, isn't that just fantastic?

I tried to shake off this nasty feeling by going for a swim, but instead of gliding elegantly through the water, I felt like I had been chewed on by a whole shiver of sharks, so I put my legs down on the seabed once more. Wait a minute, holy mackerel, can people even breathe underwater? I thought, *I'm suffocating, I'm suffocating!* Then I remembered: I had seen some of them hanging about the reef before, swimming around clumsily like fat manatees, and you could hear them breathing from a mile off, with air bubbles everywhere. Apparently, people could breathe underwater, so I could breathe easy.

But what could I eat if I was going to live underwater as a human? In the past, I had used my eight arms to catch anything I wanted. With two arms, that would undoubtedly be harder. I certainly couldn't spend all my time walking on the seabed. Legs only get in the way underwater. Useless things. Crabs, lobsters and the like had legs too, but well, I ate those for breakfast, so that just goes to show. No good at all. As an octopus, I had long ago formulated the theory that in the ocean, anything with legs would get eaten faster than anything without legs. Those with tentacles or fins were clearly better off. Legs were an evolutionary dead end.

Was I thinking all this as an octopus or as a human being? Probably still as an octopod because a human being would surely have protested loudly at this point. Maybe there was hope on the horizon. Maybe I would soon be an octopus again without all this human stuff…

UGH! "Hope on the horizon", where did that come from? What's a horizon anyway? I decided not to think about it any more and swam ponderously towards some coral. It would probably be best if I parked myself there and camouflaged myself. *"Parked"? No, don't think about it, don't think about it, not with any of your nine brains; don't question it, Vladislav Vostok, everything will be OK.*

I can explain my name, Vladislav Vostok, very quickly. There's nothing strange about it at all. You see, my mother entrusted her clutch of eggs to an old shipwreck, the *Vladislav Vostok*. I know it came from the human world, but if something stays in the ocean long enough, it loses all human qualities—for us, it was just another reef. Maybe an artificial one, but a reef is a reef.

Anyway, I and all my 80,0000 brothers and sisters, regardless of gender, are called Vladislav Vostok. Fortunately, I have not met any of them again. Just imagine the birthday get-togethers: *Allow me, Vladislav Vostok; Welcome, have you met Vladislav Vostok? Er, here's a crab for Vladislav Vostok*—and then all 80,000 of us would descend on the poor creature—what a nightmare. Fortunately, we octopuses are loners.

Was I camouflaged now? Humans seemed quite alone with their thoughts, easily distracted, quickly losing focus of what was important. As an octopus, I would have taken on the colour and shape of the coral surrounding me a hundred times over by now, but my two human arms still looked the same as before. A little hairy, a little flabby, a little… *ewww!*

Slightly upset, I plucked two coral branches from the reef. I wouldn't usually have done that, but this was a real emergency. I held them in front of my head, pulled my legs up and waved the branches gently in the current. I was thinking that from a distance, I could be mistaken for a full-grown cnidarian. Polyps (another word for cnidarians—for those who want to know everything, the word comes from the Greek and means "many-footed creature") build coral reefs, so I pretended to be one by twining my coral branches together. Totally polyp-like, I tell you.

After only an hour, I grew terribly bored of just sitting around on the reef all day, and started to get hungry. *Mmm, tuna steak would be just the thing right now, grilled medium rare, with some Worcestershire sauce... Oh, holy mackerel, did I really just think that? A what sauce? Even with my nine brains working on it, I couldn't pronounce that word correctly. And I've got nothing against tuna, but they're a bit fast and frankly somewhat out of my league as prey.*

Come on now, Vladislav V, keep it together. Just take the next crab. Stick to what you know. No sooner said than done. One of the puniest crabs was just about catchable with two arms. I grabbed the little thing and started to chew. It tasted like… hmm… like… hmm… if only I knew. Definitely not like a hamburger. *Mon Dieu,* I would have given anything for a hamburger; a steak, braised or seared; or even just a little piece of chocolate.

Hum, hum, I heard a boat roar over my head. How fast and elegant it was as it slid through the water. Much more beautiful than those terrible sharks. I had to suppress the urge to swim after it. Who knew if I would have ever caught up with it. I wasn't the fastest swimmer any more. Still, I imagined what it would be like to climb aboard and sit on the deck, all cool, legs crossed, and ask for a pair of sunglasses. How they would all stare! The people on board, I mean, who would undoubtedly recognize me as one of their own, with only two arms and legs. Maybe they would think I had somehow come back from one of the underwater playgrounds at the bottom of the sea, a survivor resurfacing from the depths of the unforgiving ocean… oh, blah, blah, blah. It was painful listening to all the gibberish thoughts running through my human mind.

Boom boom, times three, *boom boom*, times three, my three hearts were still doing their job. So at least a few of my octopus features remained. I dropped the coral branches and finally began to relax a little. Watching the colourful fish, jellyfish and all kinds of peaceful sea creatures around me felt so good, sooo good. It was wonderfully relaxing to gaze into the vastness of the sea and see everything floating and dancing through this blue paradise. Siri, set a reminder, I want an aquarium!

Aaaaagh! I wailed like a banshee, sat bolt upright and banged my head against the roof of my crevice. It was still dark outside. But, oh, holy mackerel, thank you, it had all been a dream. A dream within a dream, perhaps, which would explain my subsiding panic.

I stretched out my eight arms for a moment; everything was still there where it should be, no legs to be seen. *Vladislav, you deserve to sleep a little longer,* I think. *Or, then again, maybe it's best not to...*

SEE YOU SOON, MY DEARS!

With this octopus bedtime story, I bid you farewell. But you were a great audience on this journey into the mysterious world of the octopus. And to completely take the famous quote from Winston Churchill out of context: "This is not the end. It is not even the beginning of the end. But it is, perhaps, the end of the beginning."

As I type these lines, I am already thinking about which animal we will take a closer look at next. The jellyfish? Sharks? The aye-aye? Oh, I don't know, we'll think of something. Of course, you can also write to the publisher (you'll find the address in this book) about what you'd like to read next. And don't forget: in the meantime, write some octopus stories. That would make me very happy…

DO YOU WANT TO KNOW MORE?

I've compiled a list of some of my favourite books and films. Of course, this is only a tiny selection. A little secret aside: few people know how much you need to know to know how little you know. Werner Heisenberg already knew that. By the way, he invented "Heisenberg's uncertainty principle"—and if you can understand that, please send your explanation to me c/o the publisher. But please keep it very simple so that I can finally understand it too.

BOOKS:

✦ *Octopus, Squid, and Cuttlefish: A Visual, Scientific Guide to the Oceans' Most Advanced Invertebrates* by Roger Hanlon

✦ *Ocean* by Hélène Druvert

✦ *An Anthology of Aquatic Life* by Sam Hume

FILMS:

✦ *My Octopus Teacher* (Netflix)

✦ *Ocean Deep* (Planet Earth)

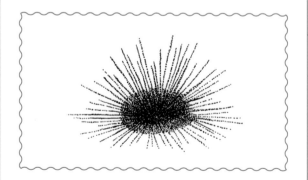

ONLINE:

✦ The most fascinating objects in space: https://www.smithsonianmag.com/air-space-magazine/weirdest-objects-universe-180976341/

Copyright © privat

Michèle Ganser, born in Aachen, Germany in 1995, studied communication design in Aachen and Mainz. She is particularly fascinated by the universe, stars and planets. She can also instantly pronounce any planet name backwards. Nrutas. Enutpen. Yrucrem. Proof enough? In her illustrations, she unusually combines exciting themes and thus creates completely new worlds. In her spare time, she enjoys reading—preferably science-fiction novels. And she can pronounce that backwards, too: slevon noitcif ecneics.

Copyright © www.detailsinn.at

Michael Stavarič, born in Brno, Czechia, in 1972, studied bohemian studies (anybody know what that is?), journalism and communication studies in Vienna. He is particularly fascinated by the idea of one day travelling through the entire universe. He would also like to be able to breathe underwater. He writes many books—for children and adults—and he has won many awards, or, if rhyming is your thing: he hoards awards. In his spare time, he gets on his inline skates. Unfortunately, he can pronounce hardly anything correctly backwards: steaks eininli. Hang on: setaks enilni (phew, made it).

Help the octopus find eight things
that allow it to hide from its enemies.

Image: page 76

Can you find all eight octopuses hiding here?

Image: page 86

Can you find all eight animals that can be dangerous to the octopus?

Image: page 96

Can you find the eight differences between the two pictures?

Image: page 120

Cut-out octopus

Pushkin Press
Somerset House, Strand
London WC2R 1LA

Amazing Octopus was first published as *Faszination Krake: Wesen einer unbekannten Welt*
by Leykam Buchverlagsgesellschaft m.b.H. Nfg. & Co. KG, in Graz – Vienna, Austria, 2021

First published by Pushkin Press in 2023

9 8 7 6 5 4 3 2 1

ISBN 13: 978-1-78269-424-3

▬ Federal Ministry
Republic of Austria
Arts, Culture,
Civil Service and Sport

Typeset by Tetragon, London
Printed and bound in China by C&C Offset Printing Co Ltd.

www.pushkinpress.com